MUSLIMS IN BRITAIN

MUSLIMS IN BRITAIN

RACE, PLACE AND IDENTITIES

• • •

EDITED BY
PETER HOPKINS AND
RICHARD GALE

Edinburgh University Press

Edinburgh University Press Ltd
22 George Square, Edinburgh
www.euppublishing.com

Typeset in 10/12.5 Sabon by
Servis Filmsetting Ltd, Stockport, Cheshire, and
printed and bound in Great Britain by
CPI Antony Rowe, Chippenham and Eastbourne

A CIP record for this book is available from the British Library

ISBN 978 0 7486 2587 1 (hardback)
ISBN 978 0 7486 2588 8 (paperback)

CONTENTS

ACKNOWLEDGEMENTS

We would like to thank a number of people who have contributed to the publication of the book, and in particular, thank you to the chapter authors for the timely and professional production of their contributions. We are both very appreciative of the encouragement and advice that Tracey Skelton offered us on our initial proposal to publish this book. Thanks to Edinburgh University Press – and Nicola Ramsey in particular – for agreeing to publish this collection and for their patience in this process. Jonathan Birt and Rachel Pain also offered very useful comments on the introduction and conclusion respectively, and we thank them for their insights. Thanks also to Jon Swords for preparing the index.

CONTRIBUTORS

Louise Archer is Professor of Sociology of Education in the Department of Education and Professional Studies at Kings College London, UK.

Jonathan Birt is a part-time Research Fellow at the Islam in Europe Unit, Islamic Foundation, UK.

Sophie Bowlby is Senior Lecturer in Human Geography in the School of Human and Environmental Sciences at the University of Reading, UK.

Claire Dwyer is Senior Lecturer in Social and Cultural Geography in the Department of Geography at University College London, UK.

Richard Gale is Research Fellow is the Department of Sociology at the University of Birmingham, UK.

Peter Hopkins is Lecturer in Social Geography in the School of Geography, Politics and Sociology at the University of Newcastle, UK.

Lily Kong is Vice-President (University and Global Relations) and Professor of Geography at the National University of Singapore.

Sally Lloyd-Evans is Lecturer in Human Geography in the School of Human and Environmental Sciences at the University of Reading, UK.

Seán McLoughlin is Senior Lecturer in Religion, Anthropology and Islam in the Department of Religious Studies at the University of Leeds, UK.

Sharmina Mawani is a Lecturer at the Institute of Ismaili Studies, London, UK.

Tariq Modood is Professor of Sociology, Politics and Public Policy at the University of Bristol, UK.

Anjoom Mukadam is a Lecturer at the Institute of Ismaili Studies, London, UK.

Caroline Nagel is Assistant Professor of Geography at the University of South Carolina, USA.

Deborah Phillips is Reader in Ethnic and Racial Studies in the School of Geography at the University of Leeds, UK.

Bindi Shah is ESRC Research Fellow in the School of Business and Social Sciences at Roehampton University.

Lynn Staeheli is Ogilvie Professor of Geography in the Institute of Geography at the University of Edinburgh, UK.

TABLES

FIGURES

CHAPTER

1

INTRODUCTION: MUSLIMS IN BRITAIN – RACE, PLACE AND THE SPATIALITY OF IDENTITIES

Richard Gale and Peter Hopkins

Introduction – British Muslim identities and the politics of writing

Researching and writing on Islam and Muslim identities has become an unavoidably political enterprise. Superficially of course, this observation is (or should be) nothing more than a professional commonplace – all research processes are inherently political, as any reflexive researcher knows. Skewed relations of power between researcher and researched are a constant of most social research situations, further complicated by cross-cutting considerations such as whether the researcher is an insider or outsider of the research participants' social network, and whether or not there are gendered, generational, ethnic or class differences – most often a combination of some or all of these – which need to be sensitively negotiated in research encounters. Moreover, these considerations do not simply evaporate on the completion of fieldwork, but carry over into the writing process, taking on new dynamics as existing codes and conventions of writing are adapted to the task of articulating particular (read selected) cultural representations. This is the salutary lesson taught by James Clifford and George Marcus in their seminal work, *Writing Culture* (1986). Indeed, as Clifford remarks in his introduction to the book '[social] science is in, not above, historical and linguistic processes', to the extent that 'the poetic and the political are inseparable' in ethnographic and other scientific writing (Clifford 1986: 2). But if a crucial part of the continuing purchase of Clifford's observations is their level of generality, they take on a particular acuteness – a difference of degree rather than kind – in contemporary research on Islam, on account of the sheer intensity of public contestation over competing representations of Muslims, both in Britain and elsewhere. Sensationalisms about the 'allegiances' of Muslims in diaspora saturate media discourse, while the titles of numerous popular (and not a few academic) books repeatedly invoke the monolith-versus-shibboleth opposition most crudely stated in Samuel Huntingdon's (2002 [1997]) 'clash of civilisations' thesis: 'Islam and the West', 'Islam and Democracy', 'Islam and Security', 'Islam and Secularism', 'Islam and Postmodernity' and so on, announce starkly the preoccupation of many commentators with the monochrome question of whether or not 'Islam' is compatible with cherished 'Western' principles. Correspondingly, it has become customary to refract discussion of Muslim identities and experiences through the lens of an increasingly ossified, post-2001 chronology, whereby 'ground zero' has become the temporal no less than spatial reference point for a scale on which key 'moments' in the unfolding of the troubled relations between 'Islam' and 'the West' – '9/11' in New York, '14/3' in Madrid, '7/7' and '21/7' in London, and so on – are plotted and chronicled. These events have become iconic tropes that organise much of the debate about Muslim identities, such that the task of navigating an analytically discriminating course in research and writing on Islam that neither under- nor overstates their significance has become at once more necessary and more complex.

None of this is of course to deny that politicised articulations of faith – Islamic, Christian, Hindu and so on – are important sociological phenomena needing to be addressed in research. Neither is it to suggest that there is any meaningful possibility for researchers to seek out putatively pre- or non-political components of Muslim identities, as a means to obviate the pitfalls of demonisation and stigmatisation of Islam that emanate from contemporary hegemonic constructions. As Talal Asad has argued (Asad 1993: 29), there is no sense in which anthropology (and by extension, other social sciences) can posit religions as 'trans-historical essences' existing independently of the specific social processes and 'domains of power' of the periods in which they manifest themselves – a point also reiterated recently by Kahani-Hopkins and Hopkins (2002) in relation to competing 'representations' of British Muslims. Our argument is rather that one of the core problems of contemporary debates about Islam concerns the highly restrictive ways in which Islam itself is constructed – without referring, often tellingly – to the views of Muslims themselves. Political pronouncements about the 'responsibilities' of Muslims in the wake of the 7 July 2005 attacks, for example, implied not only the homogeneity of Islamic identity and faith, but a corresponding uniformity of Muslim political subjectivities, which are seen to vary only on the plane of their intensity between less and rather more 'extreme' expressions (see, for example, 'Muslims must root out extremism', BBC News, 4 July 2006). Very little attention has generally been paid to the very wide variety of adaptive strategies developed and pursued by Muslims in response to changing social and political conditions in Britain (on this, see McLoughlin 2005). Indeed, the narrow application to Islam of the general – and otherwise progressive – adjective 'radical', which is taken thereby to connote 'fundamentalism' and virulent, anti-Western 'extremism', is a revealing instance of this general attenuation of Muslim political and wider social identification.

With these considerations in view, rather than strike out in bold strokes across the broad canvas of 'epoch-making' events and their assumed consequences, our primary concern in this book has been to turn the issue on its head and begin by working in miniature, building outwards from the situated practices and everyday politics in which key facets of contemporary Muslim identities are recursively engaged and negotiated. More particularly, and without imposing an unduly uniform perspective on the varied contributions to this volume, our concern has been to put together a collection that coheres around the theme of 'the spatial', construed broadly enough to encompass the notions of site, place, scale, mobility, global and local – as well as the relations between them – as they are relevant to the contexts in which Muslim identities are forged. Our argument, which is reflected amply, if implicitly, throughout the book, is that a foregrounding of 'space' and 'context' provides one useful way of transcending the tendency alluded to above of over-determining the homogeneity of Muslim subjectivities. By drawing attention to the role of particular sites as contexts of negotiation – the home, the mosque, the workplace, the neighbourhood, the Ka'ba – the various chapters of this volume analyse the ways in which differing aspects of identity are articulated and inflected under varying socio-spatial conditions. While the focus on the relationship between Islam and space maintained here is not novel (see, for example, the pioneering collection edited by Barbara Daly Metcalf, 1996), at the time of writing, it is felt that the resonance of 'space' as both an exploratory and explanatory research construct is particularly powerful.

In terms of structure, the book is organised around a set of interlocking themes, including: gender, place and culture; landscapes, communities and networks; and finally, religion, race and difference. Although this structure inevitably reflects the key themes of those contributing to this collection, they also point to trends in the ways in which geographers – and those working in related disciplines – have sought to focus upon Muslims in Britain. The purpose of this introductory chapter is to set the parameters for the contributions to the book, taken as a whole. First, we provide a descriptive overview of the historical trajectories and demographic characteristics of the British Muslim population, drawing on 2001 Census data and the findings of sample surveys. Second, we turn to a critical review of the literature on Islam and space, which we integrate into a preview of the present volume's various chapters. We conclude with a few indicative remarks, developed further in the 'Afterword', concerning the pathways that geographical and other spatially-oriented research on Muslims in Britain and beyond, might pursue in future.

The Muslim presence in Britain – historical and demographic contours

As is well known, the large majority of British Muslims trace their heritage, through one or more generations, to the South Asian subcontinent (Peach 2005). This is primarily a result of the waves of economic migration and settlement that formed an inherent part of Britain's economic reconstruction in the aftermath of the Second World War. But in view of the critical observation above concerning conceptions of history as a series of epochal 'moments', it is worth recalling that the population movements of the 'post-war era' were themselves linked inextricably to the more protracted period of British imperial rule. The 'age of empire' (Hobsbawm 1995) entailed an extensive period of social and political contact between Britain and territories with large Muslim populations, bringing in train a pattern of Muslim settlement in Britain stretching back over two centuries and more (Ansari 2004). Moreover, there were important instances in which the earlier, pre-Second World War settlement of Muslims in Britain served as a bridgehead for the later, mass migration flows. Thus Dahya (1974) reveals that the 'pioneers' arriving in Bradford and Birmingham during and prior to the war were former seamen ('lascars'), who moved inwards from port-cities that had formed their points of entry to Britain – Liverpool, Middlesbrough and Hull in the case of Bradford, and Cardiff in the case of Birmingham (Dahya 1974: 84–5, 95–6; see also Visram 1986: 34–54). These earlier groups of people were not only of South Asian, but also of Yemeni and other Middle Eastern heritage. As Ansari suggests (2004: 24), this imperial history and geography accounts to a large extent for the huge diversity of the British Muslim population. Subsequently, the British Muslim presence has been augmented through the arrival of new migrant groups, such as from Eastern Europe and Somalia (McGown 1999).

Allowing for the limitations of identity categories that presently inform British social statistics (Phillips 2007), dimensions of the diversity of the British Muslim population are reflected in the 2001 UK Census, which posed a question on religious affiliation for the first time since 1851 (Southworth 2005). As shown in Table 1.1, the Muslim population of Britain stood at slightly fewer than 1.6 million in the 2001 Census, with slightly more than 1.5 million in England, fewer than 43,000 in Scotland, and slightly fewer than 22,000 in Wales. The majority of Muslims in Britain are of South Asian heritage, with Pakistanis constituting the single largest group: 43% of Muslims in England, 33% in Wales and 67% of Muslims in Scotland were of Pakistani ethnicity. Table 1.1 also reveals substantial numbers of Muslims who identified themselves according to other ethnic categories in the Census. For example, 7.5% of Muslims in England, 4.6% in Wales and 4.4% in Scotland identified themselves as 'Other White'; 6.2% in England and 6.8% in Wales identified as 'Black African'; and 5.8% in England, 7.6% in Wales and 6.3% in Scotland identified as 'Other Asian'. The diversity of origin and heritage of Muslims in Britain is

Table 1.1 Muslims by ethnic groups in England, Scotland and Wales, 2001 Census

	England		Wales		Scotland	
	Number	Percentage	Number	Percentage	Number	Percentage
White	177,231	11.62	2,542	11.69	3,401	7.99
British	61,513	4.03	1,529	7.03	1,504	3.53
Irish	870	0.06	20	0.09	35	0.08
Other White	114,848	7.53	993	4.57	1,862	4.38
Mixed	62,496	4.10	1,766	8.12	1,367	3.21
White and Caribbean	1,340	0.09	45	0.21	-	-
White and Black African	10,209	0.67	314	1.44	-	-
White and Asian	29,663	1.95	734	3.38	-	-
Other Mixed	21,284	1.40	673	3.10	-	-
Asian or Asian British	1,124,685	73.76	14,380	66.15	33,588	78.92
Indian	131,098	8.60	564	2.59	892	2.10
Pakistani	650,516	42.66	7,164	32.95	28,353	66.62
Bangladeshi	254,704	16.70	5,006	23.03	1,669	3.92
Other Asian	88,367	5.79	1,646	7.57	2,674	6.28
Black or Black British	104,714	6.87	1,631	7.50	1,059	2.49
Black Caribbean	4,445	0.29	32	0.15	15	0.04
Black African	94,665	6.21	1,471	6.77	946	2.22
Other Black*	5,604	0.37	128	0.59	98	0.23
Chinese or Other Ethnic Group	55,761	3.66	1,420	6.53	3,142	7.38
Chinese	735	0.05	17	0.08	38	0.09
Other Ethnic Group	55,026	3.61	1,403	6.45	3,104	7.29
All people	1,524,887	100	21,739	100	42,557	100

*Includes 'Black Scottish' and 'Other Black' in the Scottish Census. [1]

further reflected in census data on place of birth: in England alone, 4% of Muslims were born in Eastern Europe and a further 6% each in both the Middle East and South and Central Africa. Above all, however, the Muslim population of Britain is British-born: nearly half of all Muslims in England (46.4%) were born in the UK. The diversity of ethnic and national

Figure 1.1 Map showing the distribution of Muslims by Government Office
Regions in England, 2001 Census

heritage hinted at in the census is cross-cut by other factors that are less easy to
quantify.

In terms of regional distribution, the map in Figure 1.1 shows the residential patterns of Muslims in England in the 2001 Census by Government Office
Regions. Above all, it reveals the extent of concentration of Muslims in the
London area, where approximately 40% of the English Muslim population
resided (Table 1.2). After London, the next largest concentrations were in the
West Midlands conurbation (accounting for 14.2%), the North West (13.4%),
and Yorkshire and the Humber (12.4%). (The map does not show the patterns

Table 1.2 Distribution of the Muslim population by English Government Office Region, 2001 Census

Government Office Region	Number	Percentage
North East	26,925	1.8
North West	204,261	13.4
Yorkshire and The Humber	189,089	12.4
East Midlands	70,224	4.6
West Midlands	216,184	14.2
East of England	78,931	5.2
London	607,083	39.8
South East	108,725	7.1
South West	23,465	1.5
Total	1,524,887	100

for Scotland and Wales on account of the fact that these countries have their own devolved governmental structures and correspondingly different regional classification systems).

Exploring these concentration patterns further, the 2001 Census confirmed what has long been known from research literature on British Muslims from across the social sciences (Dahya 1974; Khan 1977; Lewis 1994), namely that the Muslim population is not only predominantly urban, but overwhelmingly concentrated in just a few cities. The heavy emphasis on London has already been noted, while Table 1.3 indicates that the fifteen cities in the UK with the highest Muslim populations include the other capital cities of the UK, Cardiff and Edinburgh. Reflecting the earlier historical period of Muslim settlement in Britain (Ansari 2004), these fifteen cities also include the port-cities that were formerly important nodes in the British imperial economy. These were the cities – Liverpool, Cardiff and Glasgow in particular – where the so-called 'lascars', many of them Muslim, initially settled. However, most significantly, Table 1.3 reveals that three cities alone – namely London, Birmingham and Bradford – account for over half (51.7%) of the combined Muslim population of England, Scotland and Wales.

In terms of socio-economic conditions, the 2001 Census revealed the Muslim population to be disproportionately disadvantaged in comparison with the wider population. Focusing on England for the purposes of illustration, Figure 1.2 shows that, of people aged between 16 and 74 (i.e. the economically active population), a much smaller than average proportion of Muslims are within the top socio-economic categories of managerial and professional occupations: 14.7% of Muslims are within the 'higher' and 'lower' managerial and professional occupations, as compared with 27.3% of the population overall. Conversely, significantly more Muslims are either long-term unemployed or have never worked: nearly one quarter (24.1%) of Muslims are in the 'never

Table 1.3 Muslims by cities in England, Scotland and Wales, 2001 Census

City	Number	Percentage
London	607,083	38.20
Birmingham	140,033	8.81
Bradford	75,188	4.73
Manchester	35,806	2.25
Oldham	24,039	1.51
Sheffield	23,819	1.50
Leeds	21,394	1.35
Rochdale	19,248	1.21
Bolton	18,444	1.16
Glasgow	17,792	1.12
Coventry	11,686	0.74
Cardiff	11,261	0.71
Edinburgh	6,759	0.43
Bury	6,756	0.43
Liverpool	5,945	0.37

worked' and 'long term unemployed' category, as compared to 3.7% of the wider population. Examining Figure 1.2 more closely, we can see that this differential has a significant gender dimension, given the very low levels of labour-market activity among Muslim women. Thus, nearly two-fifths of this group (39%) are either long-term unemployed or have never worked, compared to 4.5% of all women and 10.3% of Muslim men. In the absence of more detailed research, however, extreme caution needs to be exercised in how these differential patterns of labour-market participation are explained. Bowlby and Lloyd-Evans address these issues in their chapter in this collection, examining competing cultural and structural explanations in the context of a discussion of Muslim women's labour-market experiences in Reading and Slough.

It is also important to note, from the point of view of the themes addressed throughout this volume, that the economic disadvantages experienced by British Muslims manifest themselves spatially. According to recent research undertaken for the then Office of the Deputy Prime Minister (now the Department of Communities and Local Government), Muslims in England and Wales are significantly over-represented in areas of relative material hardship. Thus, using the 2004 Index of Multiple Deprivation, this research showed that while Muslims constitute approximately 3% of the British population, they form slightly more than 10% of the population in areas below the bottom decile of relative deprivation (Beckford et al. 2006: 23).[2] These patterns serve as a *prima facie* indication of the linkage between segregation and socio-economic conditions, teasing away at the tendency within contemporary discourses of the 'self-segregation' of British Muslim communities, to place cultural explanations 'centre-stage' (Phillips 2006: 33–4). Recent research has also clearly demon-

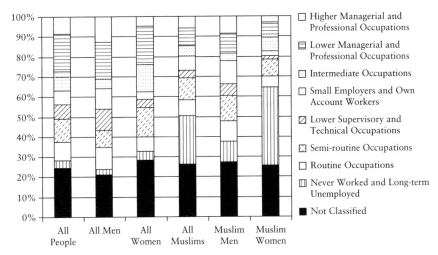

Figure 1.2 All people, all men and all women compared to all Muslims, Muslim men and Muslim women by National Statistics Socio-economic Classification (NS-SeC) in England, 2001 Census

strated that levels of segregation have been falling in recent years, undermining the contention of Trevor Phillips, former Chair of the Commission for Racial Equality, that Britain is 'sleepwalking' into a scenario of North American-style segregation (Simpson 2004; Phillips 2006; Gale 2007).

One of the many criticisms of the 2001 Census on religion is that, while it provides information on religious 'affiliation', it is of questionable value in illuminating substantive issues of interest to sociologists or geographers of religion, such as the relationships between forms of religious identity and the nature and intensity of religious beliefs and practices (Southworth 2005; Voas 2007). Nevertheless, important evidence concerning aspects of these relationships is available from national surveys, the most important of these to date being the Fourth National Survey of Ethnic Minorities conducted by the Policy Studies Institute (PSI) in 1994 (Modood et al. 1997). This revealed that for large proportions of all groups of British South Asians, religious identification was 'very important' to the way they live their lives (Modood et al. 1997: Table 9.7, 301). Significantly from our perspective, this was most evident in the case of the Muslim members of the sample, in spite of the greater ethnic diversity that characterised this group vis-à-vis the other religious designations (see Jonathan Birt's contribution to this collection for further discussion of these patterns and their wider significance).

Regrettably, the PSI study has not been repeated. However, more recent evidence of the religious commitment of British Muslims is available from the various rounds of the Home Office Citizenship Survey (HOCS), first conducted in 2001. As shown in Table 1.4, which draws on data from the 2005 survey,

Table 1.4 Cross-tabulation of 'What is your religion even if you are not practising?' by 'Do you consider that you are actively practising your religion?', Home Office Citizenship Survey, 2005 (weighted count, N = 11,927)

What is your religion even if you are not currently practising?	Do you consider that you are actively practising your religion? (%)		Total	Base
	Yes	No		
Muslim	73.5	26.5	100	355
Hindu	73.3	26.7	100	86
Sikh	70.9	29.1	100	150
Buddhist	57.7	42.3	100	38
Any other religion	47.7	52.3	100	333
Jewish	42.0	58.0	100	69
Christian	30.9	69.1	100	10,885
Refusal	0.0	100.0	100	5
Don't know	0.0	100.0	100	6

Muslims, Sikhs and Hindus exhibit a greater tendency to identify themselves as 'practising' their religion than Christians, Jews or Buddhists. Proportionally more Muslims than members of any other group said they were actively 'practising' their religion, although they were closely followed by Hindus: 73.5% of Muslims and 73.3% of Hindus identified themselves as 'practising'.

An important issue in this context concerns the ways in which different aspects of Muslim identities – religious, social and political – are reconciled. Much of the debate in this area, in Britain and elsewhere, has centred upon the practical and symbolic roles of the nation-state, allegiance to which is understood in many political quarters to be both total and incapable of division (Werbner 2000; see also Bowen 2006 on France). Of course, as Werbner has astutely observed (2000: 310–12), globalising forces in late modernity have resulted in a multitude of social, economic and political trends that increasingly transgress national boundaries, raising thorough-going questions over what it might mean to be either loyal or disloyal to the nation-state at core. Nevertheless, cherished assumptions concerning the exclusivity of the national imaginary persist, and have been debated with especial fiat in the case of Muslims. In a way that resonates strongly with Werbner's argument, Birt (2006: 9) commented soon after the attacks on London in July of 2005, that:

> [i]t would be fruitless to place loyalty to *umma* and nation in political opposition, and therefore to portray this purported dichotomy as an ever-present existential crisis of cultural identity for British Muslims. At a time when national sentiment is eroded by commodification, devolution, relations with Europe, cultural diversity, globalisa-

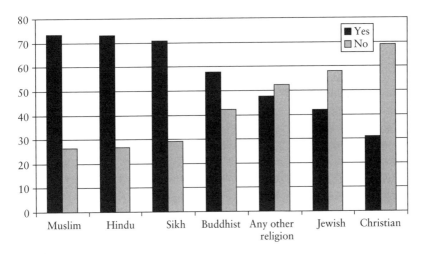

Figure 1.3 'What is your religion even if you are not practising?' by 'Do you consider that you are actively practising your religion?', Home Office Citizenship Survey, 2005 (percentages based on weighted counts in Table 1.4)

tion, even by a collective failure of the imagination, is it just or fair to expect minority groups to bear disproportionately the burdens of nationhood in moments of crisis like this?

For the purposes of intervening in this debate, it is worthwhile again referring to findings from the 2005 Home Office Citizenship Survey, which, as in previous rounds of the survey, posed a question on how strongly respondents felt they 'belonged' to Britain. As shown in Table 1.5, while the proportion of Muslims stating they belonged 'very strongly' to Britain is smaller than those of Christian and White groups (53 and 52% respectively), it is nevertheless of the same order of magnitude as the responses of other minority groups. Thus, approximately 44% of Muslims identified themselves as belonging 'very strongly' to Britain, which is entirely consistent with the responses of Hindus (42%), Sikhs (45%), and Black Caribbeans (44%). Moreover, taking the categories of 'very strongly' and 'fairly strongly' together, the patterns for Muslims and Christians differ only by a fraction of a per cent: 86.4% of Muslims and 85.9% of Christians have a 'very' or 'fairly' strong attachment to Britain. Correspondingly, only 13% of Muslims claimed to belong to Britain either 'not very' or 'not at all strongly', mirroring the Christian response across these two categories. Given that the issue addressed here arguably turns on how strongly individuals commit to the tenets of their faith, it is important to note that, even when controlling for the effects of religious practice on national identification, these relationships do not fundamentally change. Thus, of practising Muslims, 43% felt they belonged to Britain 'very strongly', and 45% 'fairly strongly',

Table 1.5 'How strongly do you belong to Britain?' by selected religious and ethnic groups, Home Office Citizenship Survey, 2005 (percentages based on weighted counts)

	White	Christian	Muslim	Hindu	Sikh	Back Caribbean	Black African
Very strongly	51.5%	53.1%	43.6%	42.3%	45.2%	44.4%	44.0%
Fairly strongly	34.4%	33.5%	42.8%	49.0%	44.0%	37.6%	40.0%
Not very strongly	10.8%	10.4%	10.8%	8.1%	9.5%	14.5%	13.6%
Not at all strongly	3.4%	3.0%	2.8%	0.7%	1.2%	3.4%	2.4%
Total	100.1	100	100	100.1	99.9	99.9	100
Base	*12975*	*10809*	*353*	*149*	*84*	*117*	*125*

while of non-practising Muslims, 47% belonged 'very strongly' and 37% 'fairly strongly' (see Maxwell (2006) for a more detailed analysis of these issues in relation to the 2003 Home Office Citizenship Survey).

What these statistical patterns suggest at the most general level is that 'the nation' is by no means a stable 'container' of identity, but, as with all identity categories, is a mutable social construct that resonates in different ways for different groups within the polity, and is subject to contextual change and (re)interpretation. In relation to Muslims specifically, while much of the public discussion of British Muslims carries the implication that the strong identification of Muslims *qua* Muslims contradicts the superordinate claims of the nation-state as the primary locus of identity, the ways in which Muslims negotiate and reconcile different strands of their identities countenance no such contradiction. The question of how different elements of British Muslim identities interleave with – without being reducible to – national identity or experiences of Islamophobia is addressed in detail by Birt's contribution to this collection.

Muslim identities through the lens of the spatial

There are various ways in which spatial approaches to the study of Islam and Muslim identities have born fruit in the form of a rapidly developing research literature. Here, while providing a synoptic account of this literature, we also indicate how the contributions to the present work both complement and extend it in significant ways.

It is important to note at the outset the ways in which the relationships between beliefs, texts and associated rituals already lend an inherent spatiality to Islamic practice. Thus, while emphatically not venerated in itself, one of the most important sites in Islam, the Ka'ba, provides the direction (*qibla*) during the cycle of five daily prayers and is the focal point of the pilgrimage (*hajj*), which all Muslims are enjoined to undertake during their lifetime, health and wealth permitting. The mosque, though not formally consecrated, takes on resonance as the place set aside for prayers, which are undertaken after ritual cleansing (*wuzu*). For Sufi-inspired devotional movements (such as the Barelwis, who have a large following among Mirpuri/Pakistani Muslims in Britain), the spiritual significance of particular sites extends to the lodges and tombs (*dargahs*) of Sufi 'saints' (*pirs*), whose 'blessing' (*baraka*) is seen to remain 'in place', even after the pir's death (Troll 1989; Sanyal 1999: 105–10; Werbner 2003). More generally, as Metcalf (1996: 3) observes, religious *practice* as opposed to rigid distinctions between 'sacred' and 'profane', provide the key: 'it is ritual and sanctioned practice that is prior and that creates "Muslim space", which thus does not require any juridically claimed territory or formally consecrated or architecturally specific space'.

The enactment in place of specific ritual observances necessarily involves engagement with prevailing social mores and environments, raising in turn important questions over the reciprocity between established practices and the meanings and significance they appear to take on under 'new' conditions (Metcalf 1996: 6–7). For instance, Werbner (1996) examines how a Sufi procession commemorating the death/rebirth (*'urs*) of a Sufi saint forms part of an ordered set of practices in Sufism to ritually sacralise a profane space (Werbner 1996: 310–11). However, in this process, it is particular *places* – in the context of Werbner's work, the 'alien' environment of British inner urban areas – that become imbued with religious significance. If Werbner's work can be seen to be concerned with the role of ritual in the extension of Islam into 'new peripheries' (Werbner 1996: 334), McLoughlin's contribution to this collection partially inverts this focus, examining the participation of British Muslims in the pilgrimage to the 'mythic homeland' of the *umma*. However, McLoughlin is likewise concerned with the infusion of an established ritual with different meanings and inflections, and reveals how, at the same time as affirming participants' beliefs, the experience of the hajj also confronts them with the fragility of notions of 'sacred community', and with the 'profane' incursions of global capitalism upon the very precincts and practices of the hajj themselves. More generally, McLoughlin's work – as Werbner's – furnishes rich insight into the relations between global cultural flows and specific locations.

There remains considerable scope for additional research on the relationship between texts, beliefs and Muslim spatial practices, particularly in view of the greater participation of different groups of Muslims in debates over Islamic sources and authority permitted by the internet (Anderson 2003; Mandaville 2007). Nevertheless, at the time of writing, the majority of research on Muslims with a spatial focus places greater emphasis on broader patterns of Muslim identity politics than on space and spirituality per se. And arguably the strongest area of development in this context is research on the relationships between space and Muslim gender identity. Important contributions here include the work of Dwyer (1999a, 1999b, 2000) and Secor (2001, 2002, 2004) on the complex negotiations entered into by Muslim women as a result of conflicting associations with female dress codes. In different ways, both of these authors indicate contextually variant attitudes towards patterns of dress, (such as between home and school in the case of Pakistani Muslim women in Britain researched by Dwyer, or different zones within the city in the case of Kurdish women in Istanbul researched by Secor). Importantly, these spatial inflections become part of the negotiation process. Other contributions include the edited volume of Falah and Nagel (2005), encompassing important work on the relationships between economic migration, domestic work and gender (Silvey 2005), and issues of Muslim women's participation in formal labour markets (Mohammad 2005; Abisaab 2005). Gender, place and culture (Section 1) is an area to which the present collection has self-consciously sought to contribute. As Deborah Phillips' chapter demonstrates, the home is a key location for young Muslim women to construct their identities and manage broader family and social relations. Alongside the significance of home spaces, the spaces of education and employment are also key locations in the lives of young British Muslims, in terms of gender identity. The chapters by Sophie Bowlby and Sally Lloyd-Evans, and by Claire Dwyer and Bindi Shah excavate issues surrounding access to the labour market and educational experiences and aspirations respectively. In both chapters, issues around the reworking of gendered expectations, the role of religious identities and the behaviours and attitudes of young Muslim women to economic relations are explored. In the final chapter of this section, Louise Archer draws attention to the experiences of Muslim boys by focusing upon issues such as masculinity, neighbourhood spaces, schooling and territoriality in the lives of Muslim youth.

There has been much research that has sought to map the locations of Muslims in Britain, primarily through census data analysis focusing specifically upon concerns about ethnic (and religious) residential segregation (Peach, 2006). This work has generated important insights into the locations of Muslims in Britain, and the relative importance of religion and ethnicity in patterns of Muslim segregation. There is, however, a need for further research to explore the everyday politics and interactions that both express and recreate such urban patterns (see, for instance, the recent work of Phillips et al. 2007). The four chapters in Section 2, on landscapes, communities and networks, make important contributions to advancing these concerns. Drawing on fieldwork in Birmingham, Richard Gale's contribution historicises the spatial negotiations that have often had to be entered into by British Muslims as means to establishing mosques and centres of religious education (*madrasas*), focusing especially on the ways in which urban planning infrastructure mediates wider contestation over the design and location of such buildings (see also Gale and Naylor 2002; Gale 2005). The chapter by Caroline Nagel and Lynn Staeheli explores the intersections between politics, public space and Muslim and Arab identities, and complicates the relationships between Muslim minorities and public spheres and spaces of society. The contributions of Sean McLoughlin and by Anjoom Mukadam and Sharmina Mawani further complement this theme through an exploration of the importance of migrations, mobilities and pilgrimages in the lives of Muslims in Britain, investigating experiences of the pilgrimage to Mecca, and the mobilities of cultural commodities respectively. The significance of locality, the influence of landscapes and the importance of geography are key themes that run throughout these four chapters as well as across many of the contributions to this book, and further work about Muslims in Britain could usefully explore the ways in which geography, locality and mobility matter. A key issue here is the specific geographical foci of research. Much scholarship has focused upon conurbations of Muslim settlement, primarily in urban England, including work in various neighbourhoods in London, Manchester and the 'northern cities'. Yet, far less attention has focused upon other cities across England, and furthermore, the devolved contexts of Scotland and Wales are often overlooked (although see Hopkins, 2008 for a recent exception).

Overall, scholarship on Muslims in Britain draws upon a broad range of disciplinary perspectives, theoretical standpoints and methodological approaches. The three chapters in Section 3, on religion, race and difference, each seek to reflect upon some of the wider academic, popular and policy issues connected with Muslims in Britain. Lily Kong's chapter seeks to situate Muslim geographies, reflecting upon historical issues relating to knowledge production and the development of geographies of religion. Tariq Modood's contribution focuses upon issues within society at large, to consider issues about multiculturalism, and Jonathan Birt speaks to questions about the formation of identities, contemporary experiences of Islamophobia and emancipatory politics in the lives of Muslims in Britain.

The principal aim of this book is to respond critically to the tendency of much political and media discussion of Muslims, in Britain and beyond, to posit a monolithic unity to Muslim political and social identities, a characterisation which fails to stand up to empirical scrutiny. Emerging from the chapters contained in the book, as well as the various sources drawn on in the preceding discussion, is a picture in which 'British Muslims' can be seen to be exceptionally diverse, in social, cultural and political senses. As a population, Muslims in Britain encompass wide differences in ethnic and national origins, as well as migration histories and trajectories, which also intersect in important ways with differences of sectarian and jurisprudential orientation (*madhab*). Important aspects of this diversity are reflected in the present volume: hence, alongside chapters focusing on Muslims of Pakistani heritage are those of Nagel and Staeheli on British Arabs, and of Mukadam and Mawani on Ismaili Shias. Moreover, settlement patterns in Britain have given rise to further diversity of experience, as these have entailed highly localised patterns of interaction with prevailing social, political and economic conditions. Of course, this should not be taken to suggest that there are no areas of experience which British Muslims share in common. In terms of identification, we have seen that Muslims profess to be actively practising their religion to a greater extent than any other religious group, while for a majority, commitment to Islam appears not to hinder identification with Britain. In terms of socio-economic experiences, it has also been shown that, on average, Muslims are much more disadvantaged than other minority groups, a pattern which is expressed and recreated in the spatial order of the specific cities in which the large majority of Muslims are concentrated. Nevertheless, as our review of existing literature has shown and as the chapters of the book further testify, such commonalities of experience as Islamophobia and economic hardship are in themselves generative of wide-ranging responses. Adapting concepts of 'space' and 'place' to form the basis of an interpretive lens enables this diversity of British Muslim experience, identity and heritage to come to the fore.

Notes

1. The Census in Scotland was conducted separately from that of England and Wales, and both are drawn on in this table. A further, parallel census was conducted in Northern Ireland, but data on Muslims in Northern Ireland is not available.

2. The Index of Multiple Deprivation 2004 gives a rank score to every lower-layer Super Output Area in England and Wales (of which there are 32,482 in total), combining weighted scores across seven 'domains', including income, employment, health and disability, education and training, barriers to housing and services, crime and living environment. Each lower-layer Super Output Area is standardised to contain approximately 1,500 people (www.communities.gov.uk/archived/general content/communities/indicesofdeprivation/216309/ accessed 14 April 2008).

References

Abisaab, M. (2005), 'Contesting space: gendered discourse and labor among Lebanese women', in G. W. Falah and C. Nagel (eds), *Geographies of Muslim Women: Gender, Religion and Space*, New York and London: Guilford Press, pp. 249–74.

Anderson, J. (2003), 'New media, new publics: reconfiguring the public sphere of Islam', *Social Research*, 70(3), 887–906.

Ansari, H. (2004), *The Infidel Within – Muslims in Britain Since 1800*, London: Hurst.

Asad, T. (1993), *Genealogies of Religion – Discipline and Reasons of Power in Christianity and Islam*, Baltimore and London: Johns Hopkins University Press.

Beckford, J., Gale, R., Owen, D., Peach, C. and Weller, P. (2006), *Review of the Evidence Base on Faith Communities*, London: Office of the Deputy Prime Minister.

Birt, Y. (2006), 'Islamic citizenship in Britain after 7/7: tackling extremism and preserving freedoms', in A. A. Malik (ed.) *The State We Are In – Identity, Terror and the Law of Jihad*, Bristol: Amal Press, pp. 3–13.

Bowen, J. (2006), *Why the French Don't Like Headscarves: Islam, the State and Public Space*, Princeton, NJ: Princeton University Press.

Clifford, J. (1986), 'Introduction: partial truths', in J. Clifford and G. E. Marcus (eds), *Writing Culture*, Berkeley, Los Angeles and London: University of California Press, pp. 1–26.

Clifford, J. and Marcus, G. E. (1986), *Writing Culture*, Berkeley, Los Angeles and London: University of California Press.

Dahya, B. (1974), 'The nature of Pakistani ethnicity in industrial cities in Britain', in A. Cohen (ed.), *Urban Ethnicity*, London: Tavistock, pp. 77–118.

Dwyer, C. (1999a), 'Veiled meanings: young British Muslim women and the negotiation of differences', *Gender, Place and Culture*, 6(1), 5–26.

Dwyer, C. (1999b), 'Contradictions of community: questions of identity for young British Muslim women', *Environment and Planning A*, 31, 53–68.

Dwyer, C. (2000), 'Negotiating diasporic identities: young British South Asian Muslim women', *Women's Studies International Forum*, 23(4), 475–86.

Falah, G. W. and Nagel, C. (eds) (2007), *Geographies of Muslim Women: Gender, Religion and Space*, New York and London: Guilford Press.

Gale, R. (2005), 'Representing the city: mosques and the planning process in Birmingham, UK', *Journal of Ethnic and Migration Studies*, 31(6), 1161–79.

Gale, R. (2007), 'The place of Islam in the geography of religion: trends and intersections', *Geography Compass*, 1(5), 1015–36.

Gale, R. and Naylor, S. (2002), 'Religion, planning and the city: the spatial politics of ethnic minority expression in British cities and towns', *Ethnicities*, 2(3), 387–409.

Hobsbawm, R. (1995), *The Age of Empire – 1875–1914*, London: Abacus.

Hopkins, P. (2008), *Islam, Youth, Masculinity*, Lampeter: Edwin Mellen Press.

Huntingdon, S. (2002 [1997]), *The Clash of Civilisations and the Remaking of World Order*, London: The Free Press.

Kahani-Hopkins, V. and Hopkins, N. (2002), '"Representing" British Muslims: the strategic dimension to identity construction', *Ethnic and Racial Studies*, 25(2), 288–309.

Khan, S. (1977), 'The Pakistanis: Mirpuri villagers at home and in Bradford', in J. L. Watson (ed.), *Between Two Cultures*, Oxford: Basil Blackwell, pp. 57–90.

Lewis, P. (1994), *Islamic Britain – Religion, Politics and Identity among British Muslims*, London: I. B. Tauris.

Mandaville, P. (2007), 'Globalization and the politics of religious knowledge: pluralizing authority in the Muslim world', *Theory, Culture and Society*, 24(2), 101–15.

McGown, R. B. (1999), *The Somali Communities of London and Toronto*, Toronto: University of Toronto Press.

McLoughlin, S. (2005), 'The state, new Muslim leadership and Islam as a resource for public engagement in Britain', in J. Cesari and S. McLoughlin (eds), *European Muslims and the Secular State*, Aldershot: Ashgate, pp. 55–70.

Maxwell, R. (2006), 'Muslims, South Asians and the British mainstream: a national identity crisis?', *West European Politics*, 29(4), 736–56.

Metcalf, B. D. (1996), 'Introduction: sacred words, sanctioned practice, new communities', in B. D. Metcalf (ed.), *Making Muslim Space in North America and Europe*, Berkeley: University of California Press, pp. 1–27.

Modood, T., Berthoud, R., Lakey, J., Nazroo, J., Smith, P., Virdee, S. and Beishon, S. (1997), *Ethnic Minorities in Britain – Diversity and Disadvantage*, London: Policy Studies Institute.

Mohammad, R. (2005), 'Negotiating spaces of the home, the education system and the labour market: the case of young, working-class, British Pakistani Muslim women', in G. W. Falah and C. Nagel (eds), *Geographies of Muslim Women: Gender, Religion and Space* New York and London: Guilford Press, pp. 178–200.

Peach, C. (2005), 'Britain's Muslim population: an overview', in T. Abbas (ed.) *Muslim Britain – Communities Under Pressure*, London and New York: Zed Books, pp. 18–30.

Peach, C. (2006), 'Islam, ethnicity and South Asian religions in London in the 2001 Census', *Transactions of the Institute of British Geographers (New Series)*, 31, 353–70.

Phillips, D. (2006), 'Parallel lives? Challenging discourses of British Muslim self-segregation', *Environment and Planning D: Society and Space*, 24, 25–40.

Phillips, D. (2007), 'Ethnic and racial segregation: a critical perspective', *Geography Compass*, 1(5), 1138–59.

Phillips, D., Davies, C. and Ratcliffe, P. (2007), 'British Asian narratives of urban space', *Transactions of the Institute of British Geographers (New series)*, 32, 217–34.

Sanyal, U. (1999), *Devotional Islam and Politics in India – Ahmad Riza Khan Barelwi and His Movement, 1870–1920*, Delhi: Oxford University Press.

Secor, A. J. (2001), 'Toward a feminist counter-geopolitics: gender, space and Islamist politics in Istanbul', *Space and Polity*, 5(3), 191–211.

Secor, A. J. (2002), 'The veil and urban space in Istanbul: women's dress, mobility and Islamic knowledge', *Gender, Place and Culture*, 9(1), 5–22.

Secor, A. J. (2004), 'There is an Istanbul that belongs to me': citizenship, space and identity in the city', *Annals of the Association of American Geographers*, 94(2), 352–68.

Silvey, R. (2005), 'Transnational Islam: Indonesian migrant domestic workers in Saudi Arabia', in G. W. Falah and C. Nagel (eds), *Geographies of Muslim Women: Gender, Religion and Space*, New York and London: Guilford Press, pp. 127–46.

Simpson, L. (2004), 'Statistics of racial segregation: measures, evidence and policy', *Urban Studies*, 41, 661–81.

Southworth, J. (2005), '"Religion" in the 2001 Census for England and Wales', *Population, Space and Place*, 11(2), 75–88.

Troll, C. W. (ed.) (1989), *Muslim Shrines in India: Their Character, History and Significance*, Delhi: Oxford University Press.

Visram, R. (1986), *Ayahs, Lascars and Princes – Indians in Britain, 1700–1947*, London: Pluto Press.

Voas, D. (2007), 'Does religion belong in population studies?', *Environment and Planning A*, 39, 1166–80.

Werbner, P. (1996), 'Stamping the earth with the name of Allah: zikr and the sacralizing of space', *Cultural anthropology*, 11(3), 309–38.

Werbner, P. (2000), 'Divided loyalties: empowered citizenship? Muslims in Britain', *Citizenship Studies*, 4(3), 307–24.

Werbner, P. (2003), *Pilgrims of Love – The Anthropology of a Global Sufi Cult*, London: Hurst.

SECTION 1

• • •

GENDER, PLACE AND CULTURE

CREATING HOME SPACES: YOUNG BRITISH MUSLIM WOMEN'S IDENTITY AND CONCEPTUALISATIONS OF HOME

Deborah Phillips

Introduction

This chapter explores the interrelationship between expressions of 'self' and the creation of 'home spaces' among young, mostly working-class, Muslim women living in a range of family circumstances in the northern textile towns of Oldham, Rochdale and Bradford. It is particularly concerned with the feelings and experiences of those moving into new spaces, but it also explores how 'self' can be expressed through the creation of autonomous home spaces within the family home.[1] While acknowledging that the concept of 'home' should not simply be conflated with that of housing, the discussion focuses on the meaning of living arrangements and housing circumstances for young Muslim women's identity. The notion of home space is used here to embrace the idea of both housing and the neighbourhood. Both may be seen as material and affective spaces that play a role in shaping everyday practices, social relations and identities of young Muslim women in Britain.

Explorations of the concept of home reveal it to be ambiguous and evocative, with multiple meanings (Rose 1993; Domosh 1998; Blunt and Dowling 2006). Home is a place that is both lived and imagined, with material characteristics and symbolic significance. Experiences and understandings of home are likely to be underpinned by social differences, such as age, gender, education, ethnicity, sexuality etc., and to vary with social, political and cultural contexts. Homes become imbued with different emotions and meanings at different times, depending on the intersection between ideas of self and family, community and other associations which help to shape a sense of connectedness and belonging. These feelings are likely to be rooted in everyday experiences at the local scale (in the family, community and neighbourhood) and may be reworked according to understandings of self that are swayed by local, national and (possibly) transnational discourses on Muslim citizenship and belonging.

The house as home is widely represented in the geographical literature as an everyday space implicated in the 'foundation of identity' and providing an 'archive of self and identity' (Warrington 2001: 368–9). The house, or dwelling-place, is particularly important for Muslim women whose everyday mobility and participation in the public (more masculine) spheres of education and work may be closely regulated (Brah et al. 1999; Mohammad 1999; Afshar et al. 2005). For many Muslim women, the domestic space plays a similar function, in terms of socialising and worship, to the mosque for Muslim men. How the dwelling-place is experienced, and what it means to those who live in it, however, is far from stable. On the one hand, the home can be a site for the performance and transformation of identity, and a place of resistance to religious, cultural, racialised and gendered norms and expectations (hooks 1990; Gregson and Lowe 1995; Fortier 2000). A home of one's own can be a place for young people to 'be themselves'. Conversely, as the feminist literature has explored, it can also be a site of oppression and disempowerment (McDowell 1999; Blunt 2005); a place where restrictive cultural traditions and patriarchal relations are re-inscribed, first by parents/in-laws and brothers, and then by husbands and other male family members. The home is viewed by many Muslims as a key space for the transmission of religio-cultural values and social practices to the next generation, a process in which women are expected to play a central role (Mohammad 2005). As Afshar (1994: 130) observes, women are viewed as 'the transmitters of cultural values and identities' and 'the standard bearers of the group's private and public dignity'.

The home-making role constructed for Muslim women can bring particular pressures and expectations of conformity to cultural norms. It can, however, also present opportunities to initiate change, especially when raising daughters. Recognising this capacity for resistance, a growing body of scholarly work has sought to destabilise essentialised representations of the Muslim female as a passive, submissive, highly regulated object (see, for example, Dwyer 1999; Shaheed 1999; Qureshi and Moores 1999; Afshar et al. 2005; Falah and Nagel 2005). This literature emphasises the complexity of processes of identification for Muslim women and the social differences (in ethnic heritage, transnational associations, education, class, locality, age) that underpin the way in which they see themselves, negotiate their sense of 'self' at home or at work, and experience feelings of local, national and Islamic belonging. British Muslim female subjectivities, Mohammad (2005: 180) contends, are not simply rooted in a religious identity but are produced across 'a matrix of discourses', ranging from the Western secular to the Islamist. Women, she argues, select from these to combine values and ideals of womanhood in the process of renegotiating a sense of self, whether this be in the context of the workplace, the neighbourhood or the home.

This chapter explores how British Muslim women's understandings of home, and the driving forces underlying the creation of home spaces, are rooted in personal and family circumstances, lived experiences of community and neighbourhood, and understandings of 'self' and 'other'. In extending the concept of home space to incorporate the neighbourhood and wider locality, the chapter touches on how women's identities may be shaped and negotiated through everyday encounters in a local setting or, in the case of areas which have perhaps never been visited, imagined local spaces.

The research context; placing young British Muslim women

Muslim women's sense of self and views of home as spaces of belonging are likely to be influenced, at least in part, by local and national media and political discourses, which have variously constructed Muslim women as victims of an oppressive Islamist regime and unaccommodating cultural 'others' (Poole 2002; Afshar 2006). The research localities of Oldham, Rochdale and Bradford have a special place in the national discourse on citizenship and belonging. All have sizable British Muslim populations of Pakistani, Kashmiri and Bangladeshi origin, which are characterised by relatively high levels of unemployment, deprivation and spatial clustering (Phillips 2006; Simpson et al. 2007). Oldham and Bradford also experienced racialised disturbances in 2001. These three multi-ethnic localities (along with places such as Blackburn and Burnley) have thus come to epitomise what are seen to be the failings of multiculturalism in the public imaginary; towns divided by racial tensions and mistrust, ethnic groups living 'parallel lives', and a lack of unity stemming from the limited spatial and cultural integration of a so-called self-segregating 'other' (Phillips 2006). While these interpretations of intercultural relations in these places have been rightly contested (e.g. Phillips 2006; Simpson 2004), they now form part of the local history of Oldham and Bradford, and help to frame British Muslims' sense of self, feelings about where they belong and where they might consider creating home spaces. Ethnic relations in Rochdale, meanwhile, were described by some local young men and women as 'not like Oldham', and 'better than Oldham', partly because of the different histories of 'rioting' and because of an active BNP presence in the latter. While racialised tensions were evident in Rochdale, barriers to social and spatial integration were perceived by its residents to be lower and more permeable.

The data presented in this chapter draw on discussions held with nine focus groups of women, three in each locality. A total of 64 women of Pakistani, Kashmiri or Bangladeshi origin, aged between 18 and 25, were involved. Most were born or had spent most of their lives in Oldham, Rochdale or Bradford. The participants were recruited via community organisations and places of work, and recruitment involved some snowballing. The focus groups were constructed on the basis of current living arrangements.

The young women participants occupied a range of positions in terms of their marital status and their experiences of family and creating home spaces. Some were single and studying at college while living at home with the extended family (6). Some single women were economically inactive or working in the family business, while others were in other types of paid employment. The remainder were married, and most were caring for young children. Some of the women lived in the parental home or that of their parents-in-law (just under half), and others owned or rented their own property.

The group discussions focused on housing decisions and aspirations, with an emphasis on feelings about moving out of the family home, possibly into different neighbourhoods. Views were elicited on the women's constructions of home and how they felt these compared with those of their parents' generation. The focus groups in Oldham and Rochdale were conducted by a Muslim woman, and those in Bradford were conducted by the (white British) author. While this will have made some difference in the way in which the women related to the group facilitator (for example, veiled women presumed the empathy of the Muslim facilitator, who wore a headscarf), there were no discernable differences in the themes emerging from the discussions. All focus groups were conducted in English, recorded and fully transcribed.

Focus groups were also conducted with young men (mostly from working-class backgrounds) in the three localities as part of the wider research project. Although the findings from these groups are not reported in detail here, they provided insights into young men's (husbands, brothers, cousins etc.) reading of home spaces and the gendering of space within them. These insights helped to frame the women's accounts of home-making. The young men in all of the groups presented gendered discourses on home and moving. Most tended to construct decisions about living arrangements, moving house and the choice of property as a male domain – in the case of married women, one which extends to fathers as well as husbands. This patriarchal decision making was explicitly acknowledged by some young women as a constraint on the creation of home spaces, although others took it for granted as 'the way we do things'.

The young Muslim men tended to talk about the everyday dwelling-spaces of the home as 'women's space'. In one focus group there was a long and animated discussion of how the addition of sisters-in-law to the household 'crowded out' young males, so that they were inclined to spend less time in the family home. The young men's construction of a domestic role for the unmarried sister and the sister-in-law was unassailable. The group agreed that a new sister-in-law provided another pair of hands to do the chores, including picking up the young men's clothes from the floor. There was general agreement from the group when one participant declared, 'it makes us lazy'. These findings are consistent with those of Dwyer (2000) and Hopkins (2007), whose exploration of masculine subject positions revealed the ease with which many young (working-class) Muslim men, perhaps unintentionally, reproduced gendered discourses of home.

In exploring the process of home-making by young Muslim women living in Oldham, Rochdale and Bradford, we will see how the creation of home spaces involves a range of strategies, including compromises, performances, resistance and accommodating varying degrees of perceived risk. All require women to negotiate a range of different subject positions in relation to their family and their wider communities of association.

Creating home spaces: home and marriage

There has been a strong tradition for young couples of Pakistani and Bangladeshi origin to remain within the extended family home upon marriage (Afshar 1994). For women, this normally involves a move into her in-laws' household and the negotiation of a set of patriarchal structures. Recent research indicates that there is still a strong demand for housing suitable for extended family living among those of Pakistani and Bangladeshi origin (Harrison and Phillips 2003). Nevertheless, social and demographic changes have also brought an increasing need for, and acceptance of, separate living arrangements. This may take the form of a separate dwelling on the same street, in which case the young women are not far from the gaze of the family, or may involve a move further afield, which affords the couple more independence.

The centrality, and the expectation, of marriage in the lives of the young women we spoke to, and its implications for their aspirations and expressions of identity, emerged clearly from the group discussions and were implicated in their narratives of self. Women were not specifically asked about their views on marriage in the focus groups. Nevertheless, discussions of where they lived, or hoped to lived, and the decisions they (or their family) made in relation to the creation of a home space were inextricably linked to the experience, expectation and timing of marriage for the majority of the women. Most participants agreed that, in their local communities, it was still very unusual for single girls to live on their own for any extended period of time. Some spoke of how young women might be permitted to live away while in higher education, although many continue to live with their parents. Girls who had moved away would generally be expected to return to the family home upon graduation to await marriage.

The women to whom we spoke displayed a range of subject positions with regard to housing and living arrangements, and with respect to the way they saw themselves in relation to family and community. However, the inevitably of marriage (for themselves and for others in their locality) was largely taken for granted. One participant in a focus group of women of Pakistani origin explained:

In our culture, our religion, we're expected to get married . . . It's not like you've got a choice . . . You're expected to go when you get married, and you're expected to get married even if you don't want to. (Pakistani woman, Rochdale)

Few women openly questioned the cultural expectation of marriage in the context of the discussion, although some talked about negotiating with parents in order to delay it.[2] There was also a recognition that expectations might change as women became more educated and financially independent. This is supported by evidence which suggests that daughters with higher levels of education are more likely to be able to negotiate parental and community concerns about independent living before marriage (Mohammad 2005; Bagguley and Hussain 2007).

Young single Pakistani and Bangladeshi women living in different localities (suburban as opposed to inner city, or more cosmopolitan metropolitan places) or those coming from more professional family backgrounds may well show a greater propensity for independent living than the women we interviewed in Oldham, Rochdale and Bradford. Nevertheless, the views expressed by women in these three localities do seem to be consistent with findings from other studies. As Kandiyoti (1993), Shaheed (1999) and Mohammad (2005) have argued, a woman's place in the Islamic home and family is strongly bound up with the ascribed role of 'mother' and 'nurturer'. The performance of this idealised view of Muslim womanhood is closely linked to a strong desire on the part of the family (and community) to guard a woman's sexual purity prior to marriage. This has repercussions for the regulation of women's lives and is implicated in the requirement for single women to stay at home. These authors argue that the re-inscription of this domestic role for women is integral to a collective (and more traditional) Muslim identity. Yuval-Davis and Anthias (1989) go so far as to suggest that the making, remaking and survival of Muslim communities, on the local and the transnational scale, may be seen as a gendered process; a reflection of the role of women as 'reproducers', in a cultural as well as biological sense.

Thus, as Mohammad (2005: 183) observes, for Muslim women 'marriage, discursively and in practice, is a key marker that shapes the trajectory of their lives'. Nevertheless, we cannot simply interpret this as constraining. As explored below, some women to whom we talked (both married and single), viewed marriage and the chance of making a new home space as a source of empowerment. For these women, marriage was perceived as enabling the expression and negotiation of identity; a route out of the parental home and a passport to greater freedom from the parental gaze. The imagined space of a different home was not so reassuring for all single girls, however. Some displayed anxiety, uncertainty and fears about future living arrangements, both in relation to living with parents-in-law (which may bring a greater loss of freedom and the imposition of another set of patriarchal expectations) and in terms of setting up home on their own.

The discussion now turns to an exploration of the circumstances in which young Muslim women have created home spaces or, in the case of women living in the family home, imagine/envisage creating a new home space.

Expressing self within the family home

The expectation that a young Muslim woman will remain within the family home until married, or live with her in-laws upon marriage, brings many constraints to the expression of self through home-making. Nevertheless, the women in our discussion groups showed that there was always room for social agency and some manifestation of individual identity through the creation of micro home spaces, even in the most difficult of circumstances. This was particularly important for women who might be expected to spend a considerable amount of time at home, under the gaze of the family.

In practical terms, there may be little physical space over which a woman living in the family home can exert control, either because of overcrowding or because she is disadvantaged by the distribution of power in the household by gender, age and/or position within the family. As Sibley (1995) and Valentine (2000) have explored, children often have limited space (either physically or symbolically) to express their individuality within the family home. Nevertheless, physical overcrowding on the scale experienced by many Muslim families in the research localities presents particular challenges. It was not unusual for discussion group participants to live in 3- or 4-bedroomed properties with up to ten family members. Single women often shared a bedroom with one or more sisters. Nevertheless, a number of these women spoke of how they found ways to stamp their personal codes on particular spaces; for example, by decorating the interiors of wardrobes, particular corners of a bedroom or a bedhead. As one women, explained, 'for me, it's the way I hang up my clothes, all neatly, with those little scented packets . . .' For married women living with in-laws, the kitchen was a potential space for the assertion of identity, although it was also inevitably a place of potential conflict between female members of the household. Micro-spaces may again assume great symbolic importance here. Arranging particular cooking ingredients or crockery, for example, were mentioned as ways of asserting control and individuality.

Women living in family homes thus adopted a range of different strategies in order to negotiate the role constructed for them and to preserve a sense of self. Some also talked of 'imagining' a home of their own. One married woman living in a household with seven adults and two children in inner Bradford explained:

> It's not that I'm unhappy or anything, but I do sometimes think, who am I? Where do I fit in? There are so many of us here, which is nice, but . . . [sentence unfinished]. I sometimes think about entertaining my mum and dad and brothers and sisters in my own place and how it would be . . . It may happen one day, inshallah.

This embodiment of the home space, this imagined space, permits the woman to reconfigure the everyday setting and to enter a liminal place, or as Soja (1996) suggested, a 'third space'. The roles that they construct for themselves may be traditional, gendered ones (e.g. mothering and entertaining) but they take place beyond the regulated space of the immediate family. They may involve 'rule breaking', like 'putting on jeans' or 'not cooking everything from first principles so that is all that you do all day', but it does not necessarily imply turning your back on your family. As explored in the next section, family connections remain of central importance to most of the women in our research areas, regardless of living arrangements.

A number of single women across the research localities had, in their view, taken steps towards materialising their dreams of a home of their own, while still living with their parents. Some had purchased properties, often with the help of their families, which they could call 'their own'. While in practice this may constitute a family investment, this material acquisition gave the young women a symbolic independence and a place of anticipated home:

> My mum and dad helped me buy. They said it is a good investment and I think it's fun to think about living there. Scary but fun. (Pakistani woman, Bradford)

Following hooks (1990), we might see the construction of both micro and imagined home spaces, however fragile or temporary, as having radical potential. hooks describes how the process of creating home spaces was important for African-American women's sense of self, transforming them into 'subjects' rather than just objects of racial oppression and discrimination. As Muslim women await marriage, or participate in a household where they may have limited power over decisions which affect their lives, they can be seen to reclaim their subjectivity through creating an autonomous space which they make their own. Some, as married women, will later take the step of moving out of the family home. The acquisition of a separate dwelling for married children is a growing reality in Oldham, Rochdale and Bradford, partly as a result of overcrowding. Thus, while young married couples may spend some time living with in-laws in the early years of marriage, growing numbers will acquire a home of their own.

Living together separately

A number of the young women in the focus groups were clear about the benefits of home-making outside the family home, although not all of them wished to make this sort of move. Those who had moved out, or wished to do so, particularly talked about the need for privacy and independence. References to being 'a person', or 'your own person' were common, signifying a desire on the part of the women to reclaim their subjectivity, to express a separate identity and to have a sense of self. A young Bangladeshi woman in Bradford, for example, commented:

As a married person, my husband's not married to the family, he's married to me, so therefore in order for me to work on my marriage I need to move out.

Moving out was also seen as a way of putting an end to conflicting roles for the women within the household. As one woman asked:

. . . are you going to act as a daughter or a wife? In your own home, you're a wife or a mother. You're a person. (Bangladeshi woman, Bradford)

The young women recognised that their views and expectations were often different from those of their parents' generation. Women in Oldham agreed that 'our parents put up with a lot more, and circumstances are different, and so we don't put up with things', while focus group participants in Rochdale talked about how moving out had become a rite of passage for many young women today, giving them 'independence . . . and some sort of responsibility'. It was, however, recognised that there would be variations between families and that not all girls would want to, or be able to, achieve such autonomy. The security, as well as the potential constraints, offered by the regulatory regime of the family was acknowledged.

The creation of a physically separate home space was viewed by many of the young women in our focus groups as providing a space in which some of the traditional Muslim constructions of femininity and womanhood could be challenged, particularly with respect to dress, religious practices and everyday behavioural norms. Some women also felt that normative constructions of men's roles and masculinity were challenged by a move from the family home, although it was thought that the strictures of family life were less pervasive for men. Several women observed that their husbands were less ready to move out of the family home than they were, commenting that they were 'too comfortable' where they were.

A number of different imaginaries and experiences of leaving the family home emerged from the focus group discussions. However, all accounts were underpinned by an explicit acknowledgement of the enduring importance of family connections. Responsibilities to parents were recognised, but so too was the need for continuing support from the wider family. The general ideal was summed up by many of these young people as '. . . not living in the same house upon marriage, but nearby'. Constructions of 'nearby', however, differed. Some women had moved to a house in the same street or within a few minutes' walk. In some of these cases, the move was as much a practical response to overcrowding as a quest for independence (although this may have been the unintended consequence). As one Bangladeshi woman living in Oldham explained, 'you've got your own separate houses, but you still spend a lot of time with the main family, like your parents or the grandparents or whoever it is'. Others had taken a decision (albeit constrained by the need for family approval) to move a little further away, beyond the immediate gaze of the family, and some had relocated beyond the established community areas to avoid the 'curtain twitching'. It was nevertheless evident that, for the most part, a move away did not equate to a desire to weaken family ties.

The continuing importance of family alongside the trend toward independent home-making emerged in a narrative of home spaces, which stretched across multiple sites of 'home'. Accounts of the lived experience of home revealed various modes of belonging to the family, which involved close associations as well as separation. Some young women perceived no dualism between the 'main' family home (a common descriptor) and their own separate home. Others simply depicted the home space as a blurring of the boundaries between two (or more) places at which they felt 'at home'. Narratives of home spaces which included the family home were intertwined with those of independence and the need for privacy. Young Muslim women portrayed themselves as capable agents, negotiating the spaces in between the family home and the separate dwelling-space they have claimed as their own. This destabilises the concept of home as a single physical entity, as exemplified in the following quote, where the duality of different sites is captured in slippages in the use of the term 'home':

> You've got your main house, and you've got your daughters and your sons, and they'll go home at night, but during the day they'll be there. The kids will be there, the grandparents will still look after the kids, and the children will go out to work. Like I always go home first, I go to my mother's house first, and then I go home afterwards. So it's just like you go to the main house and then you go to your own house . . . (Pakistani woman, Rochdale)

This making of a 'space in between' (a 'third space') performed varied functions. For some, it was a transitional space, separate but closely connected to the family. One young Bangladeshi woman living independently, for example, glimpsed her imagined self in another setting, but was not yet ready to take that risky step:

> I think when I'm more mature, secure financially, I would move out of the area into more of a nicer area . . . I'm still a bit scared, because obviously in a Muslim family you live all your life at home, you do live a sheltered life. The girls anyway . . . I wanted to start off close, ease myself out. (Bangladeshi woman, Oldham)

Other focus group participants had moved away from the Muslim community areas of Oldham, Rochdale and Bradford into what was perceived to be 'white' space (in reality, this was usually ethnically mixed rather than white). These moves were prompted by a desire for better housing, schools and neighbourhood amenities, better opportunities for inter-cultural mixing as well as a quest for greater privacy and independence. Feelings of ambivalence about crossing the physical boundaries between multi-ethnic and white space, self and other, were eased by the feeling that the home space extended back into their community.

More young British Muslims are moving into new spaces, although there are perceived risks attached. Women raised worries about racist harassment, racism, feeling 'out of place' and their capacity to fulfil their duty to transmit an Islamic identity on to their children if they lived in a 'white' area. Neighbourhoods beyond the ethnic community areas may thus be viewed as potential sites of anxiety, especially for veiled Muslim women, as compared with the relative predictability and security of inner areas.

Conclusions

This chapter reveals multiple experiences and constructions of home spaces among young British Muslim women. These extend from the micro-spaces of the bed-head to the multiple sites of home; from the act of 'leaving home' as an expression of resistance, to those who occupy 'spaces in between'. It reveals how, for these women, home can be a 'spatial imaginary', whose meaning reflects personal experiences in local contexts and extends across various scales to create and connect places. As Blunt and Dowling (2006) explore, home is not only a physical entity but also a 'state of being'.

The diversity of Muslim women's subject positions came through in this research. Our research participants had much in common in terms of age, class background, education and their experiences of living within established community areas in small, northern English, former textile towns. All regarded their Muslim faith as central to their identity, but they presented a range of different views on expressions of Muslim self, and on preferred housing and living arrangements. The recognition of different constructions of home and Muslim womanhood allows us to move beyond gendered discourses and dominant culturalist stereotypes that construct Muslim women as passive, subordinate and repressed. Some women displayed considerable agency in creating home spaces outside the family home and beyond the established community neighbourhoods. Others demonstrated their agency and resistance to family expectations in less overt but nevertheless significant ways, by creating micro-spaces that they could call their own. There were thus signs that some young Muslim women were challenging, sometimes in small ways, the places constructed for them by family and community.

It is important to acknowledge, however, that, even when there are displays of resistance, the experience of home is likely to be variable and full of contradictions. While the newly created home space can be a place for defiance and of freedom, privacy and autonomy, it can also be a place where gendered and patriarchal roles are re-inscribed through domestic rules, rituals and home-making. The chapter reveals widespread acceptance of the cultural norms of marriage and motherhood among the research participants, which contributes to the reproduction of the hetero-normative space of the Muslim home. While the expectation that British Muslim women will assume a life of domesticity is weakening as more women enter paid work, marriage may well be less negotiable. Women did not, however, necessarily view marriage as constraining; some perceived it as a route to a position of greater power in the domestic sphere. There was certainly evidence of there being room for women to makes their own spaces, even within constraining circumstances. Nevertheless, our quick glimpse at young men's views on domestic space, together with Hopkins' (2006) exploration of Muslim masculinities, suggests that gendered constructions of home and home-making remain a contested terrain.

Finally, this chapter provides insights into the role of home spaces in constructing and negotiating a place for young Muslim women in multicultural Britain. Women's experiences and expectations of home as a 'way of being' were underpinned by a number of different discursive frameworks of belonging and non-belonging. These ranged from the family and local community areas, to wider spaces of national and transnational citizenship. Women's discussions about where to live in Oldham, Rochdale and Bradford not only reflected practical considerations but also exposed feelings about 'their place' as Muslim women, through narratives of 'self' and accounts of being 'at home'.

Notes

1. The 'family home' is defined here as the home of either parents or in-laws.
2. Although marriage is taken for granted by many British Muslim women, studies have shown that women may engage in strategies to postpone marriage, at least until after higher education (Bagguley and Hussain: 2007).

References

Afshar, H. (1994), 'Muslim women in West Yorkshire: growing up with real and imaginary values amidst conflicting views of self and society', in H. Afshar and M. Maynard (eds), The Dynamics of Race and Gender, London: Taylor and Francis, pp. 127–47.

Afshar, H. (2006), 'Muslim women and the dilemma of hijab, terrorism and security in the UK', public lecture given to the Leeds Social Sciences Institute, University of Leeds, 16 November.

Afshar, H., Aitken, R. and Franks, M. (2005), Feminisms, Islamophobia and identities, Political Studies, 53(2), 262–83.

Bagguley, P. and Hussain, Y. (2007), The Role of Higher Education in providing Opportunities for South Asian Women, Bristol: Policy Press.

Blunt, A. (2005). 'Cultural geography: cultural geographies of home', Progress in Human Geography, 29, 505–15.

Blunt A. and Dowling, R. (2006), *Home*, London: Routledge.

Brah, A., Hickman, M. and Mac an Ghail, M. (1999), Thinking Identities, London: Palgrave Macmillan.

Domosh, M. (1998), 'Geography and gender: home again', Progress in Human Geography, 22, 276–82.

Dwyer, C. (1999), 'Veiled meanings: young British Muslim women and the negotiation of difference', Gender, Place and Culture, 6(1), 5–26.

Dwyer, C. (2000), 'Negotiating diasporic identities: young British South Asian Muslim women', Women's Studies International Forum, 23(4), 475–86.

Falah, G. and C. Nagel (eds) (2005), Geographies of Muslim Women: Gender, Religion and Space, New York and London: Guilford Press.

Fortier, A.-M., (2000), *Migrant Belongings: Memory, Space, Identity*, Oxford: Berg.

Gregson, N. and Lowe, M. (1995), 'Home-making: on the spatiality of social reproduction in contemporary middle-class Britain', Transactions of the Institute of British Geographers, 20, 224–35.

Harrison, M. and D. Phillips (2003), Housing and Black and Minority Ethnic Communities: Review of the Evidence Base, London: Office of the Deputy Prime Minister.

hooks, b. (1990), *Yearning: Race, Gender and Cultural Politics*, Boston: South End Press.

Hopkins, P. (2006), 'Youthful Muslim masculinities: gender and generational relations', Transactions of the Institute of British Geographers, 31(3), 337–52.

Hopkins, P. (2007), 'Young people, masculinities, religion and race: new social geographies', Progress in Human Geography, 31(2), 163–77.

Kandiyoti, D. (1993), 'Identity and its discontents; women and the nation', in P. Williams and L. Chrisman (eds), *Colonial Discourse and Postcolonial Theory: A Reader*, New York: Harvester Wheatsheaf, pp. 376–91.

McDowell, L. (1999), *Gender, Identity and Place: Understanding Feminist Geographies*, Cambridge: Polity Press.

Mohammad, R. (1999), 'Marginalisation, Islamism and the production of the "other"s' "other"', Gender, Place and Culture, 6, 221–40.

Mohammad, R., (2005), 'Negotiating spaces of the home, the education system and the labour market', in G. Faleh and C. Nagel (eds), Geographies of Muslim Women: Gender, Religion and Space, New York and London: Guilford Press, pp. 178–202.

Phillips, D. (2006), 'Parallel lives? Challenging discourses of British Muslim self-segregation', Environment and Planning D: Society and Space, 24(1), 25–40.

Poole, E. (2002), Reporting Islam: Media Representations of British Muslims, London: I. B. Tauris.

Qureshi, K. and Moores, S. (1999), 'Identity remix: tradition and translation in the lives of young Pakistani Scots', *European Journal of Cultural Studies*, 2(3), 311–30.

Rose G. (1993), *Feminism and Geography: The Limits of Geographical Knowledge*, Cambridge: Polity Press.

Shaheed, F. (1999), 'Constructing identities: culture, women's agency and the Muslim world', International Social Science Journal, 51, 61–73.

Sibley, D. (1995), Geographies of Exclusion, London: Routledge.

Simpson L. (2004), 'Statistics of racial segregation: measures, evidence and policy', *Urban Studies*, 41(3), 661–81.

Simpson L., Phillips, D. and Ahmed, S. (2007), Oldham and Rochdale: race, housing and community cohesion, Manchester: Cathie Marsh Centre for Census and Survey Research.

Soja, E. W. (1996), *ThirdSpace*, Oxford: Blackwell.

Valentine, G. (2000), 'Exploring children and young people's narratives of identity', *Geoforum*, 31, 257–67.

Warrington, M. (2001), 'The geographies of domestic violence', *Transactions of the Institute of British Geographers*, 26, 365–82.

Yuval-Davies, N. and Anthias, F. (eds) (1989), *Woman-Nation-State*, London: Macmillan.

'YOU SEEM VERY WESTERNISED TO ME': PLACE, IDENTITY AND OTHERING OF MUSLIM WORKERS IN THE UK LABOUR MARKET

Sophie Bowlby and Sally Lloyd-Evans

Introduction

In this chapter we will discuss the extent to which British Muslims have faced problems of integration into the work environment. We draw both on analyses of large-scale quantitative data sets and on our own and others' qualitative research on employees' and employers' motives, beliefs, aspirations and experiences relating to the employment of Pakistani Muslim ethnic minorities. While there are many studies examining the quantitative evidence of ethnic minorities' employment disadvantage, there are far fewer studies exploring British Muslims' experiences within the labour market. By exploring both the quantitative and qualitative data we hope to build up a more comprehensive picture of British Muslims' integration into the work environment.

The chapter is organised into two sections. In the first we discuss the quantitative evidence concerning British Muslims' employment and the types of explanation that are advanced for the differential success of distinct ethnic minority groups. In particular, we address the question of whether differences between the employment experiences of British Muslims and those of non-Muslims relate to differences in the success of particular ethnic minority groups as compared with other groups, including the white British majority, or are linked to religious affiliation. In the second section we draw on our own research with Pakistani Muslims to discuss the processes that may underlie these differences.

Is there an 'Islamic penalty' in employment?

There is now a considerable body of work that has explored the changing labour market situation of different ethnic minority groups in Britain since the 1960s. Most of this research has used either census data or large-scale surveys

[37]

of ethnic minorities. In terms of an understanding of the employment situation of Muslims today, and more specifically the likelihood of discrimination on grounds of their religion, it is important to note that, for all the studies we discuss in the following section, the data were collected prior to the attacks of 11 September 2001 and that any Islamophobia reflected in the data is likely to have intensified since then.

Many studies attempt to measure the difference between the employment outcomes that would be expected for ethnic minority individuals based on their human capital and the employment outcomes that are in fact observed. This difference is sometimes called an 'ethnic penalty' (Heath and McMahon 1997; Heath and Cheung 2006). Conceptually this 'penalty' is viewed as reflecting differences between the outcomes that would arise in a well-functioning and 'fair' labour market and those experienced by ethnic minorities. In such a market, differences in the employment success of individuals are assumed to result from differences in their 'human capital' – their skills and knowledge relevant to the labour market. An ethnic penalty may reflect factors such as: 'cultural' attributes of the group that affect their labour market behaviour; systematic differences in the economic opportunities in the places in which different ethnic groups live; or racial discrimination. The measures of human capital employed in these labour market studies include educational qualifications, age and sometimes English ability. Many studies also attempt to control for difference in the local economy by using measures of labour market buoyancy or a regional identifier.

A range of studies have shown that there are different ethnic penalties for different ethnic minority groups in Britain – although not all these studies use this concept (Modood et al. 1997; Owen 1997; Fieldhouse and Gould 1998; Model 1999, Clark and Drinkwater 2005; Simpson et al. 2006). In general, groups categorised as Pakistani and Bangladeshi, whose members are predominantly Muslim (92 per cent and 93 per cent respectively (Peach 2006)), are found to experience significant ethnic penalties in employment performance measured by rates of economic activity, unemployment and proportions in semi- or unskilled manual work. Cheng and Heath's (1993) analysis of the labour market returns on investment in education for first-generation migrants during the 1980s suggested that one process leading to the ethnic penalties they identified was discrimination based on skin colour. Indeed, most commentators argue that a significant element of these ethnic penalties results from 'racial' or 'ethnic' discrimination (for more direct evidence of discrimination see Commission for Racial Equality 1996).

The identification of ethnic penalties depends upon the identification of appropriately defined ethnic groups. Recent quantitative studies classify individuals' ethnicity using a census question which asks respondents to choose an 'ethnic group' affiliation from a predetermined list in which the categories are based partly on geographic origin or nationality and partly on colour (e.g. black African or Indian). It is widely acknowledged that the census categories may group together culturally diverse people and hence do not always identify meaningful 'ethnic groups' (Bulmer 1999). Insofar as the 'culture' of a group – in which religious practice is likely to be a significant element – may affect the ways in which members of the group engage with the labour market, the limitations of these definitions can affect attempts to identify cultural factors influencing their labour market 'success'. In the 2001 Census a further question was added in which people were asked to identify their religious affiliation. The inclusion of this question has made it possible to try to disentangle the effects of religion from those of 'ethnicity' as defined in government categories.

Peach (2006) shows that, in terms of census ethnic categories, Muslims are ethnically diverse. Although 68 per cent are of South Asian origin, 12 per cent are White, 6 per cent Other Asian, 7 per cent Black and 4 per cent 'Chinese or other'. The Muslim population is strongly concentrated in areas of economic disadvantage, young and growing rapidly; just under half are British born (46 per cent) and have poor levels of qualification compared to other groups (nearly two-fifths or 40 per cent are recorded as having no British educational qualifications, as compared to about a quarter of the total population). One of its most important characteristics is the low rate of participation of women in the formal labour market. Seventy per cent of Muslim women aged 25 and over were economically inactive, as compared to 41 per cent overall in the 2001 Census. This fact, alongside larger families, will lead to low household income. In summing up the employment situation of the Muslim population Peach writes: 'Muslims experienced the highest unemployment rates, the highest proportions of long-term unemployed and the lowest occupational profile' (Peach 2006: 645).

It appears that the Muslims of Britain are a disadvantaged population and that people from other religious groups fare better in the employment market. So – does following the Muslim faith in some way create disadvantage in the employment market or is it simply that people from ethnic groups whose religion is Islam are doing badly in the employment market for reasons unconnected with their religion? Is there an 'Islamic penalty' as Lindley (2002) suggests on the basis of an analysis of data from the 1994 National Survey of Ethnic Minorities (Modood et al. 1997)? A number of studies emphasise the complexity of the relationships and the difficulty of coming to a clear conclusion. For example, Brown (2000) found that the employment rates and job profiles of Muslims from South Asia were affected by their ethnicity. A recent study by Clark and Drinkwater (2005), while concluding that 'controlling for other factors, Muslims have lower employment rates than individuals with another, or indeed no, religious affiliation', also points out that 'separating the influences of ethnicity and religion is extremely difficult, both conceptually and empirically' (2005: 30). Religion is part and parcel of the ethnic identity of most Muslim groups and has been interwoven with the development of the cultural identity of these groups both before and after their arrival in Britain (Brown, 2000).

The quantitative studies suggest that there is some form of 'Islamic penalty'.

We suggest that a full understanding of the employment situation of Muslim ethnic minorities requires us to disentangle first, the social processes involved in 'racial' or 'religious' discrimination experienced by Muslims and second, the various ways in which religious commitment and observance, so often bound up with cultural identity and political identification, might impact upon the labour market behaviour of Muslims. It also requires us to examine the relationship between Islam, cultural tradition and women's involvement in the labour market, which we explore further in the next section of this chapter. This latter element is left largely undebated by the authors we have discussed above, apart from an acknowledgment that women's labour market participation is low among Muslim ethnic minority groups.

It is also important to consider generational differences and the role of anti-racist activism in different places (Virdee 2006). We need to understand in what ways the class origins and political activism of the first generation of immigrant Muslims are affecting the socio-economic situation and activism of young second- or third-generation British-born Muslims and how, in turn, this influences their employment prospects. We suggest that we need more in-depth case studies of the processes involved in the employment disadvantage of men and women in different Muslim groups, including smaller Muslim groups such as those from Eastern Europe, Somalia and other African countries, to set alongside the broad-brush picture that emerges from large-scale data.

In the next section of the chapter we contribute to the small body of case studies of the employment of Muslim minorities in Britain by looking at qualitative data drawn from our own studies of the employment experiences of Muslim Pakistanis in Reading and Slough, two towns in the economically successful South East. Pakistanis exemplify many of the characteristics of Muslims within Britain. Nationally, British Pakistanis have poor employment outcomes, tend to live in relatively segregated areas with high levels of deprivation, and only about 24 per cent of women over 25 are economically active. They constitute 42 per cent of the Muslim population of England and Wales (Peach 2006).

The case of Pakistani muslim workers in Reading and Slough

Between 1995 and 1996, we conducted two research projects examining the labour market aspirations of twenty-seven first-generation Pakistani Muslim female migrants living in Reading, aged between 25 and 60, and twenty-five second-generation young women aged 16–24. We conducted in-depth, semi-structured interviews with both groups of women to gain insight into the issues surrounding Pakistani Muslim women's access to paid work during their lifecourse (Lloyd Evans et al. 1995, 1996). Between 1998 and 2001, we undertook a further research project exploring the ways in which processes of racialised gendering influence young people's labour market aspirations and opportunities in Reading and Slough (Bowlby, et al. 2002, 2004). As part of this project we interviewed thirty Pakistani Muslim men and women aged 16–24 and forty-three employers – twenty-three in Slough and twenty in Reading. The employers were selectd to be broadly representative of employers in the two towns.[1] (Further details of our methodology can be found in the references above.) The interviews focused on the firms' hiring practices, with particular reference to young people, and also discussed the kinds of skills employers looked for, their assessment of the quality of applicants and the local labour market situation. Since one of the projects was focused on women, we have more information on women than on men and this imbalance is reflected in our discussion. There is an urgent need for more research with young Muslim men on issues of employability, aspirations and experiences of paid work.

The Pakistani populations of Reading and Slough are predominantly working class, with origins in the rural district of Mirpur, an area with a long tradition of out-migration for economic reasons. However, there is a small Pakistani middle class. Pakistanis in both towns are residentially concentrated in one or two areas. Both towns are in the M4 corridor west of London, with very low levels of recorded unemployment. In both, the service sector has replaced manufacturing as the dominant sector in terms of employment numbers, although Slough has retained a larger manufacturing sector. The early immigrants in both places worked largely in manufacturing and manual work and many lost employment as firms moved away or cut labour during the 1970s and early 1980s. Manufacturing firms now direct recruitment towards highly skilled engineering and white-collar employees, while the public sector, IT and software and the retail sector account for much service employment. Most employers and public sector agencies believe there is a skills mismatch in the local labour market and that the skills levels of young people are failing to keep up with the demands of local employers. Despite this, 91 per cent of the Pakistani Muslim youth we interviewed had undertaken some form of paid work.

This history and current situation in the two towns are reflected in the statistics on pages 42 and 43. In these tables the religious categories used are those defined by Census responses to a question on religious affiliation, which show both that unemployment is lower and activity rates higher than among Muslims nationally and that Muslims in both towns (who are predominantly Pakistani – 63 per cent in Reading and 82 per cent in Slough) do significantly worse than other religious groups on both measures. In particular, unemployment rates are nearly double those of the total population, with Reading Muslims faring slightly better than those in Slough. Table 3.2 gives details of the occupations of religious groups in both towns. The greater importance of manufacturing in Slough than in Reading is signalled in the figures for 'process, plant and machine operatives', but what is particularly striking is the importance of this category for Muslim men in both towns as compared both to the experience of Muslims elsewhere and to the occupational characteristics of the Christian population. For women it is 'sales and customer service occupations' that stand out

Table 3.1 Male and female economic activity and unemployment rates for selected religious groups: 2001 Census

Men aged 16+

		Reading %	Slough %	England and Wales %
Economically active				
	All people	78.58	79.11	73.80
	Christian	76.97	79.11	72.66
	Hindu	85.49	79.68	74.40
	Muslim	70.42	70.11	64.49
	Sikh	76.85	78.86	73.28
Unemployed	All people	3.01	4.23	4.29
	Christian	2.65	3.31	3.68
	Hindu	1.59	3.45	3.79
	Muslim	5.93	7.69	9.47
	Sikh	4.03	3.86	5.40

Women aged 16+

		Reading %	Slough %	England and Wales %
Economically active				
	All people	64.56	64.07	59.50
	Christian	64.20	66.93	59.20
	Hindu	58.87	61.99	59.36
	Muslim	38.06	38.05	30.88
	Sikh	64.31	69.06	59.33
Unemployed	All people	3.01	4.23	4.29
	Christian	2.65	3.31	3.68
	Hindu	1.59	3.45	3.79
	Muslim	5.93	7.69	9.47
	Sikh	4.03	3.86	5.40

Source: 2001 Census: Standard Area Statistics (England and Wales). Table S153 The religious categories are those defined by the Census from responses to a question on religious affiliation.

in a similar way. If the profile as a whole is examined, it appears that although Muslims in Reading and Slough are more likely to be employed than Muslims in England and Wales as a whole, they are also somewhat less likely to be in managerial and professional occupations and more likely to be on the lower rungs of the occupational ladder.

In our research we focused on the ways in which aspirations to engage in paid work and success in doing so were bound up with people's gendered and racialised identities. Brah has argued that 'structure, culture and agency are . . . inextricably linked, mutually inscribing formations' (Brah 1994: 152)

Table 3.2 Religion and occupation in Reading and Slough (% of population)

	Christian			Hindu			Muslim			Sikh		
MALES	Reading	Slough	E & W	Reading	Slough	E & W	Reading	Slough	E & W	Reading	Slough	E & W
1. Managers and senior officials	17.67	16.49	18.73	16.41	17.19	21.53	9.73	11.78	16.03	24.44	11.78	19.16
2. Professional occupations	15.29	9.27	10.70	41.31	24.86	22.39	13.98	10.89	12.38	14.22	12.06	12.48
3. Associate professional and technical occupations	13.12	12.28	12.96	9.65	11.72	11.12	7.64	7.55	8.07	14.22	8.13	9.23
4. Administrative and secretarial occupations	6.72	6.69	5.21	7.92	8.37	7.91	6.95	7.06	5.96	7.11	7.53	5.84
5. Skilled trades occupations	17.46	19.48	20.73	3.67	6.89	9.06	8.57	9.83	12.65	8	12.50	13.13
6. Personal service occupations	1.84	2.55	2.06	3.09	1.55	1.44	2.01	1.67	1.95	1.33	0.84	1.09
7. Sales and customer service occupations	4.93	4.21	3.71	3.86	8.82	8.78	9.96	10.38	9.35	7.56	8.03	7.80
8. Process, plant and machine operatives	9.8	14.53	13.79	4.25	9.08	8.74	21.93	23.92	17.35	12.44	19.89	18.33
9. Elementary occupations	13.17	14.42	12.12	9.85	11.53	9.04	19.23	16.92	16.27	10.67	16.57	12.93
Total	100	100	100	100	100	100	100	100	100	100	100	100
Total no. of Males	23701	16914	8766K	518	1553	149,851	1295	3286	279,194	225	2976	80,140
FEMALES	Reading	Slough	E & W	Reading	Slough	E & W	Reading	Slough	E & W	Reading	Slough	E & W
1. Managers and senior officials	11.43	11.27	10.91	9.28	9.94	11.66	5.22	5.28	9.37	15.3	7.93	11.28
2. Professional occupations	11.42	7.04	9.17	23.71	14.21	13.77	10.13	9.50	12.48	13.11	7.12	8.88
3. Associate professional and technical occupations	15.49	14.96	13.62	15.46	11.77	11.84	9.97	9.74	11.75	7.1	10.82	10.73
4. Administrative and secretarial occupations	24.39	28.38	23.32	21.31	22.14	22.31	21.68	21.06	19.89	21.86	19.56	19.50
5. Skilled trades occupations	1.76	2.03	2.42	1.03	1.22	1.49	1.90	1.82	1.78	0	3.31	2.18
6. Personal service occupations	10.79	12.39	13.37	7.56	5.32	5.62	10.44	9.15	12.02	4.92	5.47	6.49
7. Sales and customer service occupations	12.67	11.47	11.93	13.06	17.87	15.57	23.42	21.82	17.36	17.49	15.09	14.57
8. Process, plant and machine operatives	1.65	2.36	3.05	0	6.89	7.66	1.42	5.92	4.67	4.37	11.21	12.03
9. Elementary occupations	10.41	10.11	12.21	8.59	10.64	10.07	15.82	15.72	10.68	15.85	19.48	14.34
Total	100	100	100	100	100	100	100	100	100	100	100	100
Total no. of Females	21566	16044	8179K	291	1147	116,495	632	1705	122,809	183	2597	66,755

Source: 2001 Census: Standard Area Statistics (England and Wales). Table S154

producing multiply determined identities which are simultaneously racialised and gendered. Racialised and gendered social categories are not fixed but nevertheless can serve as stereotypes in relation to which individuals position themselves and which may be used by employers and co-workers in judging a person as a worker. These social categories will shape different people's ideas of what 'being Muslim' entails for men and women and will operate at a variety of scales: for example, through neighbourhood social networks; through local media and local institutions such as mosques, schools, political and leisure groups; through the national press, the internet and diasporic social linkages.

From our research with Pakistanis, we identify three interlinked sets of disadvantages which might produce an 'Islamic penalty' in the UK labour market. In all cases the socio-economic processes producing these disadvantages are bound up with locally distinctive social relations on a variety of scales including the neighbourhood, town or regional scale: (i) disadvantages stemming from restricted social networks; (ii) disadvantages stemming from employers' expectations and behaviours; (iii) socio-cultural barriers stemming from Muslim people's social situation and reactions to that situation. We now discuss each of these in turn.

Neighbourhood and networks

The quantitative studies discussed above found that even after allowing for the effect of living in a ward with high unemployment, Muslims seemed to suffer an employment penalty. At the neighbourhood scale Bauder (2001) has argued that there is a link between place-specific cultural experiences, residential segregation and labour market segmentation. In particular he suggests that 'local structures of feeling shape labour market identities' (Bauder 2001: 43). Such 'structures of feeling' include understandings of the role of paid work in men and women's lives and the desirability of different occupations. These understandings are mediated through social interactions within a particular neighbourhood. Such social interactions may also provide information about job availability and act as conduits for employers' recruitment (Hanson and Pratt 1995).

The prevalence of areas of Pakistani residential concentration in 'ethnic enclaves', the significance of maintaining close relationships within the *biraderi* (the kin and quasi-kin social network) (Peach 2007, Shaw 1994) and the importance of maintaining family honour (*izzat*) through acceptable behaviour mean that Pakistanis rely strongly on within-group and within-neighbourhood social contacts for information about jobs and ideas of what constitutes acceptable work for men and women. In our studies we found that for young people of all backgrounds the social networks of parents and friends were very important to finding the first part-time job – over half had found their first job by this route. These networks were usually focused around the neighbourhood and school. However, young Pakistanis in both towns were more likely to find their first jobs through peers or cold-calling than through family and we suggest that this reflected the lack of employment of mothers and the perceived unsuitability of fathers' occupations as a source of employment (Bowlby et al. 2004).

The social networks of an individual are central not only in creating a picture of the jobs that may be available, and socially acceptable, but also to locating a specific vacancy. Using peer-group friends for job search biases information flows, since such friends often share the same gender, ethnicity, class and neighbourhood. In both towns we found some employers had become the preserve of a particular ethnic, gender and class group for part-time work. For example, in Reading and Slough we found evidence that certain manufacturing firms had targeted Pakistani Muslim women employees in the past and employed them in textiles or in 'packing halls'. While such links can be initially advantageous, they can create problems later, when factories close or if this 'type' of work comes to be identified with Pakistani Muslims.

Among the older women in Reading, the positions of their husbands and extended family within local social networks were of fundamental importance to their incorporation into the job market. About half of our sample either had not worked in Britain or had no work experience. With the exception of the professionally qualified women we spoke to, many second-generation job seekers entered families in which paid work for women was not established. As a result, they lacked knowledge of work opportunities, recruitment processes and training schemes. Among young people, locally based experiences at school and at home were important to job aspirations, attitudes to and experiences of education, training and employment and ideas about the work opportunities for people 'like them'. For our respondents, ideas about 'good jobs' were restricted to professions that are either highly visible to parents or highly visible in their community, such as doctors, teachers, pharmacists or accountants. The construction of this yardstick leaves many young people with few alternatives and possibly a sense of failure. When talking to a number of young women in Reading sixth forms we were surprised by their limited knowledge of the professional careers they wanted to pursue. For example, one young women said she was hoping to study medicine as it seemed 'an easy option' and 'non-stressful'.

Politics and employers' expectations and behaviours

At the scale of the town we found that the politics of race and ethnicity were significant influences on the labour market, particularly in Slough. Slough is a multi-ethnic town in which the presence of non-white people and a diversity of cultural and religious practices are evident in daily life. In the 2001 Census the ethnic minority population made up 37 per cent of Slough's population, of whom 14,360 were Pakistanis. In Reading the ethnic minority population was

13 per cent in 2001, of whom only 4,000 were recorded as Pakistani. Perhaps unsurprisingly, at the time when we did our research in the late 1990s, political activity concerning race and anti-racism was less developed in Reading than in Slough. Slough employers were fairly knowledgeable about issues of discrimination and questions of ethnic and religious sensitivity. In contrast, Reading employers were ill informed and, when asked about the (lack of) employment of ethnic minorities, employers were likely to say 'they don't apply for jobs' but claimed that 'if the need arose' they would be happy to make provision for religious practices, such as prayer rooms and appropriate dress. Thus, in Reading, ignorance could lead to insensitivity and failure to try to recruit among ethnic minorities. In Slough, however, employers' claims that they recognised cultural difference sometimes slipped into stereotyped and negative views about the 'problems' posed by employing young Muslim Asians as opposed to other minority ethnic groups, as we detail below.

Firstly, many Slough employers complained that Pakistani Muslims – both men and women – often want to take a large amount of leave to return to Pakistan at short notice or take leave too often for religious celebrations such as Eid. Furthermore, Slough employers linked their experiences to the widespread national discourse that presents Muslim women as passive subjects, controlled by male family members and unable to participate fully in the paid labour market. These employers claimed that the demands of the family take precedence over the demands of the job, especially for women, and that parents did not take daughters' employment seriously. This essentialisation of Muslim women as a homogeneous group cast them as 'problematic' employees who are likely to be less flexible and committed than others. While we spoke with some young women whose paid-work careers were restricted by parents, family attitudes varied immensely: our interviews showed wide variability in the extent and severity of these restrictions, whereas Slough employers tended to talk as if negative experience they had had with specific employees applied to all.

Young Muslim men can also be subject to a different set of discourses that identify them as potential troublemakers, due to press reports of fighting and inter-ethnic tensions, which we found to be commonplace in Slough. Both Pakistani women and the few Pakistani men we spoke to said that finding work was more problematic for the young men than for the young women. For example: 'One thing, it's harder for boys to get jobs than girls . . . because boys, especially Asian boys, Pakistani boys in Slough, haven't you heard of them, Slough boys? – they've got bit of a reputation for being trouble . . .' (young Pakistani woman, 17, Slough).

Secondly, Muslim women are often perceived by employers as 'not fitting in' with corporate identities in terms of dress, appearance and styles of communication. The growth of service occupations has resulted in the increased salience of the cultural attributes and working identities of potential employees. Employees are required to have self-presentation, communication styles and social ambitions that are 'acceptable' within the environment of the firm and in its relations with the public (Duster, 1995). People who are seen as strongly different in 'manners' and social style are likely to be disadvantaged in such labour markets. For example, jobs in the retail sector may require a certain look, an image to which some Muslim women may not conform. One of our young respondents said:

> I think [my employers] believe that they [Muslim women] don't look as professional as somebody else. I mean when they show you the uniforms and the pictures that they have in their magazines . . . it's like their way of doing it, she has nice little earrings, normally a bobbed hairstyle, perfect make-up, its always the same sort of colours, they've got their ideas of the same colours of shoes and tights they prefer too. They've got their idea of the image they are looking for and Asian girls don't fit it. (Young woman in employment with high street retailer)

Recent political controversy over the rights of Muslim women to wear the veil has heightened sensitivities around dress and appearance. While many employers now allow women to alter uniforms to accommodate the wearing of trousers or hijab, the debate over the acceptability of veils continues. Hopkins and Patel (2006) report that increasing numbers of British Muslim women are reasserting their Islamic identity by adopting the hijab. For many, the hijab is a form of resistance against male attention, which allows them to move freely in public places, but also against Islamaphobia (Hopkins and Patel 2006, Dwyer 1999). Hopkins and Patel (2006) found that women who are 'visibly' Muslim are more likely to report discrimination in the labour market than those who adopt a more western appearance when they are in public spaces. For others, conforming to a more western appearance is a survival strategy that enables them to feel more accepted in the labour market.

Without conscious attempts to resist the tendency, demands that employees are socially acceptable to employers and co-workers tend to perpetuate the gender, ethnic and class characteristics of existing employees. These demands lead firms towards socially 'safe' employees – in the south-east of England we suggest these will be people who can use broadly middle-class, 'English' styles of communication. One young second-generation woman gave this account of being interviewed for a job as a shop assistant in Reading:

> she [the person interviewing her for the job] said 'you seem quite westernised to me', I was going 'thank you' [ironically], she goes 'you don't mind wearing the overalls that come to the knee', and I said 'I don't mind' . . . it's just a natural assumption that you will mind.

Also, our employer interviews suggest that the image of the 'good' young employee is not only white English and 'middle class' but also 'feminine'. This leaves non-white young men in a potentially difficult situation where they are especially likely to have difficulties in obtaining employment and associated work experience.

Socio-cultural obstacles to employment – gendered working identities

Education, training and qualifications

Previous research has shown that education and academic qualifications are highly valued in Muslim families living in the UK. Although Pakistani Muslim women have lower economic participation rates than other ethnic groups, there is a marked improvement in the academic attainment and work aspirations of second-generation women. Moreover, women with further education seem more determined to work and manage childcare than those without (Dale et al. 2002; Tyrer and Ahmad 2006).

However, qualifications do not guarantee appropriate employment. Among the twenty-seven first-generation female migrants in Reading, we identified a group of middle-class women who identified themselves as 'professional'. In Pakistan they had established themselves as professional workers, but they found on arrival in Britain that their qualifications and work experience were not recognised. For example, one respondent had to work as an 'unqualified' teacher for several years till her professional status was finally recognised. Several of the professional women took over ten years to gain entry into the professions they left in Pakistan and to be established in professional Reading networks.

Among the young women born in the UK, aged 16–25, academic qualifications were generally considered important and education represented a path for social mobility for many individuals and their families. Academic aspirations among young women and their parents were often polarised between families that wanted their daughters to qualify in medicine or law and those who only aimed for the secondary labour market. If unable to attain a place in professional training, some very capable young women were relegated to low-paid office and retail work. Parents, particularly mothers who have not experienced paid work, can lack understanding of the wider UK labour market and this can impact negatively on the employment prospects of their children. Dale et al. (2002) report similar findings in Oldham.

Teachers' attitudes towards the career prospects of young Muslims are also important. There was a consensus among our young interviewees that some teachers have a stereotypical image of 'young Muslim women' as submissive, uninterested in work and prevented by family or community pressures from pursuing a career. In such cases, girls argued that they were channelled into traditional caring and vocational roles, regardless of ability. One woman said:

> throughout the whole school time I was under the impression that I'm not going to become anything. I ain't going to be able to do anything [paid work] so why bother, so it was a big doss.

The educational attainment of young Muslim boys is often similar to that of young white working-class boys and they face similar obstacles to the labour market. Some of the young Muslim boys we spoke to had experienced low expectations from teachers – 'she told me to be a builder or a taxi driver' (Pakistani man, 19). Young men talked about the pressure from parents for them to stay at school to improve their job chances but found that parents' desire to help them with job choices was limited by parents' lack of knowledge about training and career options. These findings are supported by other research studies (Dale et al. 2002; Tyrer and Ahmad 2006) which argue that, while education is a vehicle for mobility, the stereotypical attitudes of many teachers and career advisors and parental lack of knowledge can have a negative impact on the aspirations and attainment of Muslim youth.

For young women and men, participation in work experience can be a valuable method of gaining labour market experience, challenging preconceived ideas about different jobs. Work experience can provide 'something of an insight into the field of work, showing you what's out there in the big wide world' (young woman in Reading). Disappointingly, we found that young Pakistani men and women had lower participation rates in school work experience schemes (57 per cent and 62 per cent) than white men (68 per cent) and women (75 per cent). Discussions with agencies involved in work experience placements in Reading and Slough suggest that it is becoming more difficult to find placements for pupils from schools with high number of Asian students.

Family, community and attitudes to paid work

Attitudes of family and the wider community are central to the formation of all young people's ideas about work and acceptable occupations. Among Pakistanis, men are expected to enter the labour market, but the importance of the idea that women are caregivers and reproducers can lead to different expectations.

Most women believed that parenting should take precedence over personal career aspirations. All but three of the first-generation women over 25 undertook the main responsibility for the household and childcare and did not expect or desire that this might change. The majority of our respondents who had experience of paid work had fluctuated between part-time and full-time work while their children were young. It is important to note, however, that four professional respondents and three older, less-well-educated women were the main breadwinners of their household. Due to the lack of childcare provision, social networks and assistance in the household, the problems faced by most British women in combining motherhood with paid work are magnified for the women we interviewed. One respondent commented that in Pakistan other household members assist with housework and childcare when women want to engage in paid work, but 'it doesn't work like that here'.

Many of the first- and second-generation younger women with families were happy to stay at home with their children if they were financially secure. By contrast, many older non-professional women sought paid work as a financial survival strategy for their families and were willing to consider most jobs, regardless of status. Listening to their accounts, it became clear that they had been redefining their gender roles – which had been focused on the home and highly influenced by the norms in their class and place of origin – by adopting the dominant British view which says that 'it is good for women to work'. However, many of these women who were seeking work for the first time lacked experience, confidence and skills.

The role of paid work in women's lives thus depended on how the paid work available locally was seen by the women, and those around them, to relate to their roles as wives. Women are expected to make a home for the husband, socialise the next generation and provide care to the husband's extended family. Paid work is usually secondary to these obligations. For example, one married women we interviewed said that unsuitable work for a Muslim women was 'any work which undermines women's ability to run the home'. Some women commented that their families feared that a 'working woman' could bring shame on them as a public advertisement of the inability of the husband to provide sufficiently for his family. In addition, the current provision of childcare for preschool-age children is unacceptable and unaffordable for many families.

However, contrary to the ideas held by many employers, family obligations do not mean that women do not want to work, rather that they are less likely engage in paid work until their families are older and they will then seek part-time, flexible jobs. In their research, Tyrer and Ahmed (2006) also stress the importance attached to women's 'right to choose' paid work. However, for many women, family responsibilities tend to channel them into low-paid service sector work with little opportunity for career enhancement and training, regardless of their skills and qualifications.

Working identities and notions of acceptable work

For individuals and families it is increasingly important to maintain acceptance within the Muslim community, since the outside, white, non-Muslim world is becoming more hostile. Within Muslim communities a high premium is put on maintaining cultural solidarity and the moral values of Islam. The lax sexual morals of white society are seen as a major threat to the maintenance of a distinctive Muslim culture and women's behaviour is central to cultural differentiation from mainstream white UK society. Mixing with men who are not kin in a situation that is not adequately controlled can compromise such values. Although all the young women we interviewed intended to work or were working, in both Reading and Slough our interviewees spoke of pressure on parents from the 'community' to ensure that daughters behaved acceptably. These attitudes affect the nature of the working environment that is considered suitable for women. Jobs in feminised sectors such as education – 'there is not so much involvement with males in the school environment' – were often preferred to 'office environments, where there is a freer mixing of the sexes is not so suitable'.

This pressure leads to limitations on paid work. For example: 'I'm quite lucky to work as well because I'm Asian and there's a lot of Asian people that are not allowed to work, like my friends here, hardly any of them work' (young Pakistani woman, 16, Reading, interviewed at school). Some women, as with Dwyer's interviewees (Dwyer 1999), counterposed a religious identity based on informed reading of the Qur'an, which they endorsed, to a 'cultural' identity as Pakistani, which they wished to challenge. This strategy allowed them to question the undesirability of paid work for women. Many of these women wore the hijab with western dress that conformed with Islamic principles.

In contrast, for the young Pakistani men, entering paid work, especially to become a doctor or lawyer – occupations few had the educational qualifications to attain – was an expected part of their gendered and racialised identity. The large South Asian community in Slough gave legitimacy to South Asian employment: 'Slough is a very Asian oriented town . . . it's easier for Asians to get work'. However, the size of the community seemed more helpful to young Pakistani women than men. There are more press reports of Asian young men as belligerent, disaffected and difficult in Slough than in Reading, even though there is no evidence that the incidence of disaffection among young Pakistani men is actually greater in Slough.

In contrast, the visibility of young Muslim women in Slough as employees encouraged others and, specifically, made them feel that wearing shalwaar kameez or the hijab was acceptable to employers. In Slough the greater size of the Pakistani community provides more, and more varied, 'role models' of working Pakistani women for both parents and daughters so that the 'risks' of nonconformity appear less in Slough than in Reading. However, some young women in Reading said the small size of Reading's Pakistani population made 'community policing' less effective than in Slough – 'everyone knows your business there'. Although negative images of young Pakistani men were less prevalent in Reading than in Slough, some felt a lack of acceptance by white groups and a sense of isolation through not living in a large Muslim community. In both towns some young men had aspirations that seemed out of line with their qualifications, and for these there is a risk that frustration of their aspirations may result in involvement in petty crime.

Conclusions

We suggest that in western labour markets, Muslim communities are subject to a particular form of 'othering' that can be partly attributed to the highly visible expressions of their religious identities and also to the high value accorded to spending time on religion and family relationships. Visible religious markers such as dress and appearance, notions of appropriate social behaviour and gendered roles are inextricably bound to the working lives and identities of Muslim workers. Current 'racial discrimination' against Muslims may be linked to a fear of terrorism that makes employers more hostile to overt expressions of 'Muslimness' such as wearing the hijab or full beards, or praying during the working day. Moreover, in a society that places such high value on 'work', economic productivity and wealth, it is sometimes difficult for employers to understand communities that so explicitly value religion and family. These two factors combine to produce an 'Islamic penalty' within the UK labour market that manifests itself in a number of ways:

Firstly, ideas held by employers about employability skills, stereotypes of the role of work in Muslim families and a distrust of people who express visible religious difference are being translated into a discourse which identifies Muslim employees as 'unskilled' and 'problematic'. Secondly, this discourse is highly gendered and creates particular barriers for Muslim women, who can be seen as 'reluctant' workers in the UK labour market. More recently, young Muslim men may be seen as 'undesirable' and potentially 'subversive'. Thirdly, there are sociocultural barriers to participation in paid work common to working-class groups but exacerbated by a lack of knowledge of the range of current job opportunities and poor social networks for job seekers. As we have sought to highlight, these processes will produce different barriers to work in different places. In multicultural spaces like Slough, a significant Pakistani Muslim community can work to reduce the impact of 'othering' by employers and agencies as Muslim workers become more visibly represented in the local labour market and help to build social networks. However, such representations do not always work to reduce negative stereotypes held by employers and may indeed perpetuate barriers to work based on narratives about the experiences of employing Muslim workers. This is in opposition to places like Reading, where 'othering' is more simplistic and based on a lack of awareness and understanding of ethnic and religious diversity.

Notes

1. Nomis and Census data on the economic structure of the two areas was used to ensure that the firms were broadly representative of the variety of firms in the area, in terms of both size and sector. Firms were selected from a list provided by Thames Valley Enterprise (the local Training and Enterprise Council), supplemented by firms listed in the Yellow Pages. In Reading letters of invitation were sent out to firms and followed up with a phone call. In Slough firms were contacted via the local Education-Business Partnership in return for our involvement with a questionnaire survey of the skill requirements of firms in the Slough area. Two training agencies and two private recruitment agencies were also interviewed. The majority of the interviews were tape-recorded and subsequently transcribed.

References

Bauder, H. (2001), 'Culture in the labour market: segmentation theory and perspectives of place', *Progress in Human Geography*, 25(1), 37–52.

Bowlby, S., Lloyd-Evans, S. and Roche, C. (2002), 'Becoming a paid worker: images and identity', in T. Skelton and G. Valentine (eds), *Cool Places: Geographies of Youth Culture*, London: Routledge.

Bowlby, S., Lloyd-Evans, S. and Roche, C. (2004), 'Youth employment, racialised gendering, and school-work transitions', in M. Boddy and M. Parkinson (eds), *City Matters: Competitiveness, Cohesion and Urban Governance*, Bristol: Policy Press.

Brah, A. (1994), '"Race" and "culture" in the gendering of labour markets', in H. Afshar and M. Maynard (eds), *The Dynamics of Race and Gender: Some Feminist Interventions*, London: Taylor and Francis.

Brown, M. S. (2000), 'Religion and economic activity in the South Asian population', *Ethnic and Racial Studies*, 23(6), 1035–61.

Bulmer, M. (1999), Question Bank Topic Commentary on Ethnicity, http://qb.soc. surrey.ac.uk/topics/ethnicity/ethnicitymartin%20bulmer.pdf [The Question Bank is an ESRC-funded internet social survey resource based in the Department of Sociology, University of Surrey.]

Cheng, Y. and Heath, A. (1993), 'Ethnic origins and class destinations', Oxford Review of Education, 19(2), 151–65.

Clark, K. and Drinkwater, S. (2005), *Dynamic and Diversity: Ethnic Employment differences in England and Wales, 1991–2001*, IZA Discussion Paper No. 1698, Forschungsinstitut zur Zukunft der Arbeit (Institute for the Study of Labour), Bonn: University of Bonn.

Commission for Racial Equality (CRE) (1996), *We Regret to Inform You . . .*, London: Commission for Racial Equality.

Dale, A., Shaheen, N., Kalra, V. and Fieldhouse, E. (2002), 'Routes into education and employment for young Pakistani and Bangladeshi women in the UK', *Ethnic and Racial Studies*, 25(6), 942–68.

Duster, T. (1995), 'Postindustrialisation and youth employment: African Americans as harbingers', in K. McFate, R. Lawson and W. J. Wilson (eds), *Poverty, Inequality and the Future of Social Policy: Western States in the New World Order*, New York: Russell Sage Foundation.

Dwyer, C. (1999) 'Veiled meanings: young British Muslim women and the negotiation of differences', Gender, Place and Culture, 6(1), 5–26.

Fieldhouse, E. A. and Gould, M. I. (1998), 'Ethnic minority unemployment and local labour market conditions in Great Britain', *Environment and Planning A*, 30(5), 833–53.

Hanson, S. and Pratt, G. (1995), *Gender, Work and Space*, London: Routledge.

Heath, A. and Cheung, S. Y. (2006), *Ethnic Penalties in the Labour Market*, Research Report No. 341, Leeds: Department for Work and Pensions, Corporate Document Services.

Heath, A. and McMahon, D. (1997), 'Education and occupational attainments: the impact of ethnic origins', in V. Karn (ed.) *Ethnicity in the 1991 Census*, London: TSO.

Hopkins, A. and Patel, K. (2006), 'Reflecting on gender equality in Muslim contexts in Oxfam GB', *Gender and Development*, 14(3), 423–35.

Lindley, J. (2002), 'Race or religion? The impact of religion on the employment and earnings of Britain's ethnic communities', *Journal of Ethnic and Migration Studies*, 28(3), 427–42.

Lloyd-Evans, S., Bowlby, S. and Mohammad, R. (1995), *Pakistani Women's Experience of the Labour Market in Reading: Barriers, Aspirations and Opportunities, Report I*, University of Reading in Association with the Pakistani Community Centre, Reading (available from the authors).

Lloyd-Evans, S., Bowlby, S. and Mohammad, R. (1996), *Pakistani Women's Experience of the Labour Market in Reading: Barriers, Aspirations and Opportunities, Report II*, University of Reading in Association with the Pakistani Community Centre, Reading (available from the authors).

Model, S. (1999), 'Ethnic inequality in England: an analysis based on the 1991 census', *Ethnic and Racial Studies*, 22(6), 966–90.

Modood, T., Berthoud, R., Lakey, J., Nazroo, J., Smith, P., Virdee, S. and Beishon, S. (1997), *Ethnic Minorities in Britain: Diversity and Disadvantage*, London: Policy Studies Institute.

Owen, D. (1997), 'Labour force participation rates, self-employment and unemployment', in Karn, V. (ed.) *Employment, Education and Housing Among Ethnic Minorities in Britain*, London: Her Majesty's Stationery Office.

Peach, C. (2006), 'Muslims in the 2001 Census of England and Wales: gender and economic disadvantage', *Ethnic and Racial Studies*, 29(4), 629–55.

Peach, C. (2007), 'Sleepwalking into ghettoisation? The British debate over segregation', in K. Schonwalder (ed.) *Residential Segregation and the Integration of Immigrants: Britain, the Netherlands and Sweden*, Discussion Paper Nr. SP IV 2007–602, Berlin: Wissenschaftszentrum Berlin für Sozialforschung (Social Sciences Research Centre Berlin) (www.wzb.eu).

Shaw, A. (1994), 'The Pakistani Community in Oxford', in R. Ballard (ed.), Desh Pradesh: The South Asian Presence in Britain, London: Hurst.

Simpson, L., Purdam, K., Tajar, S., Fieldhouse, E., Gavalas, V., Tranmer, M., Pritchard, J. and Dorling, D. (2006), *Ethnic Minority Populations and the Labour Market: An Analysis of the 1991 and 2001 Census*, Research Report 333, Corporate Document Services for DWP (available at: www.dwp.gov.uk/asd/asd5/rports2005–2006/Report333.pdf).

Tyrer, D. and Ahmad, F. (2006), *Muslim Women and Higher Education: Identities, Experiences and Prospects*, Liverpool: Liverpool John Moores University and European Social Fund.

Virdee, S. (2006), '"Race", employment and social change: a critique of current orthodoxies,' *Ethnic and Racial Studies*, 29(4), 605–28.

RETHINKING THE IDENTITIES OF YOUNG BRITISH PAKISTANI MUSLIM WOMEN: EDUCATIONAL EXPERIENCES AND ASPIRATIONS

Claire Dwyer and Bindi Shah

Introduction

Young British Muslim women remain a topic for unrelenting public and media debate in the UK. The debates sparked by a newspaper article by cabinet minister Jack Straw about the wearing of the *niqab*[1] are testament to the critical focus upon gender and equality within a broader sphere of public debate about the 'integration' of Muslims in Britain. Yet all too often in these debates 'Muslim women' remain a discursive category framed by the over-determined signifier of the veil (Dwyer 1999b). Our starting point in this chapter is that a discussion of the experiences of young British Pakistani Muslim women must distinguish between 'Muslim woman as a category of discourse and Muslim women as concrete historical subjects with diverse social and personal biographies and social orientations' (Brah 1993: 443). We explore this diversity by focusing specifically on the topic of the education and career aspirations of a group of young British Pakistani Muslim women interviewed in Slough in 2004 as part of a wider project on the educational experiences of young British Pakistanis.[2] Our analysis responds to current debates about the increased representation of young Muslim women in further and higher education and the workplace (Dale et al. 2002a and b; Ahmad 2001; Ahmad et al. 2003; EOC 2007). We focus on the contexts within which educational experiences and aspirations are negotiated, emphasising that gender, ethnicity, class, religion and racism interrelate as 'contingent relationships with multiple determinations' (Brah 1993: 443). The discussion illustrates the extent to which gendered identities are being debated and negotiated, yet also emphasises the structural contexts within which these negotiations are made.[3]

Framing studies of British Muslim women, education and employment

Our analysis of the educational aspirations and experiences of these young women draws much from earlier work on young South Asian Muslim women which explored the ways in which 'race' and 'culture' work in the gendering of labour markets (Brah 1993; see also Brah and Shaw 1992). The theoretical framework developed here challenges the pervasive culturalist explanations which suggest that Muslim women are prevented from taking up paid employment by Muslim men. Brah suggests that neither culture nor structure can be privileged over the other and instead that they should be seen as dynamically interrelated. Such a framework does not deny the impact of patriarchal discourses in the lives of young South Asian Muslim women (Afshar 1994; Ali 1992; Mohammad 2005a) but, crucially, such discourses are not theorised as analytically separate 'cultural constraints'; rather, they are articulated within a wider social formation.

Scholarship on young British South Asian Muslim women has concentrated predominantly on their experiences of education and work in the context of broader concerns about the under-representation of young Muslim women in higher and further education and the labour market. Research focused at the level of the school has considered the ways in which young women negotiate the expectations of teachers and peers as well as family and community pressures (Archer 2002; Basit 1997; Haw 1998; Shain 2002). There is an emphasis on the extent to which many young Muslim women are articulating 'high educational and career goals' (Basit 1997: 429) which are often supported by their parents and which may challenge teachers' 'culturally held stereotypes' (Haw 1998: 136). A range of recent studies highlights the growing numbers of young South Asian Muslim women in higher education (Ahmad 2001; Tyrer and Ahmad 2006; Hussain and Bagguley 2007) and celebrates the achievements of women who have overcome both institutional and communal pressures to pursue their education.

While empirical evidence points to the growing educational achievements of young British Asian women there is debate about how these should be interpreted. Indeed what emerges is recognition of the diversity of experiences of young British Muslim women (Shain 2002; Abbas 2003). Some authors see the pursuit of higher education by young Muslim women as evidence of the renouncement of 'traditional' values and practices (Bhopal 1997, 1998), while others (Ahmad 2001) argue that aspirations to higher education and employment cannot always be read as a challenge or resistance to parental values. It is clear that educational aspirations are often negotiated, as Basit suggests: 'parents are amenable to their daughters' desire to work if they are able to attain a good education and go into a career perceived as safe and respectable: one which does not jeopardise the safety and reputation of these young women' (Basit 1997, 428).

Mohammad (2005a) argues that the enduring significance of patriarchal and community constraints for young Pakistani Muslim women should not be under-estimated, and indeed these have increased with the rise in Islamism. Like Ali (1992), she is ambivalent about the trade-off between acceptable forms of conformist Muslim femininity in pursuit of higher education. While Mohammad recognises increasing aspirations towards higher education among young Muslim women she argues that they are harder to achieve for girls from working-class families whose parents are not educated and that those who go to university are more likely to have educated parents (Mohammad 2005a: 197).

Earlier work on South Asian women and employment (Brah 1993) emphasised the extent to which women faced barriers in entering the workforce both because of patriarchal attitudes and because of discrimination. She also emphasised the difficulties for women in balancing domestic labour with paid work outside the home. More recent work by Dale et al. (2002a and b) shows much higher levels of labour market participation among the Pakistani Muslim women studied and cites the importance of increasing levels of education. She suggests that women with qualifications are more likely to work after marriage and will negotiate this with future partners or in-laws. The data analysed by Dale et al. (2002a and b) showed that the presence of children was a significant factor influencing whether or not women worked, although they speculated that, as more qualified women entered the workforce, they would choose to stay on after they had children. Dale et al. (2002b: 22) emphasise that 'negative and out-dated stereotypes of Muslim women held by employers' remain a significant barrier to employment, a concern also raised in a survey by the Equal Opportunities Commission (2007). It is clear that choices about paid work for South Asian Muslim women are made through the negotiation of a range of interrelated factors and are influenced by class and location (Lloyd-Evans and Bowlby 2000).

Research context and methodologies

The empirical material discussed in this chapter was collected as part of a broader project which sought to understand the divergent educational experiences and academic and employment outcomes of young Pakistani men and women in a comparative study of Bradford and Slough. This chapter draws specifically on thirty-one interviews and a group discussion conducted with young women aged between 16 and 27 in Slough. Slough, a town in the southeast of England, has a population of 119,067 of whom 12 per cent identified themselves as having a Pakistani heritage in the 2001 Census. Slough was chosen as the site to conduct the research as a town with a significant ethnic minority population of Pakistani Muslim heritage and where the local authority and Muslim organisations have raised concerns about the educational achievements of Pakistani Muslim pupils. While overall unemployment levels are lower than the national average, Pakistani Muslim populations in Slough are primarily located in the wards with the highest deprivation indices and unemployment rates.[4]

In recruiting participants for the research we sought to recruit both young people who might be defined as educationally 'successful'[5] and those who were deemed 'less successful'. Our sample matched those in education aged 16–23 with those in the same age range who were either employed or unemployed. Respondents were recruited and interviewed by Bindi Shah[6] from a range of locations: youth and community centres, local schools, voluntary organisations, a job-skills training centre, the local university and universities around London; among participants on Slough Borough Council's Modern Apprenticeship Programme; and through snowball techniques. Our sample includes ten university students (studying at local universities such as Brunel and Thames Valley University as well as universities in London including University College London),[7] ten who were in full-time employment (including four who were on the Modern Apprentice Scheme at Slough Borough Council); six who were still at school and three who were at a further education college. Two were economically inactive, and of those in school or further education colleges, six were working part time. As these details suggest, our sample is more heavily slanted towards women in education and employment than might be true of this age group as a whole in Slough, but this partly reflects the emphasis of our study and our recruitment strategy. However, this emphasis in our sample should be borne in mind. The focus of our interviews centred on the young women's educational experiences and aspirations and their current or future employment expectations. We were particularly interested in what had shaped their decision making and experiences.

Four case studies

To frame our discussion and illustrate some of the key themes emerging from the interviews with the young women we draw mainly on the narratives of four respondents. These interviews were chosen as they are representative of common themes related to education, employment and negotiations around gender roles and religious identities across the interviews. By focusing on the experiences of four young women in this way we hope to give a stronger sense of the personalities behind our analysis than by using a broader range of individual quotes. We provide a short description of each of the young women before further developing some of the key themes in the next section.

Alia

We first met 20-year-old Alia, who is a full-time Information Systems (computing) student at Westminster University, at the Slough Community Saturday

School[8] where she is a volunteer teacher of GCSE[9] science and maths. Since the school is held in the mosque she was wearing *shalwar kameez* and *dupatta* scarf, although when we later met her at college she was in jeans and T-shirt with no scarf. She initially failed the 11+[10] exam and attended a school outside Slough, in Windsor, rather than going to the failing local school. However, she later transferred to a Slough grammar school to take her A levels. She is the first child in her family to go to university. While her father, who works in a factory, had little education in Pakistan, her mother grew up in the UK and although she left school at 16 now works as an education support worker in a school. Alia plans to go into IT when she graduates and work as a project manager. She hopes to get married three or four years after graduating and already has someone in mind. She would like to continue working after marriage but is keen to start a family too.

Rana

Rana is 22 and currently works full time for the Slough Borough Planning Department although she does not yet have a permanent job. She has a degree in Business and IT with Multi-media from Buckingham Chiltern University College. Like Alia, she did not pass her 11+ and went to a poorly performing local school before transferring to another, better, local school for GNVQ[11] and A levels. Rana became very interested in her religion while in the sixth form and opted to wear the hijab. She explains that her immediate family was not very religious but that she has had an influence on them and her brothers, particularly, are becoming more interested in Islam. She is the only one in her family with a degree: her sister left college to get married, although she is still working; both her brothers left school after GCSEs; and neither of her parents is well educated. Her aspirations for the future are to get a permanent IT job, probably with the local authority, which she considers a good employer. She expects to get married and continue working after marriage, as that is the experience of her friends. However, if she has children she would work part time, if her in-laws were available to do the childcare.

Sultana

Sultana is 19 and a full time student of Finance and Accounting at Brunel University. Unlike the other subjects in our case studies, although she was born in the UK, her education before the age of 12 was in Pakistan. Her older sister and brother have degrees, but her younger brother left school after his GCSEs. She intends to qualify as an accountant and to practise, but is unsure whether this will be in the UK or Pakistan, as at the moment her parents intend to retire to Pakistan, where one of her brothers lives, and she is undecided whether she would choose to remain in the UK without them. She expresses ambivalence about marriage, citing the evidence of her broader extended family that marriages are not happy. She says that she will probably get married, although the person must be a strong Muslim. She wears the hijab.

Huma

Huma is 19 and is on the Modern Apprentice Scheme[12] at Slough Borough Council, where she is studying for NVQs in administration and IT. Although she enjoyed school she reflects that she did not take it seriously and describes the poor reputation of her local neighbourhood school which she attended, having failed the 11+. However, after her GCSEs she was encouraged to stay on to do a GNVQ in Business Studies and her teacher told her about the Modern Apprentice Scheme. She is now very enthusiastic about the skills she has learnt, and intends to stay in an administration role either at the council or in another public sector body. A major role model is her sister, who works as a hotel receptionist. She describes her parents, who grew up in Britain but are not highly educated, as being strongly supportive of her aspirations. She is a practising Muslim but describes her parents as 'liberal' and expresses concern about what she sees as Islamic influences from outside Slough-for example, those handing out leaflets in the street. She expects to have an arranged marriage with relatives from Pakistan, as her sister and brother have done, but says there is no pressure on her to get married soon. Like her sister, she expects to continue working after marriage.

Educational experiences and negotiations

The educational experiences of these four young women highlight simultaneously the challenges for young British Pakistani Muslims in accessing good education and the value attached to education by these young women. Like many of our respondents, all of these young women described failing the divisive 11+ exam, which meant that they were unable to attend the higher-achieving grammar schools in Slough. While the local comprehensive school was seen negatively by respondents because of poor teaching or the disruptive behaviour of other pupils, particularly boys, it was also seen in positive terms as an 'Asian' school. In contrast, Alia, who went to a state girls' school outside Slough, was somewhat ambivalent about the experience:

> To be honest, when I was there I hated it because the majority were white, and we had about 200 girls, and about twenty of us were Asians . . . I felt really alienated.

For those respondents who went on to study in the sixth form, the choice to stay at school was emphasised as providing more structure and support than being at college. When it came to tertiary education, all three of the students described here have remained in the family home and commuted to university. Although Sultana was offered a place in Bristol and the family went to visit the area, thinking that she and her mother might move there, they preferred to remain in Slough and for Sultana to commute from there to Brunel University. The popularity of local universities for ethnic minority students in general, and girls in particular, has been emphasised in other studies (Hussain and Bagguley 2007) and it was clear from our study that young women were more likely to go to a local university. Reflecting on the choice between Buckingham Chiltern and Westminster University, Rana explains:

> the reason was the course and the location, if I go to uni in London, by the time I get home I'm going to be too tired to study, or I'm going to be travelling in the dark.

It was also clear that while some respondents did travel by train or bus to work or college, others relied on their parents to provide transport:

> He [father] doesn't want me to come by bus, because it takes an hour, so he comes all the way from Windsor, he has a business, a restaurant, so he comes all the way to pick me up. (Sultana)

Although it was not made explicit in our interviews, these decisions about where to go to university and how to travel between home and work or college are indicative of negotiations between young women and their parents about how much independence they have. In particular, the role of fathers in driving the young women might be read as a strategy to monitor or safeguard their behaviour, although none of the respondents made this claim.

Reflecting on their experiences at school, most respondents emphasised that girls were harder working than boys. As Rana explains:

> Boys were more into having fun rather than studying, whereas the girls were more into getting their coursework done and handing it in on time.

Interviewees agreed that working hard at school was important because of the opportunities it provided in the future. Huma explains:

> I think girls take education more seriously than boys, because boys know that when they're finished, they can just go and do this, they don't care, and girls know we don't want to work in retail, we want to go and do something.

This distinction between young men and young women was made even more explicit by another respondent:

boys take it for granted as I said before and they just want to have a little bit of a laugh, and so they don't do as well as girls. Whereas girls want to impress their parents, especially their dads and say to them, 'look, we can be someone else'. Because they know that if they screw up, they will not get a chance to do it again, . . . they know that if we don't pass this time round, we're not going to get further and we're not going to get to uni. (Fauzia, 17, studying A levels at a further education college)

Fauzia articulates a view that resonated with that of many respondents: educational success was a vehicle by which young Pakistani Muslim women could win respect and approbation from their parents, particularly their fathers. In contrast to some of the young men we interviewed for whom going to college was little more than a social activity, young women worked hard to gain the opportunity for further study. The young women also talked about the value of supportive peer cultures of other motivated young women at school, as Alia explains:

we were all quite academically orientated, so it helped, because I didn't have friends that I knew were going to get married at the age of 18 as soon as they finished A levels, they were all going to university and do a degree.

Employment experiences and aspirations

As the discussion above suggests, a key finding from the overall study was the emphasis placed on education by the young women we interviewed. All of the young women saw gaining qualifications as a means by which they could have good employment prospects. For Huma, gaining qualifications through the Modern Apprentice Scheme gives her the opportunity to do office work, which she sees as a higher-status, more independent job than working in retail like some of her peers:

If you don't have good GCSEs you won't get a good job anywhere. I've always liked office work and to be independent. I thought this is a good opportunity for me to go and get a good job, because once you've got your GNVQ Level 2 and 3 you get jobs that earn £15,000 a year. Basically, I've seen people work in retail, and I'm not saying it's bad, but I know I'm too good to work in retail, I've got the brains, and I've done my GCSEs . . . here I get experience, we work here like a full-time employee and take on responsibilities.

All of the respondents emphasised that being educated gave you better employment prospects and contrasted this with the experiences of their parents. As Sultana explains:

[to get a qualification] is very important, especially when I looked at people in Pakistan who are not educated and are having such tough lives, all they can do is cleaning, servants, so it built me up to think that education is important. . .My mum said, 'Look at your dad, working in the Mars factory, if he had studied more, it would have been easier for him.'

Alia, too, echoes this view:

I think because themselves, they've never been to university and now because I'm going, it's their way of achieving something themselves, and when my dad tells people that I'm doing a degree he's just so proud, so proud you know.

Good job prospects were valued not simply in terms of how much money you earned but also of the respect given to you and your family if you had a good 'professional' job.

Respondents emphasised the support they received from their parents, both mothers and fathers, to pursue their education. Educated children confer status on a family and it was not the case that only the ambitions or success of sons were favoured (Ahmad 2001). As Rana says:

when we meet up with friends he [her father] will say to them 'my daughter [has] done this degree', they all talk about their children, 'what did your children do?', so at least he's got one child who has actually gone to university and things like that, so yeah, he is proud I would say.

It is clear that educated daughters are a source of pride and even, as Ahmad (2001) suggests, cultural capital. A recurring theme in the interviews, and one which begins to complicate fixed assumptions about patriarchal Pakistani family structures, was the degree of independence possible if you have an education and the prospect of a good job. Respondents pointed out that a good education gave you 'insurance' and the ability to earn your own money if your marriage failed, drawing on examples of relatives or neighbours:

I've always got my degree to back me up, especially as the divorce rates are so high, they [her parents] know that if ever something like that happened to me, I've always got my degree to fall back on. Especially my dad, he always says to me 'God forbid, if anything ever happened to you, you've always got your degree to fall back on'.(Alia)

Increased levels of education among (some) Pakistani Muslim women offer an insight into the ways in which gender roles and expectations may be renegotiated (cf. Dale et al. 2002a). For some respondents, education and work provided greater financial independence or a sense of security for the future. A theme developed elsewhere (Ahmed 2001), although not made so explicit by our respondents, is that better-educated women will be able to secure more-educated partners. This is hinted at by Alia, when discussing her mother's support for her education:

> My mum's from here and my dad's from back home [i.e. Pakistan], and I can see the conflict that they've had and I know my mum wouldn't want me to go through the same, that's why she's really trying to educate me well.

While all these young Pakistani Muslim women expected to enter the workplace, there was surprisingly little discussion of the possibility of barriers to their labour market participation or any expectations of racialised or gendered prejudices towards them. This is in spite of considerable evidence that Muslim women face marked disadvantage and discrimination in the workplace (see EOC 2007). However, the young women were aware of how their ambitions challenged stereotypes. Alia, describing her ambitions to work in IT after her graduation, brings up this issue:

> There's so much hype about Muslims at the moment. To get into an IT firm and get a job, being a girl, I think that's going to be a big thing in itself for me . . . they reckon that we are oppressed and by showing that I've done the degree, and I've got a 2.1 and I'm going to come into the big, wide world and I'm going to do a job. It's going to be a big thing.

It is perhaps worth reiterating the importance of the local authority as an employer of two of these young women and the extent to which they saw the local Borough Council as being a good employer for Asian women.

Negotiating normative gender roles

As we suggested above, discussion of increased educational and employment opportunities for British Muslim women has often centred upon the extent to which this is paralleled more broadly by changing gender roles. This is a complex debate and we concur with Avtar Brah's sensitive foregrounding of the ways in which structure and culture interrelate in the analysis of patriarchy and gender relations (Brah 1993: 443). First, it is fair to say that all of the young women discussed above describe the ways in which they have negotiated their aspirations of education, work and independence with their parents. Earlier we suggested that patriarchal control might be evident in the ways in which daughters were driven to and from college. Certainly, all of the respondents emphasised that it was important to build up trust and confidence from their parents. As Rana and Huma explain:

> Some parents say 'if my daughter goes to college' or 'if my daughter goes to university, she might get into the wrong crowd and she might start doing things against

Islam' . . . because I've built up that trust and they trusted me so they were fine, they supported me all the way.(Rana)

My parents will support me whatever I want to do, whatever I decide, they will support me . . . trust and stuff, they know we're not like that . . . like my sister works in the hotel, she sees so many Pakistani girls come in with men . . . (Huma)

These comments suggest that these young women recognise the need to protect their 'respectability' and guard against forms of gendered performance that could be observed and interpreted as bringing disrepute on themselves or their family (cf. Dwyer 1999a and b; Mohammad 2005b). Trust appears both hard won and perhaps provisional. All of these respondents also cited examples of friends who were not able to carry on with their education or enjoy equal independence as they had:

I've seen parents, like my own friends' parents, like N., they're really different, they don't give her that freedom, they did, but I think she broke their trust. (Huma)

I know one of my friends, her dad is really strict. Soon as she finished her A levels, he took her back home and got them married, they came back here, they're doing degrees, but they got married to people that are uneducated, really uneducated, and I just think that it's so unfair.

There is thus some evidence for the argument (Mohammad 2005a; Ali 1992) that expanded educational and employment opportunities for some young Pakistani Muslim women are secured only through careful adherence to normative gender roles. However, it was also true that young women in the workplace were ready to contest narrow views of gendered respectability, as Huma explains:

In Islam, talking to boys is not wrong, I don't know why other people think talking to boys is wrong. Obviously you have to talk to boys, in your career, you have to go socialising with men in your departments.

As indicated above, Dale et al.'s (2002a and b) study of employment opportunities for Pakistani Muslim women emphasises that the lowest workplace participation rates are for women with children, and considers whether increasing levels of education and employment among young women might affect these rates over time. In view of this, it is perhaps significant that each of the young women described here expected that they would get married and to that extent held normative views about their expected gender roles. As Alia explains, while she wants to develop her career in the next few years, marriage will follow after that:

I want to get a good IT job, get a respectable job status, and just work my way up for a few years. For Pakistanis, it all comes down to marriage, it's such a big thing . . . they're OK for me working for the next few . . . my dad's like 'you're not allowed to get married for another couple of years, like three or four years'.

While marriage was expected, it was also considered with some reservation by some respondents. Sultana expressed ambivalence about the possibility of finding a suitable partner:

the experience of marriages that I have seen, have all been bad, like not really bad, like not everyone got divorced, but from all my aunties, none of them have ever said that they love their husband.

For all respondents, while marriage was inevitable, they suggested that in the same way as they had negotiated educational choices they would also negotiate expectations about marriage partners in terms of whom they chose and how they would live after marriage. Asked about the future, Huma says:

having a good job, if however I do get married, being independent, having a nice house, not staying with my parents all the time and having their support, I need to be independent . . . mainly, it's having a really good job, something that I can look back and say 'well I did good for myself'.

This negotiation would also include continuing to work after marriage and children. For Huma, her older married sister, who is the main breadwinner and working as a hotel receptionist, is an important role model:

I think she'll still have a career [when she has children], because there's people at her work, like, English people, they've got three or four children, they still made a career, they still manage, you can, and she'll always have her mum and dad to support her.

As Huma suggests, while attitudes may be changing, the extended family remains key in providing childcare among British Pakistani Muslim families (cf. Dale et al. 2002a and b). In general, the young women we interviewed did not contest normative gender roles. Indeed Rana, while trying to explain that women should have the opportunity to develop a career, also expresses the view that the nurturing of children is an important role for women:

No one should tell her what to do or how to do it, but then again she should understand that there's more to life than a career basically. You get more reward like bringing up children and things like that . . . women should work and you shouldn't make them stay at home [but] it's not inferior being a housewife . . . I would class that as something good, at the end of the day you're nurturing your children, you're not just abandoning them and leaving them for the man to bring up, or the childminder or leaving them in a nursery.

Similarly for Alia, the first of her family to go to university and with a strong desire to be a trail blazer as a Pakistani Muslim woman in the workplace, there is still a strong adherence to prescribed gender roles. Indeed, when asked about the importance of education she gives an answer that not only expresses individualised achievement (although she does mention this) but also reinforces the extent to which education enables her to better fulfil the prescribed role of a mother:

> I think education has got to do with everything, I know for me, because my mum and dad have always said to me 'you're going to be the wife, you're going to look after the home' . . . it makes sense because I'd want to give my own experiences to my own children.

Alia's remarks might seem to echo the findings of Afshar (1989a and b, 1994) about Pakistani Muslim women deferring their own independence but investing in their children. However, it is also true that a combination of economic and cultural processes has opened up new spaces for Pakistani Muslim women. If Alia's views are read as a reinforcing of normative gender roles they can also be contextualised by the reflections she makes about 'how far' women should go in pursuing a career:

> I think in moderation, because I've seen a lot of girls that have done Masters and stuff, they're 35 and not married, and they really regret it. When they should have got married they were just so into education and they looked for someone of the same match. And Pakistani men aren't really as educated as the women, then it's so difficult, and they'll just stay spinsters for the rest of their life, and then they regret it.

This fear of not finding a suitably educated partner is also expressed by Ahmad's (2001) respondents and suggests the extent to which young working-class Pakistani Muslim women like Alia are negotiating new forms of gender relations.

Contested religious identities

In the final section of this chapter we want to reflect briefly on how the young women we interviewed talked about their religious identities. As previous work (Dwyer 1999a and b) found, the young women, although all identifying as Pakistani Muslim, held a range of attitudes towards Islam and the relationship between religious and ethnic identities. For some of the respondents, like Huma, a religious identity was part of a broader cultural or ethnic identity.

Huma was resistant to broader 'community' attitudes and also particularly sceptical about expressions of Islamic revivalism:

> As long as you follow Islam, read the Qur'an, respect your parents, who cares what people think . . . I don't really care what the community thinks, I just care about my parents . . . When you go to the high street there's all these Asian people there, especially Pakistanis handing out Islamic [pamphlets] . . . there's Islamic exhibitions, people protesting, I don't believe in that.

In contrast, Rana, who embraced a more self-consciously devout Muslim identity when she was in the sixth form, places her Islamic identity at the centre of her life. When asked about how she measures success, she emphasises that education or status should never displace religious identity:

> I might be a good Muslim, that would be better for me than to have a degree and be really educated and be at the top and have no faith, and have no Islam in my life. If I had a choice, I would take uneducated [i.e. choose not to be educated].

Indeed, for Rana education should be valued not for what employment or status it might promise but for the possibilities that it has given her to develop a better understanding of her faith:

> Maybe my education has helped me, because obviously you need intellect, you need to be intellectual to look into your religion and look into what's right and wrong. It's not that [i.e. because] I was born into a Muslim family that I've chosen my religion, basically I've actually looked at it and I thought 'this makes sense' so maybe if I wasn't educated I wouldn't have actually pondered on my purpose in life.

Alia expresses a more ambivalent perspective. She is comfortable with her Muslim identity and, reflecting on her experiences teaching at the mosque school, she says:

> and I think it keeps me in touch with my religion as well and that's a big thing obviously, being in a western society, it's really easy to go astray.

However, she is also aware of the ways in which she confronts contested values about appropriate performances of observant gendered Muslim identities (see Dwyer 1999b), as she explains:

> I know at the mosque, a lot of the teachers are obviously quite old men. And one of the teachers, he sees me on Saturdays, and I've got the hijab on, he sees me at the train station and I haven't got it on, and he just gives me some dirty looks . . . you know they're really twisted.

For Alia, the experience of going to university has given her a new opportunity to think through her identity as a young British Pakistani Muslim woman.

> It's really important for Asians, because we have a lot of cultural stuff in us, and it's important we understand our culture. And also because obviously I'm a Muslim, and there's so much hype in the media. And I think a lot of young people feel like they're just following the crowd, or like lost sheep following the rest of them because they are Muslims, and they've got to believe everything else. I think it's really important that they go to university, look at everything else around them and then understand why they're following their belief, and that's what's helped me.

Conclusion

In this chapter we have drawn on findings from a study of attitudes towards education and employment among young British Pakistani Muslim women to explore how they are negotiating 'new' identities. As we stated at the outset, our sample is specifically drawn from a group of young women who are involved in education or the workplace but come largely from working-class backgrounds and are often the first generation in their family to go on to further or higher education. While our findings are biased towards this group of higher-achieving young women, these are not young women from middle-class families, where there has been a much longer trend of participation in higher education for Asian women. However, we also accept that our sample does not include young women who have not been successful in persuading teachers or parents that they should stay in education or resist early marriage (Shain 2002).

Our findings provide some evidence for the extent to which a new generation of Pakistani Muslim women are forging new opportunities through increased levels of participation in further and higher education. Our discussion illustrates the ways in which these opportunities sometimes require negotiations around performing 'respectable' or 'safe' gender roles which for some young women may be a more self-consciously religious identification. Yet our findings also suggest that working-class families, with little experience of education, support the greater opportunities for education and work for their daughters. Indeed, there is evidence that families may invest more in their daughters than in their sons as girls begin to outperform boys at school and the labour market is more receptive to female workers with 'soft skills' (McDowell 2003; Dwyer et al. 2008). These findings raise important questions for this emerging generation of young British Pakistani Muslim women in terms both of how they will negotiate their future roles in the workplace and of how new forms of gender relations may be forged. As we argue elsewhere (see Dwyer et al. 2008), there are challenges for young working-class Pakistani Muslim *men* with few skills or qualifications to fulfil their expected gender roles as breadwinners and they may, as Macey (1999) suggests, seek another source of masculine pride in reasserting patriarchal control over sisters and wives. Our work perhaps provides some evidence that, as young women gain greater financial and educational independence, they will have the resources to shape new forms of potentially more egalitarian gender relations.

While religious identities were not a central focus of our research, our findings provide evidence for the persistence of faith as an important source of identity, articulated in a variety of ways. For some young women a more self-consciously Islamic identity is important in demanding new opportunities, while for others there are risks attached to the ways in which religious identities may be imposed upon them. If dress remains an over-determined signifier of identity for young Muslim women it is also true that even in Slough (a much less obvious place of politicised Muslim identity than, for example, Bradford) multiple-gendered performances of religious identity are possible.

Notes

1. In October 2006 Jack Straw, Labour Member of Parliament for Blackburn and Leader of the Commons, wrote an article in the *Lancashire Telegraph* raising his concerns about meeting constituents who wore the full face veil or niqab, arguing 'I felt uncomfortable talking to someone "face-to-face" who I could not see'. He argued that 'wearing the full veil was bound to make better positive relations between the two communities more difficult. It was such a visible statement of separation and of difference.' (http://politics.guardian.co.uk/homeaffairs/story/o., 1889231.00.html accessed 2 April 2007)

2. The research was part of a wider project, 'Gender, Social Capital and Differential Outcomes', funded by the Leverhulme Programme on Migration and Ethnicity based at the Migration Research Unit, Department of Geography, University College London and the Centre for the Study of Ethnicity and Citizenship, University of Bristol. The research team included Claire Dwyer, Tariq Modood, Gurchathen Sanghera, Bindi Shah and Suruchi Thapar-Björkert and ran from October 2003 to September 2005 with research carried out in Slough and Bristol. For more details see www.bris.ac.uk/Depts/Sociology/leverhulme. While this paper draws on the Slough interviews see Sanghera and Thapar-Björkert (2007) for a discussion of some of the Bradford data.

3. We are indebted to all the young women who gave up their time to be interviewed for this research and to the many people and agencies who facilitated access to these interviewees. In addition to the helpful comments from the editors, this chapter has benefited from comments from audiences at seminars at the universities of Lancaster, Brunel and the West of England.

4. Slough's ethnic minority population is over-represented (25–30 per cent) in the inner urban wards of Chalvey, Central, Baylis and Stoke.

5. For the purposes of the larger research project we adopted dominant notions of educational success, in terms of gaining GCSEs or A levels and entrance into further or higher education. However, we also recognise, as we have discussed elsewhere (see Dwyer et al. 2008), that this normative model can be criticised and indeed many of the young people we interviewed rejected this normative definition of 'success'.

6. All of the interviews were conducted by Bindi Shah, transcribed and coded using the computer package Atlas-ti. All names have been changed. See Shah (2007) for more reflections on the research practice.

7. Of the young women at university, they were studying a range of social science and teaching courses (such as Psychology, Sociology and Philosophy, and Education and Science), business and law-related courses (such as Business and Management, Law, Information Systems with Business Management, and Finance and Accounting), and science-related courses (such as Biomedical Sciences, and Nursing).

8. The Slough Community Saturday School is a supplementary school run by volunteer teachers to help raise the standards of achievement of, particularly, Pakistani Muslim children (although it is open to all) in Slough. Parents pay a nominal fee for the school, which is held in the Stoke Poges mosque and includes national curriculum subjects, English, Maths and Science, as well as 'Personal Development Philosophy' and Islamic Studies.

9. General Certification of Secondary Education. Public examinations taken in Year 11 the final year of compulsory education. Advanced Levels are taken in school Year 12 (A/S) and Year 13 (A).

10. A particular feature of the Buckinghamshire Education System is the 11+ exam, which is an exam taken by children in the final year of primary school and is used to select the most academically able students to attend competitive 'grammar' schools. Although widely criticised, this competitive entry scheme remains in some educational authorities in Britain. Considerable debate remains about the difficulties for working-class children to access the best state schools in Britain because of the mobilisation of different forms of social and cultural as well as economic capital by middle-class parents (see Ball 2003).

11. National Vocational Qualifications (NVQs) are work-related, competence-based qualifications.

12. The Modern Apprentice Scheme, supported by the Learning Skills Council, is a scheme where young people are sponsored by an employer to study for national awards while also gaining work experience and a wage.

References

Abbas, T. (2003), 'The impact of religio-cultural norms and values on the education of young South Asian Women', *British Journal of Sociology of Education*, 24(4), 411–28.

Afshar, H. (1989a), 'Gender roles and the "moral economy of kin" among Pakistani women in West Yorkshire', *New Community*, 15, 211–25.

Afshar, H. (1989b), 'Education: hopes, expectations and achievements of Muslim women in West Yorkshire', *Gender and Education*, 1(3), 261–72.

Afshar, H. (1994), 'Muslim women in West Yorkshire: growing up with real and imaginary values amidst conflicting views of self and society', in H. Afshar and M. Maynard (eds), *The Dynamics of 'Race' and Gender: Some Feminist Interventions*, pp. 127–50.

Ahmad, F. (2001), 'Modern traditions? British Muslim women and academic achievement', *Gender and Education*, 13(2), 137–52.

Ahmad, F., Modood, T. and Lissenburgh, S. (2003), *South Asian Women and Employment in Britain*, London: Policy Studies Institute.

Ali, Y. (1992), 'Muslim women and the politics of ethnicity and culture in Northern England', in G. Sahgal and N. Yuval-Davis (eds), *Refusing Holy Orders*, pp. 101–23.

Archer, L. (2002), 'Change, culture and tradition: British Muslim pupils talk about Muslim girls' post-16 "Choices"', *Race, Ethnicity and Education*, 5(4), 359–76.

Ball, S. (2003), *Class Strategies and the Education Market: The Middle Classes and Social Advantage*, London: RoutledgeFalmer.

Basit, T. N. (1997), ' "I want more freedom, but not too much": British Muslim girls and the dynamism of family values', *Gender and Education*, 9(4), 425–39.

Bhopal, K. (1997), *Gender, 'Race' and Patriarchy: A Study of South Asian Women*, Aldershot: Ashgate.

Bhopal, K. (1998) 'How gender and ethnicity intersect: the significance of education, employment and marital status' *Sociological Research Online*, 3(3), 1–16.

Brah, A. (1993), '"Race" and "culture" in the gendering of labour markets: South Asian young Muslim women and the labour market', *New Community*, 19(3), 441–58.

Brah, A. and Shaw, S. (1992), *Working Choices: South Asian Young Muslim Women and the Labour Market*, Department of Employment, Research Paper 91.

Dale, A., Shaheen, N., Kalra, V. and Fieldhouse, E. (2002a), 'Routes into education and employment for young Pakistani and Bangladeshi women in the UK', *Ethnic and Racial Studies*, 25(6), 924–68.

Dale, A., Shaheen, N., Fieldhouse, E. and Kalra, V. (2002b), 'Labour market prospects for Pakistani and Bangladeshi women', *Work, Employment & Society*, 16(1), 5–26.

Dwyer, C. (1999a), 'Contradictions of community: questions of identity for British Muslim women', *Environment and Planning A*, 31, 53–68.

Dwyer, C. (1999b), 'Veiled meanings: British Muslim women and the negotiation of differences', *Gender, Place and Culture*, 6(1), 5–26.

Dwyer, C., Shah, B. and Sanghera, G. (2008), 'From cricket lover to terror suspect- challenging representations of young British Muslim men', *Gender, Place and Culture*, 15(2), 117–36.

Equal Opportunities Commission (2007), *Moving on up? The Way Forward*, Report of the Equal Opportunities Commission's investigation into Bangladeshi, Pakistani and Black Caribbean women and work, London: EOC.

Haw, K. (1998), *Educating Muslim Girls: Shifting Discourses*, Buckingham: Open University Press.

Hussain, Y. and Bagguley, P. (2007), *Moving on Up: South Asian Women and Higher Education*, Stoke-on-Trent: Trentham Books.

Lloyd-Evans, S. and Bowlby, S. (2000), 'Crossing boundaries: racialised gendering and the labour market experiences of Pakistani migrant wives in Britain', *Women's Studies International Forum*, 23(4), 461–74.

McDowell, Linda (2003), *Redundant Masculinities?* Oxford: Blackwell.

Macey, M. (1999), 'Class, gender and religious influences on changing patterns of Pakistani male violence in Bradford', *Ethnic and Racial Studies*, 22(5), 845–66.

Mohammad, R. (2005a), 'Negotiating space of the home, the education system and the labour market: the case of young, working-class, British Pakistani Muslim women', in G. W. Falah and C. Nagel (eds), *Geographies of Muslim Women:Gender, Religion and Space*, London: Guilford Press, pp. 178–202.

Mohammad, R. (2005b), 'British Pakistani Muslim women: marking the body, marking the nation', in L. Nelson and J. Seager (eds), *A Companion to Feminist Geography*, Oxford: Blackwell, 379–397.

Sanghera, G. and Thapar-Björkert, S. (2007), '"Because I'm Pakistani . . . and I'm Muslim . . . and I am Political" – gendering political radicalism: young femininities in Bradford', in T. Abbas (ed.), *Islamic Political Radicalism*, Edinburgh: Edinburgh University Press, pp. 173–91.

Shah, B. (2007) 'Place, space and history in the research process: reflections from Slough', paper presented at panel on Feminist Research Methods at the American Sociological Association Meetings, New York, 11–14 August.

Shain, F. (2002) *The Schooling and Identity of Asian Girls*, Stoke-on-Trent: Trentham Books.

Tyrer, D. and Ahmad, F. (2006), *Muslim Women and Higher Education: Identities, Experiences and Prospects: A Summary Report*, Liverpool: John Moores University and European Social Fund.

RACE, 'FACE' AND MASCULINITY: THE IDENTITIES AND LOCAL GEOGRAPHIES OF MUSLIM BOYS

Louise Archer

Introduction

British Muslim young men occupy a sensationalised and demonised position in contemporary British society – indeed, we might describe them as the new folk devils of the British imagination. Popular discursive constructions of British Muslim young men coalesce around homogenised and stereotypical representations of dangerous and angry fundamentalists who engage in burning books (the Rushdie affair), rioting (e.g. in Bradford, Oldham) and planning, advocating and/or carrying out acts of terrorism (11 September 2001, 7 July 2005, summer 2006). In short, they are popularly feared as the archetypal 'outsiders within' – those who cannot be trusted and whose loyalty to the nation-state, and to the values and ideology of 'Britishness', cannot be counted upon.[1]

These representations and panics raise important social justice questions. Extending Skeggs' (2004) theorisation of the representation of working-class subjects in public life, I would argue that British Muslims are being increasingly subjected to a narrow 'forced telling of the self' within popular and media discourse. For instance, it has become a common practice within news and current affairs reporting to parade an endless series of Muslim individuals, spokespersons and community representatives who are asked to explain their identities and to define their own positions vis-à-vis the various events and issues in question. This is not limited to Muslim men, as witnessed in autumn 2006, when fierce debates erupted around the wearing of the *niqab*, a debate in which Muslim women have been impelled to explain and situate themselves and their religious identities/practices through a simplistic, narrow dichotomy (wearing the veil vs not wearing it[2]). As with the coverage of 9/11 and the London bombings, this media coverage has demanded that Muslims position and justify themselves by taking up either 'pro' or 'anti' positions within a narrowly framed discourse.

These practices – propelled by the popular preoccupation with 'dangerous' Islam – have rendered Muslims hypervisible within public life. Indeed, it is currently difficult to watch, listen to or read any news that does not contain some reference to or concern with Muslims/Islam in some form. Paradoxically, however, the narrow parameters within which this preoccupation takes place are also rendering Muslims profoundly 'invisible'. By this I mean that the terms of reference and debate within which Muslims are 'allowed' to speak and appear remain incredibly narrow. Muslims continue to be denied the opportunity to be represented (or to represent themselves) in terms of a complex, holistic and heterogeneous humanity. It is this narrowness of representation that generates a profound representational invisibility (West 1993). Hence the widespread hypervisibility of Muslims across news and current affairs is not balanced by (for instance) a 'normalised' presence within popular soaps, literature, reality TV, comedy and dramas/films. Indeed, where Muslims are represented within popular cultural forms, these tend to be narrowly focused on specific themes (e.g. national 'belonging', religion and culture and particularly 'culture clash'[3]).

In other words, Muslims tend to be represented only in terms of their 'Muslimness' – they do not appear as 'normal' members of British society and the 'British public'. It is thus my contention that the current media panics are enacting a form of representational violence on Muslims in Britain – calling into question the identities, values and behaviours of *all* Muslims and demanding that they be displayed and opened up for scrutiny. The aim of this audit of Muslim subjectivities is either to provide reassurance to the non-Muslim majority or to enable intervention and policing of potential 'danger'.

This chapter aims to challenge popular representations of British Muslim masculinities by opening up ways of thinking otherwise about the young men's identities and self-representations. To this end, I draw upon a conceptualisation of identities as multilayered and 'culturally entangled' (Hesse 2000) constructions, located within complex axes of structural inequalities. Arguments are illustrated using data collected as part of a wider study on 14- to 16-year-old British Muslim pupils' ethnic and gender identity constructions (Archer 2001; 2002a; 2002b; 2003). This project involved focus-group discussions with sixty-four young people (thirty-two boys and thirty-two girls) from four schools in a northern town in England ('Mill Town'). Half of the interviews were conducted by the white, middle-class female author (LA) and the other half were conducted by one of two British Asian women researchers:[4] Tamar (TD), who self-defines as Pakistani Christian (and who conducted the bulk of the interviews) and Nessa (NS), who identifies as British Pakistani Muslim (and who conducted one boys' discussion group).

The chapter reflects upon the data gained from the boys' discussion groups. All of these discussion groups were conducted around the mid-1990s. Obviously this is now marked as a historical period that contrasts somewhat starkly with the current post-9/11 climate, yet it also contains some interesting parallels which, I believe, render the data relevant to current debates. Notably, the boys were constructing their identities in the wake of the Salman Rushdie affair (a point discussed directly in the data that follow). The Rushdie affair has been defined as a pivotal point in British race relations (Modood 1992), sparking national debates around race, religion, citizenship and 'belonging'. It similarly evoked representations of 'dangerous' Muslim masculinity and impelled Muslims to 'tell' their identities in relation to the events and issues raised. In this sense, we might see useful parallels between the location of these young men at this particular point in time, and young Muslims in today's post-9/11, post-7/7 climate.

Before moving on to the substantive analyses, it is worth reflecting on the data selection made in preparing this chapter. Readers will notice that there is an emphasis upon some of the boys' more 'sensationalised' accounts – which is, of course, somewhat paradoxical to the position outlined above and my critique of narrow, sensationalised representations of Muslim masculinity. My aim in selecting, for instance, boys' constructions of 'hard' Muslim masculinities is precisely in order to engage with dominant popular representations. The analyses aim to engage with and challenge these sensationalised accounts through the presentation of alternative readings and more complex understandings of the boys' multiple performances of Muslim masculinity. It is hoped that this form of 'defusing' of dominant narratives around Muslim masculinity may then facilitate the space for more 'mundane' and less sensationalised accounts to be brought into the discursive arena (e.g. see Archer 2003).

As I have detailed elsewhere (Archer 2001; 2003), the boys in this study claimed specifically Muslim identities and located themselves within a discourse of *umma* – which they constructed as a global network of Muslim brotherhood. They resisted both Britishness and Pakistani/Bangladeshi identities, claiming that these are 'just where you're born'.⁵ However, at the same time, they constructed identities that were very much rooted in their local areas. In the next section, the chapter discusses the importance of space/place to the boys' experiences and identity constructions: firstly in relation to the wider Mill Town locale and then specifically within schools. The final section considers the boys' constructions of symbolic discursive territories (through one group's discussion of the Salman Rushdie affair), with attention drawn again to how even these symbolic spaces are grounded within localised relations and spaces.

Segregated places – contested spaces

The local area

Questions of geographical segregation have long been raised in relation to debates around ethnic integration and inclusion. These issues were highlighted particularly in a controversial address by Trevor Phillips, Chair of the Commission for Racial Equality, in which he warned that Britain is 'sleep-walking to segregation' (22 September 2005). In a sensationalist critique of what Phillips termed 'anything goes multiculturalism,' he argued that the focus on 'multi' culturalism needs to be redressed with greater integration and shared values. In particular, the speech criticised residential segregation between communities and warned against the dangers of ethnic 'ghettoes'. South Asians, but particularly Pakistanis (who are predominantly Muslims) were singled out as especially (and increasingly) residentially segregated groups (however, see D. Phillips 2006 for critique). Pre-dating Trevor Phillips' critique by some years, the boys in my study also described Mill Town as an ethnically segregated locale. However, they discussed the issues in somewhat more complex terms that would seem to elude some of Phillips' proposed solutions (e.g. his suggestion to bring together segregated groups of young people in common spaces, such as summer camps, to develop mutual respect and common values).

Across the study, boys described Mill Town as geographically racialised, segregated into 'white' and 'black' areas. The four schools that they attended were located in contrasting parts of the town – yet all were in predominantly 'white' areas. For instance, Hightown School was up on a hill in a leafy, white, middle-class residential suburb, whereas Westfield School was located in the middle of a fairly 'run-down' white, working-class residential estate. The vast majority of the boys lived in the predominantly Muslim residential area in the centre of town ('Barnton') and travelled out to their schools. While they described the areas where they lived as 'crowded', 'dirty', 'untidy', 'cramped', 'damp', they were also valued as 'friendly' and 'safe' ('there's no racism cos its all black', Javed). In contrast, the white areas of town – both the working-class white 'estates' and the middle class suburbs with 'open space and gardens' – were experienced as risky and unsafe, being 'violent' and 'racist'. In other words, they mapped their local terrain into 'safe' and 'unsafe' spaces similarly to the black urban boys in Westwood's (1990) study.

Jagdip: Some of the areas like –
Naseem: There's some areas really bad –
Sham: There's some areas there's a lot of violence.
Naseem: Not so much the black but the white area –
Sham: Yeah, that's racist.
(Lowtown School, TD)

LA: So have you experienced racism in Mill Town?
Rahan: Loads.
LA: Loads? Like what sorts of things?
Rahan: Its like everyday life.

LA   Everyday?
Wajit: You get racism everywhere in [Westfield area].
(Westfield School, LA)

The boys recounted how their daily commute into these areas to go to school
required them to negotiate numerous experiences of verbal and physical racism.
For instance, boys at Hightown school had to navigate longer routes home to
avoid being assaulted:

Deepak: This area, at home time you can't walk through the short-cut. Go
            around there are you're gonna get KO'd, man.
Abdul: Cos it's pretty racist round here, it's a pretty racist area.

Another boy, Gulfraz, descibed how his father (a taxi driver) would drop him
at school, which, as his friend Abdul explained, was to protect him from the
dangers of walking through the local area as a visible minority ethnic boy:

Gulfraz: I go in a car with my dad – I go to him err drop me here and there –
Abdul: . . . so he just looks foreign, innit? [if] he comes round here yeah,
            he just get caned, cos these [white] lads are pretty racist!
(Hightown School, TD)

Racist incidents were not solely restricted to the boys' excursions into 'white'
areas – as the boys suggest in the following extract, they would be sporadic
'raids' by organised white racist groups into the predominantly Muslim areas
of town ('Barnton'):

TD: What – what about your parents and family? Have they had any
            racism?
Yasser: A lot.
Shabid: A lot.
Yasser: Like the NF spotted them –
Tam: Was there, was there a National Front – National Front thing here?
Yasser: Yeah a lot have been beaten down.
Shabid: Yeah quite a lot of people from uh like . . . once my uncle got
            chased . . . and my other uncles came out . . . for back-up.
Yasser: And most of Barnton must have come outside – they – all used to
            come round outside my dad's – when my dad all finished praying
            in the mosque – and they used to come – they all used to go chasing
            . . . grab 'em.
Abdul: Cos they know – . . . that there's a part where there's more
            Asians . . . there's there's no white person or anyone yeah to hassle
            yer –

Yasser: But that's why they used to come *down* there! The Asians . . . they
           want to like take over (Abdul: Take over). *Now* they [whites]
           won't come because . . . all our big brothers, they all grown up and
           they [are] older and there's too much of us, innit? (TD: Yeah) Like
           our fathers . . . they used to – if they being racist they'd pick a fight.
(Eastfield School, TD)

As the above extract illustrates, the boys constructed these incidents within
a highly masculinised social sphere, in which white male protagonists were
pitted against the 'Asian' boys and their extended male networks of brothers,
fathers and uncles. The boys' accounts evoked strong notions of gendered and
racialised territoriality – of 'our' and 'their' spaces that are constantly contested, threatened and defended. Within the account, hegemonic masculinity
appears to play an important role in both the causes of, responses to and the
perpetuations of racisms. This is particularly notable in Yasser's suggestion that
these areas were attacked by white groups in an attempt to stop them becoming more powerful within the town ('But that's why they used to come *down*
there! The Asians, they want to like take over'). Boys and their male relatives
engaged in 'fighting back', a practice that enables young men to assert themselves as embodying powerful, hegemonic masculinities ('*Now* they won't come
because . . . there's too much of us, innit?').

The theme of 'taking over' – as a key factor within the perpetuation of inter-
ethnic violence – was also reiterated by boys in discussion groups at other
schools. For instance, the Hightown boys argued that hegemonic masculinity
demands the protection of 'face' – notably, ensuring that they are not seen to
be 'weak'. One key element of this involves being seen not to tolerate racist
name-calling (being 'called like, Pakis'), but responding with violence:

TD: Why – why do you think it'll never change?
Deepak: It'll never change because they the people that –
Gulfraz: Like all the white people –
Abdul: [If we're] called like 'Pakis' and that, and you know we – we're not
           gonna say oh – we're not gonna say 'yeah, yeah', you know?

The notion of white racism as a perceived response to Asians 'taking over'
is returned to in the next section, on schools. The point I would like to note
here, however, is that these discourses of masculinity are closely enmeshed with
wider racialised discourses. For instance, the notion of Asians 'taking over'
echoes 1970s Powellian rhetoric around 'immigrant invasion'. Within this discourse, contestations over 'territory' and social power are grounded within
exclusionary notions of 'Britishness', in which Asians are positioned as 'not
belonging' (Gilroy 1991) and illegitimate 'owners' of space within British
society. These 'neighbourhood nationalisms' (Cohen 1988) are thus enacted

through conflicts over the defence or claiming of particular spaces against racialised others.

As the data extracts illustrate, the boys aligned themselves with a discourse of hegemonic masculinity that positions the only 'manly' way to engage with racism as to 'fight back'. These constructions of 'hard' masculinity were also distinctly racialised and constructed within a global context – being shaped with particular reference to fantasies of hegemonic black (US/African/Caribbean) masculinity. For instance, Abdul and Fazaan evoked America as a 'hard' space within which black groups are able to assert power and 'stand up for themselves' by virtue of their enactment of 'rough' and violent masculinities:

Abdul: No – uh, racism's getting worse here . . . I – I think it's probably getting better in America because in America you can play rough . . . there – very rough there – and they used to have – know what I mean – organisations uh – of – you know what I mean – killing more black people and that – but it's getting better there –
Fazaan: All Asian people should think like that.
TD: You think Asian people need to become more aggressive and more angry about things?
Abdul: Yeah – stick up – uh, stand up for themselves and not stand in the corner.

Even when Tamar later attempted to move the discussion on, Abdul returned enthusiastically to his thesis that the way forward for Asians is to embody and perform 'hard', hegemonic 'black' masculinities, epitomised for him by the boxer Mohammed Ali ('Get Muhammed Ali hhh! Know what I'm saying?! [. . .] because he – he just have to *look* at himself . . .'). These mythologised hyper(hetero) black masculinities were evoked as the epitome of 'hard', hegemonic masculinity, echoing wider popular discursive constructions of 'cool' black masculinity (e.g. Archer and Yamashita 2003; Majors and Billson 1992). The boys also located themselves in relation to a racialised mapping of the country, constructing London as where 'Nazis' and the BNP are, while viewing Bradford as 'rough' and able to 'stick up for . . . the black's rights'.[6]

Abdul: . . . in London, the Nazis are there!!
Deepak: You should know! You're from London!
TD: It's not – no – I think it's . . . a bit, . . . uh it's easier.
Deepak: No BNP there and that?
TD: They are, but uh it depends where you live, I mean, where I live it's fine.
Fazaan: Are they any like racist fights –

TD:	Not, not as much as here, cos – cos I mean, I – I grew up in Bradford –
Fazaan:	Bradford? Bradford's rough.
TD:	Which is rough?
Abdul:	You had the riots, hh!
TD:	Yeah, exactly –
Fazaan:	And they stick up for them, the blacks' rights.

The boys' identification of Bradford as 'rough' points to a conflation of discourses around social class, masculinity, 'race'/ethnicity, religion and region. The exchange between Tamar and the boys also highlights differences of gender, age and class: Tamar contests their construction of London (as a stronghold of Nazis/BNP), explaining that 'where I live it's fine'. She hints at differences between her current life-world (as a young graduate professional, living in a reasonably leafy and affluent area of London) and that of her youth, growing up in a working-class family in Bradford. The differences between Tamar's and the boys' lived geographies are not only in terms of the different physical areas they inhabit, but also in their temporality (e.g. fighting as more a part of school-aged young people's daily landscapes) and gender (fighting as bound up with performances of masculinity).

In the discussion groups, Tamar was frequently asked to reveal where she 'came from'. I discuss this elsewhere as exemplifying the boys' performances of masculinity and their attempts to position Tamar (and themselves in relation to her) as one of 'our' women (see Archer 2002a, 2002b; 2003). Discovering that she comes from a Pakistani family and grew up in Bradford was always a source of surprise and fascination to the boys – not least because they tended to read Tamar's accent and appearance as 'other' than their own normalised constructions of Muslim/Pakistani femininity. In particular, they assumed she was southern, middle-class and sometimes that she was 'Indian' on account of her accent and dress/appearance. The boys' mythologisation of Bradford as epitomising a 'hard' ('rough') form of Muslim identity ('they stick up for . . . the blacks' rights') thus shifted Tamar's positioning within the discussion group – providing her with potentially more symbolic status. A number of the boys responded to these shifting dynamics by attempting to assert themselves even more strongly[7] so as to align themselves with 'hard' Muslim masculinities.

It is important to note that these 'hard' Muslim masculinities were not performed consistently or unambiguously by these boys – they all recognised tensions and paradoxes within such performances and they also constructed themselves in ways that contradicted such performances. For instance, elsewhere in the discussions boys constructed themselves as sensitive and/or as achievement focused (see Archer 2003). Furthermore, not all the boys in the study claimed to value or aspired to perform these 'hard' masculinities. Indeed, several boys argued that 'fighting back' is not a good response to racism and a number of boys (but particularly those from Lowtown and Westfield schools who were interviewed by either me or Nessa) suggested that they preferred to 'ignore' racism. For instance, Rahan (Westfield School, LA) suggested that the apt way of dealing with racist comments is 'you just look at them'. Wajit (Westfield School, LA) also agreed that while 'you get racism everywhere in [area] . . . you normally just ignore it'. These more restrained responses did not simply mean that these boys experienced less racism than those who advocated more angry or violent responses – they recounted experiencing a similar level of daily insults and abuse ('they do loads of things – throwing eggs at our windows, throwing rubbish in our garden', Majid, Westfield, NS). Rather, they point to a diversity of performances of British Muslim masculinities. Moreover, the increased prevalence of the 'ignore it' discourse within groups conducted with the white researcher underlines the situatedness of the discursive production. For instance, it invites questions regarding the role of power and the potential for whiteness (together with other axes of social difference) to silence or facilitate the production of particular discourses.

Moreover, there was no simple dichotomy between those boys who enacted or valued 'hard' Muslim masculinities and those who did not. Rather, I would suggest that the discourse of 'hard' Muslim masculinity provided a key reference point for all the boys' identities – providing a powerful and seductive attraction by virtue of its hegemonic appeal – against which the boys navigated and negotiated a range of identity positions and responses. This often resulted in contradictory positionings; for instance, Imran and Gufter (Lowtown School, LA) described with some pride their performances of some of the symbols of 'gangster' masculinity. They claimed to be in gangs and they took some delight in explaining aspects of their 'gangster' style, e.g. wearing 'baggy pants' (Imran) and 'bopping' ('walk with a broken leg', Gufter) – which they performed for the interviewer. Yet elsewhere in the discussion, Gufter derided other Asians for 'acting black' ('You get these *Asian* people who . . . they think they're niggers, you know? . . . they hear about it and they think it's fashion') and Imran agreed that such people were victims of popular media culture ('too much films, innit?', Imran).

Gufter: Different . . . but most Asian kids will go looking for fights you
           know they [try] to be like black . . . you know they try talking
           black as well . . . like 'I'm a nigger don't start with me!' . . . But
           they're not! But . . . they, they just they just . . . weird! Thick!

Imran: And the . . . the only word that they use is innit 'man!' . . . man!
           hhh!

Gufter: [laughs] Talk weird! [laughter] It's like the black people they do it
           because . . . that's the way they (Jamil: Been brought up) brought
           up . . . whereas here they do it because they think . . . right 'I'm a
           black'. Its fashion they try to do it like that.

(Lowtown School, LA)

Boys like Wajit (Westfield School, LA) who had elsewhere espoused 'ignoring' racism also admitted to being in local gangs for 'protection' and 'back-up' (Wajit). Hence the boys took up shifting positions in relation to discourses around 'hard' Muslim masculinity that were negotiated across discursive and material contexts as they navigated their lives within their local areas.

In school

While all the boys from across the discussion groups talked at length and in some detail about the racisms that they experienced within public areas and spaces in Mill Town, their accounts of racisms and racialised relations within school were more varied. Broadly speaking, the boys at Eastfield and Hightown schools were more likely to describe incidences of racism and tense relations between ethnic groups (pupils and/or teachers) than boys at Westfield or Lowtown schools. Before discussing these points in greater depth, it is worth first noting here a few of the characterising features of each school, to help situate and contextualise these analyses. Lowtown School had the highest proportion of minority ethnic pupils, at around 80–90 per cent, the majority of whom were from Bangladeshi backgrounds. Hightown School had the lowest proportion of non-white pupils (approximately 20 per cent), most of whom were from Pakistani backgrounds. Eastfield and Westfield schools recorded roughly similar proportions of minority ethnic pupils (33 per cent and 42 per cent respectively), most of whom were from Pakistani backgrounds. At the time of the research, Lowtown, Eastfield and Westfield schools were all recording below the national average for five or more A-C grades at GCSE, whereas Hightown School was slightly exceeding the national average.

It was also notable that the strongest and most vigorous accounts of racism within schools were produced in discussion groups with Tamar, rather than with me (see Archer 2002a, 2002b for discussion). Boys at Eastfield and Hightown schools (but particularly those interviewed by Tamar) perceived their schools to be characterised by racialised forms of micro-segregation. That is, while Muslim and white pupils attended each school and coexisted alongside one another in many of its spaces, the boys highlighted a range of ways in which subtle forms of segregation were played out. For instance, they pointed to separation in classroom seating patterns and the use of communal areas at break times and lunchtimes. Indeed, a number of pupils' photographic diaries[8] also reinforced this point.[9] Yasser, for instance, suggested that 'black and whites don't sit together' in class or at break times:

TD: If you were like head teacher what do you reckon you'd do? How
          do you think you'd change things at school? . . . Do you reckon
          you'd change anything?
Yasser: I'd change racism . . . I'd change racism.

TD: You'd change racism? How do you reckon you'd do that?
Yasser: At the minute – black and whites don't sit together.
(Eastfield School, TD)

Yasser went on to explain how particular social spaces in school were known as either 'white' or 'black' – for instance, he and his (Muslim) friends did not use the common room at school because this was a 'white' space ('none of us hardly go in there! It's all the whites', Yasser). In Hightown School, as researchers, Tamar and I also noted the striking physical segregation of a couple of key classes, notably the running of parallel classes in French (all white pupils) and Urdu (all Muslim pupils).[10] Across the discussion groups, boys also suggested that they spent most of their social time within school in male, Muslim friendship groups.

However, these issues of 'segregation' resist any sort of simplistic interpretation. For instance, the boys confounded potential readings of themselves as 'excluded' by white pupils from particular spaces in school (e.g. the potential interpretation that Yasser and his friends are being denied access to the social resource of the common room). Instead, Yasser reframed the common room as a refuge for white pupils – a place where they retreat from their more powerful Muslim male peers who dominate the school space – rather than a place that Muslim boys were denied access to ('they're scared of us aren't they!' Yasser).

Of course, any such example will produce a multitude of readings (for instance, some of the boys' white peers might produce quite different counter-readings). What is particularly interesting about Yasser's comments is the ways in which he seems to be evoking and mobilising a 'hard', hegemonic form of Muslim masculinity to position himself/Muslim masculinity as powerful within the school space. This form of masculinity stands in stark contrast to previous dominant educational discursive constructions – which positioned Asian boys as 'soft', 'little' and 'effeminate' (e.g. see Gillborn 1990; Connolly 1998). In addition to drawing its power from hegemonic forms of masculinity, this construction is also given discursive weight by wider moral panics around 'dangerous' Muslim masculinity. It is thus rendered a particularly potent and seductive form of masculinity for boys to mobilise within the discursive 'jockeying for position' (Edley and Wetherell 1997) associated with 'doing boy' in school. For instance, boys recounted deploying race/racism as a weapon within their jostles to be 'cock of the school'. Recounting spectacular tales of fights also provided spaces for bonding and mutual recognition as part of a process of 'doing boy' – enabling collective boundaries to be drawn between 'us' and 'them'.

This intermeshing of discourses around 'race', racism and masculinity is also illuminated in Yasser's reflection that he feels racism cannot be changed or ameliorated within school because (he argues) it is an expression of resentment and subordination on the part of white pupils/boys in response to Yasser and his friends' strengthening masculinities:

TD: Why do you think that you can't change?

Yasser: Cos you look down at the Year 7 now . . . and the other years . . .
           it's not that you know I think its gonna carry on like that . . . I'm
           not saying that oh – 'we're the hardest' or anything (TD: Uh huh),
           but it's like have you noticed the blacks mostly that are taking over
           more and more? . . . And racism is just going to carry on and carry
           on . . . There's never been whites since I joined school that have
           taken over has it? . . . I think the British listen to quite a lot of us
           now (TD: They do?) I think they got used to it . . . (TD: Mmm)
           you get the odd few who don't like . . . who give you cheek.

(Eastfield School, TD)

Here, Yasser picks up on his earlier theory that white racisms develop and
solidify in response to growing status and power among Asian pupils. However,
as his final remark indicates – this hegemony is only partial. While 'talking
tough' and engaging in violent counter-attacks in response to racist taunts provided several of the boys with the tools for constructing 'hard' Muslim masculinities, the boys also recognised the limitations of these identities. In
particular, they recognised that their performances held ambiguous value
within the school space – while they were valued by the boys themselves and
generated masculinity capital within male peer groups, as illustrated below,
their ability to enact these responses was determined by each situation and
context. Furthermore, these performances brought the boys into conflict with
teachers and school rules.

TD: Um, at school, I mean, do you get a lot of racism at school?

Gulfraz: Yeah, too much.

Deepak: You know, we walk around, we walk around school.

Gulfraz: And they call you names.

Deepak: Last week . . . this lad, he called me and that . . . I mean . . . he got
           too much racist . . . if I'd wanna, I'd have broke his nose and that,
           but he was with his mates . . . that's why I didn't do nothing – [but]
           if I'd wanna, I'd have killed him.

Gulfraz: If they say anything then you can just cane them.

TD: Yeah.

Deepak: But then again, if you do do summat, and they get a beating,
           then you get the blame for it – even if they started it. Nah, just can't
           beat the white guy. The white guy is straight, the black lad's messed
           up.

(Hightown School, TD)

Hence Deepak and Gulfraz suggest that the efficacy of violence as a
response to their experiences of racism is dependent upon context and can thus

be a risky strategy. They recognise that school rules are organised to punish/prohibit violence as a 'solution' or appropriate response to racism – much to their apparent chagrin. Their feelings of powerlessness are compounded by their perception that white boys are protected by the school institution. As Deepak says: 'just can't beat the white guy. The white guy is straight, the black lad's messed up'. This comment echoes bel hooks' (1992: 89) analysis that black masculinity has been conceptualised within dominant discourses as psychologically 'fucked up'. It is perhaps also notable that Deepak's assertion was made several years before the Macpherson (1999) report brought the notion of institutional racism more directly into the popular public consciousness.

Of course, not all pupils by any stretch felt that their schools were institutionally racist spaces – and Lowtown School in particular prided itself on fostering a clear anti-racist ethos. Indeed, boys at Lowtown School described their school as a space where racism is 'not allowed', and hence experienced it as distinct from other areas of Mill Town. However, as illustrated in the excerpt below, beyond the physical boundaries of the school, pupils could experience quite different relations with their classmates.

TD:	Do you change when you come to school?
All:	No.
Sham:	Don't think so . . . s-some people.
Jagdip:	Cos usually we all go round together at home.
Sham:	It depends, some people are. Like some people are here and er they talk to us like, summat. It depends, you know? Cos there's a bit of racism, like I said, but not in school, you know, when you go outside. You see, they [white pupils] wouldn't talk to you, wouldn't if they were with their mates – like I mean white guys.
Said:	Like when they're here they're really quiet, but like when they're with their friends, parents, they talk and all that.
Sham:	Yeah, yeah!
TD:	What about you? Are you like, I mean would you talk to them outside school if you see them?
Sham:	Yeah (All: Yeah). We did, but they ignore us! And then they come in school and you know, they try and hide it, [we say] 'How come you didn't say hi?', [they say] 'Oh I didn't see ya'. But we *know* it's really –
TD:	How does that make you feel?
Sham:	Not bad, I guess it's just *life*, it's – everyone has to put up with things . . . if they do that the next day as well then I say 'Why did you do that?', he says 'Cos I didn't see ya', I go '*No*, you're racist, aren't you?'. So . . . innit.

(Lowtown School, TD)

Sham's account underlines the difficulties inherent in attempts to challenge racisms within society. While his school has managed to create a space in which racisms are 'not allowed', it is unable to carry this beyond the boundaries of school as a geographical and temporal site. Sham's account also poses pertinent questions for today's debates around integration and inter-cultural relations – and suggests that there are few easy answers.

Symbolic territories: race, face and space

In this final section I would like to consider perhaps the most contentious extract to emerge from the discussion groups. This emerged from the group conducted by Tamar with boys at Hightown School. The Rushdie Affair was not a topic on the interview schedules, but it did emerge in two of the groups conducted by Tamar, who then probed the pupils' views on it.

TD: What do you think about um the umm Salman Rushdie thing?
          [Boys excitedly talk over one another]
Abdul: Man need to be killed, innit!
Gulfraz: I'm gonna kill him.
Fazaan: I, I'll kill him!
TD: You'd kill him?
Abdul: I – I'll kill 'im . . . if I see him now.
Fazaan: I'll kill 'im as well.
Abdul: . . . he did it for publicity, that's what he did it for, to get . . . well known and that. That's what he did it for, to make a bit of money and that . . . but I tell ya, I not going to give a fuck if I get to uh . . . jail and get killed whatever, I not really give a fuck – but if I see that guy, man . . .
TD: Why do you think it's so bad, what he did?
Abdul   Because –
Gulfraz: Because –
Abdul: Because he offended our religion! . . . know what I mean? He uhh, he took the mick out of our religion . . . all the white people must have been laffing and that [at] all the Bengalis (Fazaan: Yeah the Sikhs) yeah, uh . . . I tell you, when I see that guy . . . he's gonna get chopped up!

(Hightown School, TD)

This extract can be read in a number of different ways. For instance, the boys' talk could be read as an instance of angry ('fundamentalist') young men espousing violent and extreme views (e.g. they suggest that they would 'kill' Rushdie because 'he offended our religion' and Abdul asserts that he would be willing to go to prison or be killed himself). Hence the extract might be taken as evidence to support public concerns about the rise of radicalism among young British Muslims.

However, the extract might also be read as an indication of the discursive production of masculine identities through intermeshing discourses of 'race', religion and gender. The boys are able to draw on 'hard' performances of British Muslim masculinity and might be read as engaging in verbal tests of toughness with one another (Brown 1998; Archer 2001) as part of the process of 'doing boy' both to one another and to the interviewer. The discursive power and strength of their performances are thus not linked to, or dependent upon, 'real' actions. While these masculinities are constructed within a specifically racialised and religious (British Muslim) frame of reference, they also clearly evoke the tenets of a potent form of hegemonic masculinity, through appeals to toughness, bravery/fearlessness, danger, combat and action. The deployment of such discourses enables the boys to assert themselves as powerful men (to each other and to the researcher) not only through their espousal of hegemonic masculinity but through their claims to racial/religious authenticity, which is achieved through their positioning of themselves as defenders of the honour of their religion.

Consideration might also be given to the situatedness of the boys' discourses – notably both the boys' accounts and our own experiences as researchers of markedly more strained inter-ethnic relations within this particular school at the time of the research (see Archer 2003). Furthermore, Abdul specifies Rushdie's offence as not principally a matter of malignity or blasphemy, but in distinctly localised terms, as an assault on the collective 'face' of Muslims, causing other ethnic and religious groups ('the white people . . . the Sikhs') to 'laugh' at him and his friends. This, again, suggests a possible reading of the extract as exemplifying racialised, hegemonic entanglements – in which the boys seek to resist 'softness'/less powerful positionings through the production of specifically racialised forms of masculine 'hardness'.

Conclusions

In this chapter I have argued that Muslims are increasingly subject to a forced telling of the self in UK public life. Drawing on data from a study of Muslim young people in the mid 1990s, I have attempted to draw some parallels between then and contemporary events – suggesting in particular that while there are, of course, considerable differences between the contemporary post-9/11, post-7/7 world and the post-Rushdie era of the study, there is a pertinent parallel, in that both are times in which young Muslims, but particularly young Muslim men, are being forced to situate (and explain) themselves in relation to wider, negative (demonising) discourses around 'fundamentalist', 'dangerous' Muslim masculinity. The chapter has drawn attention to the role of space/place in Muslim boys' identity constructions, discussing in particular the racialisation of residential local areas and of relations and spaces within schools. In response to narrowly framed public panics around Muslim masculinity, I have attempted to open up potential readings of the boys' identity discourses. In particular, it has been argued that Muslim boys' constructions of racialised, religious identities need to be understood as integrally bound up with the production of masculinities and processes of 'doing boy'. As such, this chapter aims to challenge the public exoticisation of Muslim masculinity and it is hoped that it will contribute to the ongoing search for more liberatory 'third spaces' in researching social difference (Cohen and Ainley 2000; Reay and Mirza 2001).

Notes

1. The construction of a Western–Muslim cultural dichotomy underpins many of the commentaries on these events. For instance, in his statement to Parliament denouncing the 7 July terrorist attacks (11 July 2005: www.number-10.gov.uk/output/Page7903.asp), Prime Minister Tony Blair mounted a defence of an imagined, homogenised Britishness of 'our values' and 'our way of life' – despite the perpetrators' being born and raised as British citizens.

2. I would further argue that the debate has been configured such that women who do not wear the niqab are rendered 'reasonable', 'integrated' and 'British', whereas those who wear it are positioned as 'unreasonable'/radicalised, 'separatist' and other/anti-British.

3. E.g. The films *Bend it Like Beckham* and *East is East*.

4. A reflexive account of interactions of 'race', gender and class in the production and analysis of the data can be found in Archer (2002).

5. Hence they appeared to contest some of the claims made within contemporary citizenship debates.

6. The boys' use of political blackness as a unifying identity position from which to talk about racisms is discussed elsewhere, see Archer (2001, 2003).

7. For instance, some boys stated that women in Mill Town would not be 'allowed' to dress like Tamar (Tamar was, in her own view, fairly conservatively dressed, wearing a long-sleeved top and long skirt).

8. In the wider study, a number of pupils (but mostly girls) also completed photographic diaries. Pupils were provided with an instant camera and were asked to take photographs over a 24-hour period representing 'A Day in My Life'.

9. For instance, a number of pupils' photographs depicted distinct seating patterns, organised along both ethnic and gender lines, within particular classes and social spaces, e.g. in the playground or in the school canteen.

10. Indeed, we also experienced feeling segregated ourselves – we had asked to go in to a couple of classes to observe and talk with pupils and were surprised that I was shown in to the all-white French class and Tamar to the Urdu class.

References

Archer, L. (2001), ' "Muslim brothers, black lads, traditional Asians": British Muslim young men's constructions of race, religion and masculinity', *Feminism & Psychology*, 11(1), 79–105.

Archer, L. (2002a), ' "It's easier that you're a girl and that you're Asian": interactions of race and gender between researchers and participants', Feminist Review, 72, 108–32.

Archer, L. (2002b), 'Change, culture and tradition: British Muslim pupils talk about Muslim girls' post-16 "choices" ', *Race, Ethnicity and Education*, 5(4), 359–76.

Archer, L. (2003), 'Race', Masculinity and Schooling: Muslim Boys and Education, Buckingham: Open University Press.

Archer, L. and Yamashita, H. (2003), 'Theorising inner city masculinities: "race", class, gender and education', *Gender and Education*, 15(2), 115–32.

Brown, L. M. (1998), 'Voice and ventriloquation in girls' development', in K. Henwood, C. Griffin and A. Phoenix (eds), *Standpoints and Differences*, London: Sage.

Cohen, P. (1988), 'The perversions of inheritance: studies in the making of multi-racist Britain', in P. Cohen and H. S. Bains (eds), Multi-Racist Britain, London: Macmillan.

Cohen, P. and Ainley, P. (2000), 'In the country of the blind: youth studies and cultural studies in Britain', *Journal of Youth Studies*, 3(1), 79–85.

Connolly, P. (1998), *Racism, Gender Identities and Young Children: Social Relations in a Multi-Ethnic, Inner-City Primary School*, London: Routledge.

Edley, N. and Wetherell, M. (1995), *Men in Perspective: Practice, Power and Identity*, London: Prentice Hall/Harvester Wheatsheaf.

Gillborn, D. (1990), *'Race', ethnicity and education: teaching and learning in multi-ethnic schools*, London: Unwin Hyman.

Gilroy, P. (1991), *There Ain't no Black in the Union Jack*, Chicago: Chicago University Press.

Hesse, B. (2000), Un/Settled Multiculturalisms, London, Zed Books.

hooks, b. (1992), *Black Looks*, London: Turnaround Press.

Macpherson, W. (1999), *The Stephen Lawrence Inquiry*, London: The Stationery Office.

Majors, R. and Billson, J. M. (1992), *Cool Pose: The Dilemmas of Black Manhood in America*, Lexington: New York Books.

Modood, T. (1992), *Not Easy Being British*, Stoke-on-Trent: Trentham Books.

Phillips, D. (2006), 'Parallel lives? Challenging discourses of British Muslim self-segregation', *Environment and Planning D: Society and Space*, 24 (1) 25–40.

Reay, D. and Mirza, H. (2001). 'Black supplementary schools: spaces of radical black-ness', in R. Majors (ed.), *Educating Our Black Children: New Directions and Radical Approaches*, London: Routledge, pp. 90–102.

Skeggs, B. (2004), *Class, Self, Culture*, London: Sage.

West, C. (1993), 'The new cultural politics of difference', in S. During (ed.), *The Cultural Studies Reader*, London: Routledge.

Westwood, S. (1990), 'Racism, black masculinity and the politics of space', in J. Hearn and D. Morgan (eds), *Men, Masculinities and Social Theory*, London: Unwin Hyman.

SECTION 2

• • •

LANDSCAPES, COMMUNITIES AND NETWORKS

BRITISH ARAB PERSPECTIVES ON RELIGION, POLITICS AND 'THE PUBLIC'

Caroline Nagel and Lynn Staeheli

Introduction

In October of 2006, a public debate erupted in Britain over comments made by Labour MP Jack Straw about his veiled female Muslim constituents. Straw stated in an interview that he had asked women to remove their face coverings when speaking to him in order to enhance communication between them. Denying any objection to a simple headscarf, Straw stated that he felt uncomfortable speaking to someone he could not see, reasoning that covering the face defeated the purpose of meeting in person rather than over the telephone or by e-mail. Moreover, he urged his veiled constituents to consider the consequences their religious garb had in terms of creating 'parallel communities' and feelings of 'separateness'. 'Communities', Straw argued, are 'bound together partly by informal chance relations between strangers, people acknowledging each other in the street, being able to pass the time of day, sharing just experiences in the street, and that is just made more difficult if people are wearing a veil . . .' (BBC 2006). The veil, Straw suggested in his comments, is not simply another form of difference to be encountered in the everyday life of communities, but rather, an impediment to shared experience.

Shortly after the Straw episode, a case emerged in which a young Muslim teacher was suspended from her job for refusing to remove her face covering. The case was brought to court amid a chorus of commentaries by Labour ministers about the dangers of religious extremism, the oppression of Muslim women, and the threat to social harmony posed by overzealous Muslims. This sudden preoccupation with Muslim women's headwear seems curiously out of place in Britain, where, in contrast to France, headscarves have not generated a great deal of controversy. But, at the same time, these recent incidents reflect misgivings about the integration of the country's Muslim communities, who are mainly of South Asian origin, that have been building since the Rushdie Affair in 1989. The outbreak of violence in the summer of 2001 between Asian and white youths in three northern towns, the bombing of the London underground in 2005, and the foiling of a plot to blow up passenger jets in 2006, have led to expressions of concern by public officials about the 'self-segregation' of British Muslims and their seeming unwillingness to adapt to mainstream British life. These concerns have coalesced in a discourse of social cohesion which places the onus of integration on (Muslim) minorities, and which signals the marginalisation of public discourses of multiculturalism (Back et al. 2002; Lewis and Neal 2005; Yuval-Davis et al. 2005).

British Muslims have had remarkably little say in constructing their own public identity in the midst of these debates, in part because of the strength and momentum of negative stereotypes, and in part because of the government's reliance on a small number of voices to represent the entire Muslim 'community' (Gilliat-Ray 2004). Where British Muslims *have* been given a voice, their differences in terms of political views and social attitudes, and indeed of religious and cultural practices, become apparent, as do their frustrations at being constantly positioned as outsiders (Kahani-Hopkins and Hopkins 2002; see also Lewis 1994; Klausen 2005). This chapter attempts to destabilise dominant narratives of British Muslims as standing outside the public realm by analysing the relationship between religious and public identities held by activists who are simultaneously Arab, Muslim, British and participants in the public realm.

The chapter begins with a brief discussion of the role of 'difference' in the public sphere and in the construction of 'the public.' We argue that religious identities in general, and Muslim identities in particular, are uneasily incorporated into western conceptualisations of the public sphere. We show that discourses about western secular liberalism and Islam pivot on several dichotomies – public/private, East/West, rational/irrational, cultural/political – that people must negotiate, and we explore these negotiations from the perspective of British Arab activists.

We argue, specifically, that many activists attempt to bring Arab identities into the public sphere and that they encourage other community members to do so, as well. But being (for the most part) Muslim, their religious identities are also brought into public view. This is not because they attempt to politicise their religion, but because Islam has been politicised in 'other' public discourses, including those that operate in public policy, in the broader community of British Muslims, and in the stereotypes held by the 'public' at large. In this context, we argue, many British Arab activists often attempt to validate Islam as a matter of faith and culture, but not as the basis of politics. In so doing, these activists distinguish between public and private spheres while also acknowledging the simultaneity of religious and secular identities.

The neutral public, the problem of difference and the 'Muslim Challenge'

Jack Straw's views on the violation of societal norms by fully veiled Muslim women speak to a variety of tensions inherent in ideas of 'the public' as it has been conceived in western liberal democracies. The idealised public sphere celebrates the unmediated interaction between strangers and the free expression of diverse opinions and views among rational individuals (see Habermas (1989) for one characterisation). In practice, however, this conceptualisation of the public relies on the marginalisation or concealment – socially and spatially – of those whose differences are seen to undermine the public's inherent neutrality and rationality (Marston 1990; Young 1990). Women, for instance, have been seen historically as embodying irrationality by virtue of their reproductive roles, and thus have been excluded from male-dominated spaces of paid employment and politics (Pateman 1989; Walby 1994; Lister 1997). Likewise, black and minority ethnic groups have been placed outside of the public on account of their 'inherent' racial characteristics (Jackson 1987), an exclusion enforced through myriad systems of segregation and discrimination. While some of the ways in which exclusion is enforced are social, a wide variety of government policies serve to hide difference (e.g. through regulations that sustain segregation or that limit access to public spaces (Anderson 1988)) or encourage assimilation of cultural, ethnic and linguistic differences (e.g. through immigration and citizenship policies (Sassen 1999)).

As these examples indicate, the liberal public is predicated on the construction, enforcement, and regulation of social differences in order to create a veneer of neutrality and inclusiveness. It would be a mistake, however, to see the social distinctions that frame the public as static and inflexible. History is replete with struggles to alter and to expand the public and to contest exclusion from public spheres and spaces (Mitchell 1995). Feminist and civil rights movements, for instance, have resulted in fuller (though by no means complete) incorporation of women and minorities into the public sphere by extending the franchise to them, outlawing discrimination against them, and increasing their access to the workplace and the political sphere (Staeheli and Cope 1994). The advent of multiculturalism, as well, can be seen as expansive by recognising and incorporating – rather than denying – difference in the public sphere. In all of these examples, the many dichotomies structuring the public – public and private, rational and irrational, national and foreign, among others – have been renegotiated and, to some extent, reformulated through the political mobilisation of subordinated groups.

Yet differences that frame understandings of the public are not eliminated through mobilisation so much as they are reconfigured in relation to new 'challenges' that confront societies and publics. In many western societies today, the so-called 'Muslim challenge' (Klausen 2005) relates, in part, to common conceptions of the political nature of Islam and the influence of radical religious

extremism on the politics of the Muslim world (Eickelman and Piscatori 1996).
For western societies, the path to modernity has been marked by the delegit-
imization of religious authority in the political process and, to varying degrees,
the legal separation between the religious and the political (or 'church and
state') (Salvatore 2004). Religion, in this sense, has been confined, along with
other forms of irrationality, into the realm of private life.[1] The presumed lack
of distinction between religion and politics in the Muslim world, therefore, sig-
nifies inherent irrationality, anti-modernism and backwardness – a conception
reinforced by the constant stream of media images of suicide bombers, behead-
ings and burqas that flow from the Muslim world (A. Ahmed 1992).[2]

In western states, Muslim populations have come to be viewed as intensely
problematic, especially in light of the growing visibility of Muslims in public
space through the wearing of headscarves, the construction of mosques, and
requests for the provision of prayer spaces in universities and workplaces
(Dwyer 1993; Ehrkamp 2006; Salvatore 2004). An overt Islamic identity represents for many a threat to the neutral public by a religious tradition that is
often claimed to be the antithesis of liberalism, rationality and modernity (see
Said 1978; L. Ahmed 1992). Crucially, Muslims are often perceived to be pur-
posefully defying the neutrality and secularity of national societies and exclud-
ing themselves from the public by marking themselves out as different; in this
regard, Jack Straw's views are consistent with those of the broader public in
many western societies. Under these conditions, the balance between freedom
of religious expression and secular liberalism has become a contentious issue
(see Soysal 1997; Turner 2002). Increasingly, the response to Muslim visibility
and political claims in many European countries has been the scaling back of
multiculturalism – which has been blamed for the flourishing of radical Islamic
identity – and the reassertion of 'core national values' and assimilationist aims
(Joppke 2004; Lewis and Neal 2005).

Debates about the appropriate role of Islam in the public sphere (and the
limits of multiculturalism) are especially pronounced in state schools, which are
key sites for the reproduction of citizens (Dwyer 1993; Dwyer and Meyer 1995;
Mitchell 2003). In France, for instance, concerns about the radicalisation and
non-integration of Muslims have fuelled ongoing debates about the wearing of
headscarves in schools, leading to a ban on all religious attire. In formulating
the ban, French officials asserted the primacy of '*laïcité*' over individual religious freedom and the primacy of public neutrality over the right to express
'communitarian' difference (Bowen 2007; Thomas 2006). In Britain, no such
principle of *laïcité* governs the running of schools, and rows over headscarves
have been relatively rare. Nonetheless, the place of Islam in the school system
has become highly contentious as the state – which has long supported
Catholic, Anglican and some Jewish schools – attempts to expand the provision of public education through 'faith schools'. While the state has agreed to
maintain a small number of Muslim schools, discussions about increasing the

number of these schools have been fraught with concerns over Muslim self-seg-regation, extremism and the oppression of women (Gokulsing 2006; Modood and May 2001).

School controversies, therefore, are indicative of the highly problematic position of Muslim minorities in public and in the collective imagination of western nation-states. Overall, there is a pronounced tendency in public discourse in the West, perhaps most openly in Europe, to interpret the political claims of Muslim minorities in terms of the imposition of a fundamentalist, anti-modern Islam on a historically Christian, secularised, rational public. Seen in this light, 'Muslim' behaviours and practices are under the constant scrutiny of politicians, news reporters, teachers and social commentators who evaluate such behaviours and practices in terms of Muslim (dis)loyalty, (non)integration, and (un)assimilability (Werbner 2000).

Complicating Muslim public identities

The stereotype of Muslims assuming an identity that is religious above all else and that is incompatible with the secularised, modern public sphere belies the highly variable ways in which Muslims practise and conceive of relationships between religion and politics and between cultural difference and membership in the public. Macleod's (1991) groundbreaking study of the 'new veiling' in Egypt, for instance, indicates that Muslim women, particularly in the lower middle classes, have adopted religious dress for a variety of reasons, not all of them obviously religious *or* political. For some, Islamic fashions allow women to save money; for others, covering becomes important for young women who wish to work and study, but who also wish to avoid harassment on public transport and in the public spaces of congested cities. A key point made in Macleod's account and others is that the meanings and intents attached to particular 'Muslim' practices are multilayered and situated in localised political and social contexts. Above all, these practices represent a negotiation of the many dichotomies – modern/traditional, religious/cultural, public/private, female/male – that structure people's social and spatial mobility.

Recent research on Muslim minorities in the West has also explored the complexity of Muslim practices and identities and the different ways in which religious identity and belief enters into the formation of public and private identities. Dwyer's (1999) research on British Muslim fashion, for instance, examines the ways in which young Muslim women use the contested space of the school to fabricate, quite literally, new hybrid identities, undermining the static, unitary notions of Muslimness and Asianness that they encounter both in society at large and in their families. A rather different example is Kurien's (2001) description of Muslim Indian activists in the United States, who have positioned themselves explicitly as 'secularist' in opposition to the nationalist tendencies of their Hindu counterparts. For Indian American Muslim activists, secularism is central to the discourse of India as a multireligious, multi-ethnic, and multicultural entity, and they promote this secularism in their attempts to influence US foreign policy toward India and in their efforts to build an identity in the US in conjunction with other Muslim American groups.

These diverse examples caution against any single, essentialist reading of Islam as 'challenging' western notions of secular, liberal democracy, or of Muslims as constituting a population unwilling to engage with 'mainstream' society or to enter the public realm. Clearly, it is important to recognise the growing importance of religious claims on political life and on public space in many national contexts and the challenge to secularism posed by politically assertive religious movements, including Christian movements. But it is also important to recognise the variability of such claims and the different ways that individuals relate their religiosity to political participation, identities and citizenship.

In the remainder of this chapter, we wish to unsettle the apparent dichotomies that frame many western perceptions of Islam. We argue that 'secular' and 'religious,' 'public' and 'private,' 'personal' and 'political,' are not clearly demarcated spheres; they are, instead, sets of meanings and opportunities, often inscribed in particular spaces, that people interpret, appropriate and transgress in everyday life (Staeheli 1996). We focus, in particular, on the ambivalence expressed by British Arab activists toward 'Muslim' as a public and a political identity. While levels of personal religiosity vary significantly among our interviewees, in most instances, they reject a 'British Muslim' identity, which they regard as inherently politicised and as non-representative of their own feelings about religion and politics. Our interviewees do wish to challenge stereotypes of Islam, to rehabilitate the public image of their religion, and to situate themselves as citizens and legitimate members of the public. But their efforts to do so are tied up with a broader effort to validate Arab cultural identities in Britain, rather than to create a public, Muslim identity. This particular negotiation, we wish to suggest, destabilises mainstream conceptions of Islam, and at the same time draws upon and rearranges the array of dichotomies – public and private, personal and political, extremist and rational – employed in everyday discourses about Muslims and Islam.

Being Arab, being Muslim

The forty Muslim British Arabs[3] interviewed for this study were identified through their involvement in Arab-oriented organisations – i.e. those organisations with a remit to address, serve or promote people from Arab cultural backgrounds.[4] These individuals, who include both first- and second-generation British Arabs, participate in a wide variety of community activities, including charity and humanitarian work, community organising, social and cultural events, and political lobbying. Some of their activities are oriented toward the Arab world itself, while others focus more on developing local communities and fostering community participation in local and national politics. Many study participants are involved in multiple organisations, and a small number reported involvement in Muslim organisations, including both national lobbying groups, such as the Muslim Council of Britain, and smaller, mosque-based groups. On the whole, they are highly educated and have a professional status, reflective of the well-off economic position of British Arabs relative to other minority groups and even to the majority society (Al Rasheed 1996), though it should be noted that several of the interviewees come from and continue to serve the most disadvantaged segments of the British Arab population, namely, Moroccans, Yemenis and Iraqi refugees.

In the interviews, study participants were asked to explain political identities, their sense of community, their understandings of concepts like citizenship and multiculturalism, and the geographies of their political activities. We did *not* ask specific questions about religious faith, observance or mosque attendance, but issues of religion came up frequently as interviewees explained their sense of identity, their understandings of 'community' and their views on the major problems facing British Arabs. We also asked interviewees whether they identified with the category of British Muslim and what this category signified to them. It is clear from the interviews that British Arab activists are cognisant of the often negative meanings about Islam that circulate in public discourse and of perceptions of Muslims as breaching the boundary between private religiosity and public life.

As we illustrate below, our respondents' ideas about the proper place of religion in everyday life reflect their careful and thoughtful consideration of how their personal beliefs fit into wider debates about extremism, integration and citizenship. The relationships between faith, identity and politics they describe are complex, and even contradictory. Religiosity is an important motivation for our respondents, but that does not mean their activism is necessarily focused on Islam or religion. Rather, faith remains intensely personal and private for most of our respondents, even as it shapes the way they view the world and how they participate in the public realm. Because of the politicised nature of debates about Islam in Britain and because of their relationship with Asian Muslims there, most of our respondents eschew a political identity as British Muslim, and instead promote an identity as British Arab. The paradox they confront, however, is that, in order to promote an identity and a set of political claims as Arabs, they have to recognise the cultural association between Islam and Arabness. In their public political activity, then, they attempt to validate Islam and to educate British society about Islam. In so doing, their private identity becomes public, and to some degree, political.

Faith as a private, not public, identity

For some of our interviewees, Islam is an important motivating force for activism, and some see their religious faith as closely tied to their reasons for becoming involved in community organisations and affairs. For instance, Amal,[5] an Iraqi exile who has lived in several countries, identifies herself quite emphatically as a 'Muslim woman' and describes her work to promote Iraqi art as spreading the 'peace that Islam advocates in the Qur'an'. Her identity is a complex blend of religion and nationality: she is a Muslim woman, identifies her nationality as 'citizen of the world', and promotes Iraqi art specifically. Another strong statement of faith as a motivation for activism comes from Rafik, a Yemeni-Arab community leader, who sees community participation as 'a very basic principle of the Muslim faith'. When asked about issues facing his community, he speaks about discrimination, reduced life chances for Yemenis, and the lack of recognition of and support for the community by government. In order to redress these issues, he wants the state to fund Islamic education in schools, in spite of the hesitancy of local authorities. He describes state provision of Islamic education, in part, as a matter of fairness. Muslims, he remarks, 'are taxpayers, and they pay their dues to the government agencies and the local authorities, and they feel unfairly treated by not giving them back the recognition and services they need'. But his preference is not for purely Islamic schools, but rather to have 'state-run schools providing cultural and religious education to different faith groups, by tutors and teachers from the same community backgrounds'. This would be education not just about Islam, but also about Judaism, Buddhism, Hinduism, Sikhism and Christianity. In the case of Muslims in particular, he argues this is important so that children 'grow up as British Muslims, with no need to adopt ideologies from outside. They will be British citizens, they will be brought up with accepted and approved values and principles'.

In both of these examples, our respondents rooted their activism in faith, arguing both that their faith provides a resource or model for positive social change and that it was important to be active *as* members of a faith community in order to dispel misunderstandings of Islam and to redress discrimination against Muslims. It is important to recognise, however, that while Islam is a motivation for them, it is not the singular focus of their politics. Islam, their knowledge of the religion and their experiences of being Muslim shape their goals and what they wanted to achieve. Their goals and aspirations, however, are not for a politicised form of Islam in Britain or elsewhere.

Islam as a private identity

Many interviewees regard themselves as devout and observant, but they tend to place religious belief firmly in the private realm and to see their religion strictly as a matter of personal faith. Indeed, they speak disparagingly about 'broadcasting' religious beliefs and thrusting religious identities into public spaces and spheres. An example of this sentiment comes from Shadi, a young man of Lebanese origin involved in charity fundraising, who suggests that publicising Islamic beliefs puts Muslim minorities at odds with dominant social practices in mainstream spaces such as the workplace:

> [Being Muslim] is a private identity. I think, as well, there is no need for these behavioural people or extreme Muslims to go out there and try to spread the word that 'Islam is the correct way and the way forward'. I think that everyone should do what they want with their religion, but keep it to themselves and their families. If I want to practise, I practise in my own time. I wouldn't like to see a Muslim colleague of mine asking for time off to go and do his prayers. I won't like to see that kind of stuff. I would feel they are putting in a bad name. Especially since he is Muslim and living in the UK, he has to respect the rights of the UK and stick with the rules. If he is not happy, go back home.

Another example of the private nature of religion is Suha, a young British-born woman of Iraqi heritage, who describes her religion as individualistic and personal.

> I'm Muslim, but the thing is that my understanding of my religion is very much an individual relationship. I don't fall into any particular school. Because I grew up in isolation from other Muslims, I developed my own relationship with God . . . You can always consult an Islamic scholar or an Islamic academic who has read more than you, who can show you different view points, but you're responsible for your own belief. And I'm quite [proud] of my religion. I wouldn't say I'm out there [makes a trumpeting sound]; you can't really tell who is a true Muslim. I would never shout about it, but maybe that's a result of growing up in isolation.

Viewing their own faith as private, individualistic and moderate, these interviewees remark negatively on the politicisation of Islam, and they oppose the way in which, from their standpoint, some Muslims have thrust Islam into public debate. In particular, several study respondents remark negatively on the transformation of political issues such as Palestine and Iraq into religious struggles. For instance, Ghazi, a community activist in Liverpool, speaks with concern about the infusion of political issues with religious content in his community and in the wider Muslim world:

> [You] get the rise of the neo-right within the community, who are the children who have been influenced by certain elements within the community that focus on the religion. Unfortunately people ignored this in the early 1980s, and now we get a product. This is not only in the Yemeni community but the other Muslim

communities worldwide – people who are disillusioned with what's going on out there and are anti-western. Yes, there is suffering and there are issues that need to be addressed, but sometimes, for example, the Palestinian issue or the Iraq issue feeds into the Bush administration, and that feeds that culture of hate.

Najwa, a young British-born woman of Palestinian origin, similarly criticises the politicisation of religion and the Islamicisation of politics, especially with respect to the Palestinian issue, which has been important to her own political consciousness. As part of this discussion, she comments negatively on the adoption of the hijab by some Muslim women in Britain, arguing that the hijab has become a political and cultural statement rather than a symbol of personal religious devotion. Describing her encounters with young Muslim women at university, she states:

> At university, there were some girls who, one day they'd show up with the hijab and whatever, and I'd be like, 'Why do you go from clubbing every five minutes to – hello [exaggerated] – wearing a headscarf?' I got the sense with a lot of them that it was religious and spiritual to a certain extent, but it was much more some kind of cultural identity that they wanted to adopt, much more because they almost disagreed with the West politically – what was happening with the Palestinians, for example – and they wanted to reject everything cultural, as well.

These interviewees, therefore, distinguish their own religiosity from one that is political, overt and, by implication, extreme. Their criticisms of certain types of Muslims and certain ways of practising Islam reflect an awareness of and sensitivity to common perceptions of Muslims as disrespectful of boundaries between public and private realms which, in turn, places them at odds with western society.

While our interviewees generally disapprove of the politicisation and radicalisation of Islam by some Muslims, they are also critical of the politicisation of Islam by the dominant British society and the transformation of private faith into a matter of public debate and controversy. An example of this view is Rafiya, a young, British-born woman of Yemeni heritage who wears a hijab but who, like many other interviewees, insists on the privacy of her faith. Rafiya speaks passionately about 'feeling British' and argues that her visible religiosity represents only a minor divergence from the 'British way of life'. The problem with the hijab, from her perspective, is that non-Muslims construe it as a public, political statement of religious and cultural difference. Thus, she states:

> I think that's what a lot of people in this country see as negative things – the Muslims forming their own little community groups and they don't want to do what we do. I think maybe it's their ignorance. They feel threatened by the Muslims because they

don't know what that community is about, so that kind of ignorance has a negative effect on so-called multiculturalism and social cohesion. When I was at university, a lot of the students there were asking questions like 'why do you wear the scarf?' and when I gave them the answers – a lot of them obviously haven't grown up in diverse areas – they said that they didn't know this and wouldn't have dared to ask somebody because they thought that I might be offended.

In a variety of ways, then, our interviewees attest to the privacy of their own faith and disparage the ways in which religion has been inserted into the sphere of politics and public debate, whether through the actions and public behaviours of Muslims themselves or through the prejudices of non-Muslims toward Muslim practices. Their views signify a self-conscious response to the relentless association between Islam and political extremism. But they also signify the accommodation and affirmation of a particular notion of the public realm and the appropriate place of religion and religious identities within it.

Promoting Arab – not British Muslim – identities

Accompanying this insistence on religion as a private identity is an overwhelming rejection of a 'British Muslim' identity, which most study participants associate with the politicisation of Islam as described above. Several study respondents object to the British Muslim category because of the negative meanings attached to it by the media in the wake of the Rushdie Affair, the 2001 urban disorders, the 7/7 attacks, and so on. The British Muslim category has, for these interviewees, been irretrievably sullied by stereotypes about politically radical, extremist Islam that circulate in public discourse. Habeeb, a community leader in Sheffield, describes these negative meanings, while insisting on the need to privatise all identities with the exception of one's identity as a citizen. He states:

> This term, I feel, has become controversial because it has been abused by the media and it's been used more as a stereotype more than a reference – the perceptions, sometimes, are stronger than the realities. The controversy [surrounding this term] has created a completely wrong perception about it. Within the social context of my life, I want to be referred to as a British citizen and that's enough for me. These other layers of identity, I don't think they're important to anyone. They're very important to me, of course, but to anyone else, I'm only a citizen and I want to be referred to as this.

Others see the term British Muslim as synonymous with British Pakistanis, who, while professing the same faith, have different political aims and interests from British Arabs. Yemeni-born Munif, for instance, rejects the term British Muslim because

It identifies me with a group that I'm not entirely sure I believe in what they do. Every time I have a chance to talk to them about what they do, the response I get is not convincing to me. But I am a Muslim, a Yemeni, an Arab, and I associate myself with that.

As Munif's quote indicates, many of our interviewees see themselves as different from 'British Muslims' in terms of their political agendas and objectives and in terms of their cultural practices and religious attitudes. Some are quite explicit in their critiques of British Muslim variants of Islam, arguing that Asians' lack of understanding of Arabic – the language of the Qur'an – means that their faith and religious identity is based more on learning Islamic texts by rote than through interpretation of meanings. Again, a key theme that emerges from the respondents is the sense that their Islam is flexible, individualistic and private.

Our respondents, then, draw distinctions between Arab, Asian and, perhaps, British Islam. These distinctions are accompanied, as well, by statements of ecumenicalism, which many of our interviewees see as integral to Arabness. Study participants, in other words, tend to view Arabness as a multi-faith identity that requires a toned-down and more flexible conception of Islam than that associated with either Asian or British Muslims. A comment repeated in several interviews is that there are Christian, Jewish and Muslim Arabs. While modern Arab culture is infused with Islam – something noted by our Christian Arab respondents – Arab culture is not synonymous with the Islamic faith. Community leaders often emphasise that their organisations include Arabs of all faiths, and that the religious events that they sponsor – for instance, the celebration at the end of Ramadan – are open and intelligible to non-Muslims, and even to non-Arabs. These practices are often linked to a recognition of the history of shared traditions and common places of worship in Arab societies. Interviewees, for instance, refer to their comfort and familiarity with Christian churches and their sense that all religions are ultimately the same. Ramia, an Iraqi Shia active in women's organisations, describes her personal ecumenicalism in the following terms:

I am not extremist when it comes to religion, of course, but I fast, I pray. But at the same time I don't mind going to the church to pray. I believe that when I say 'I know I'm a Muslim', but it doesn't mean that I have to be like 'Wow, I'm something special!'

In another instance Leyla, a young British-born woman of Palestinian-Syrian origin, describes her view of all religions as sets of cultural practices and traditions as much as beliefs, and her wish to instil this perspective on religion in her children. She states,

I don't intend to raise my kids just knowing about Islam. They will know about all the religions. Sometimes it's nice to have, not a set of rules, but an identified practice.

Practices and traditions, even when it's not to do with religion, are lovely things. They create community, and it's part of the culture, not just the religion. So people like to have these set practices, and I think that's what religions do.

The seemingly contradictory emphases on ecumenical and non-religious identities are central to the creation of an Arab identity that is distinguishable from a British Muslim identity. It is this Arab identity, rather than a British Muslim (or simply Muslim) identity, that most of our interviewees see themselves as publicising and politicising, and that they tie explicitly to concepts like citizenship.

In asserting a public, Arab identity, interviewees are insistent that their identities not be submerged by an Asian-dominated British Muslim identity in the political sphere. Instead, they suggest, British Arabs must seek their own representation based on a specific Arab identity and Arab political interests, rather than religion. Tareq, the British-born son of Egyptian parents, argues, for instance:

> I am very aware that the state of Islam in Britain is Asian, it is not Arab, and when there are spokespersons on TV, nine times out of ten they are Asian. That's not a bad thing, but they do not represent me, and nor does the Muslim Council of Britain . . . but the government is talking to them because they represent the Asian Muslim community and that is the community that matters here. We don't really matter in the same sense.

In another example, Wajih, a Yemeni-born community activist in London who is a member of a large British Muslim organisation, describes the need to mobilise British Arabs and to promote British Arab identity in public forums and local councils. He describes his disappointment about the lack of Arab representation on a committee formed recently by the Home Office to tackle extremism, stating that authorities were 'treating Arabs either as part of the Asian community or of the Muslim community in general. They are not talking to Arabs as a separate identity.' He continues, 'From a democratic point of view, Arabs should be represented better by those who can speak the mind of the British Arabs.'

Being a British Arab and the public validation of Islam

Our interviewees, however, cannot escape the fact that Arabness is culturally bound up with Islam. In order to present themselves and their communities as fully participating in British society, therefore, they attempt to validate Islam by educating the British public – as well as Arab communities – about the religion and its connection with Arab culture. Yet the advancement of Arab identities, for many activists, also rests upon public discussion of an identity they would often prefer to be seen as private. At the same time, validation of Islam for these activists often means separation from a British Muslim identity, which, they argue, publicises and politicises religious affiliation. And so they confront a paradox: what they view as a private matter – their religion and faith – has to be brought into the public sphere through cultural and educational programmes that present a particular view of Islam.

The strategies they follow reflect their awareness of local political controversies about the (non)integration of British Muslims and wider discourses about the politicisation and radicalisation of Islam. This awareness becomes intertwined with their understandings of the historically multi-faith nature of Arab societies and, in a few cases, with their personal experiences of being raised in mixed Muslim-Christian Arab families. For our interviewees, the multiculturalism of the Arab world is a precursor to European multiculturalism. They argue that Arabs, perhaps more than other Muslim groups, are open, tolerant, cosmopolitan and suited to membership in the West. Indeed, for many of our interviewees, it is the West, and not they, who have reneged on the commitment to cultural openness and religious tolerance. Yet, while these narratives of Islam and Arabness emphasise tolerance and flexibility, they also rely upon distinctions between different kinds of Muslims and the ways in which they place their faith in the public sphere. Their negotiations of 'public' and 'private' and 'religious' and 'secular', therefore, rest on the simultaneity of identities and beliefs that otherwise seem incapable of occupying the same political space. These negotiations reflect the complex and contradictory nature of the relationships between religiosity and the public sphere, rather than enduring binaries or dichotomies.

Conclusions

This chapter has attempted to complicate common perceptions about the relationship of Muslim minorities to the public spheres and spaces of western societies. For many politicians and other public figures and commentators, Muslim minorities pose a threat to national societies by the claims they make in the political sphere. Muslim minorities in many respects have been construed as a group that is both unable and unwilling to conform to national culture and that violates the division between private faith and public life in secular, western society. This account has focused on the multiple dichotomies upon which this narrative rests – public/private, Islam/West, religious/secular, and so on – and which Muslim minorities must negotiate in formulating their political identities and activism. For the British Arab activists we interviewed, this negotiation involves formulating a distinctive sense of religiosity that is simultaneously personal and private, that is not the basis of politics, but that must be explained in public in order to participate in the public sphere.

This account, we hope, goes some way towards adding complexity to the characterisations about Muslims that we find not only in public discourse, but also in academic scholarship. Scholars have made many valuable efforts in recent decades to debunk pervasive negative stereotypes of Islam and Muslims (e.g. Eickelman and Piscatori 1996; Esposito 1999). But this literature does not fully address the diversity of political positions and identities found among Muslims, or the instability of 'Muslim' as a political category. Likewise, recent investigations of Muslim transnationalism (for instance, Bowen 2004), while expanding our understandings of the social and geographical fields in which Muslims create identities, provide only a limited view of the ways in which Muslims conceive of religion and its relationship to public identities and spaces. The political identities of Muslim people are almost inevitably tied up with political events in the Muslim world and with globalised narratives about the supposed 'clash' between Islam and the West. Yet, at least for Muslim immigrants and minorities in the West, questions about integration are never far from the surface, and any investigation of Muslim identities must consider the diverse ways in which religious identities enter into the negotiation of social membership within national and local spaces.

NOTES

1. This is not to say that religion does not enter into politics in western societies. Religiously minded individuals and groups have often brought particular claims to the public sphere in modern western societies (for a review, see Kunzman 2005). Most notable in recent years have been Christian evangelical movements, which have had an increasingly important influence on US politics. Nonetheless, most western societies have experienced a marked decline in religious observance and in the authority of religious institutions on people's everyday behaviours, signified by the precipitous decline of mainstream churches. For many in Europe and North America, 'religion' has not disappeared altogether, but has been replaced by more individualistic conceptions of spirituality (Bruce 2002).

2. The growing demand for a 'return' to Islamic principles in societal governance is, in fact, an important phenomenon many parts of the Muslim world, born of the failure of western-oriented development agendas to deliver material well-being to rapidly expanding populations (Woltering 2002; Esposito 2002). But no single, enduring relationship between religion and political establishment has existed historically in the Muslim world (Ayubi 1991), and even contemporary Islamist organisations vary significantly in terms of their political objectives vis-à-vis the state (Esposito 2002). More importantly, despite a resurgence of religiosity and religious expression in many Muslim countries, the depth of people's commitment to particular political agendas is far from certain (Macleod 1991). The subtleties and complexities of politics and Islam and Islamism, however, tend to be lost in western public discourse.

3. We interviewed forty-two British Arab activists for this study, but two of these identified themselves as Christian Arabs.

4. Some of the organisations were identified with a particular Arab nationality, such as Iraqi or Yemeni. But many of these nationally defined organisations, in fact, serve the general Arabic-speaking/Arab-origin population. We encountered several community centres and organisations who have changed their name in recent years to reflect the diversity of their clientele and members.

5. All names are pseudonyms to protect the confidentiality of respondents.

References

Ahmed, A. (1992), *Postmodernism and Islam: Predicament and Promise*, New York and London: Routledge.

Ahmed, L. (1992), *Women and Gender in Islam*, New Haven: Yale University Press.

Al Rasheed, M. (1996), 'The other-others: hidden Arabs?', in C. Peach (ed.), *Ethnicity in the 1991 Census*, London: HMSO, pp. 206–20.

Anderson, K. (1988), 'Cultural hegemony and the race-definition process in Chinatown, Vancouver, 1880–1980', *Environment and Planning D: Society and Space*, 6, 127–49.

Ayubi, N. (1991), *Political Islam: Religion and Politics in the Arab World*, London and New York: Routledge Books.

Back, L., Keith, M., Khan, A., Shukra, K. and Solomos, J. (2002), 'New Labour's white heart: politics, multiculturalism, and the return of assimilation', *The Political Quarterly*, 73(4), 445–54.

BBC (2006), 'In quotes: Jack Straw on the veil' [quote originally made on BBC Radio 4 'Today' programme], accessed 6 October 2006, at http://news.bbc.co.uk/1/hi/uk_politics/5413470.stm.

Bowen, J. R. (2004), 'Beyond migration: Islam as a transnational public space', *Journal and Ethnic and Migration Studies*, 30(5), 879–94.

Bowen, J. R. (2007). *Why the French Don't Like Headscarves: Islam, the State, and Public Space*, Princeton, NJ: Princeton University Press.

Bruce, S. (2002), *God is Dead: Secularization in the West*, Oxford: Blackwell.

Dwyer, C. (1993), 'Constructions of Muslim identity and the contesting of power: the debate over Muslim schools in the United Kingdom', in P. Jackson and J. Penrose (eds), *Constructions of Race, Place and Power*, Minneapolis, YMN University of Minnesota Press, pp. 143–54.

Dwyer, C. (1999), 'Veiled meanings: young British Muslim women and the negotiations of difference', *Gender, Place and Culture*, 6(1), 5–26.

Dwyer, C. and Meyer, A. (1995), 'The institutionalization of Islam in the Netherlands and in the UK: the case of Islamic schools', *New Community*, 21(1), 37–54.

Ehrkamp, P. (2006), '"We Turks are no Germans": assimilation discourses and the dialectical construction of identities in Germany', *Environment and Planning A*, 38, 1673–92.

Eickelman, D. F. and Piscatori, J. (1996), *Muslim Politics*, Princeton, NJ: Princeton University Press.

Esposito, J. L. (1999), *The Islamic Threat: Myth or Reality?* Oxford: Oxford University Press.

Esposito, J. L. (2002), *Unholy War: Terror in the Name of Islam*, Oxford: Oxford University Press.

Gilliat-Ray, S. (2004), 'The trouble with "inclusion": a case study of the faith zone at the Millennium Dome', *The Sociological Review*, 52(4), 459–77.

Gokulsing, K. M. (2006), 'Without prejudice: an exploration of religious diversity, secularism, and citizenship in England', *Journal of Education Policy*, 21(4), 459–70.

Habermas, J. (1989), *The Structural Transformation of the Public Sphere*, Cambridge, MA: MIT Press.

Jackson, P. (ed.) (1987), *The Idea of 'Race' and the Geography of Racism: Essays in Social Geography*, London: Allen and Unwin.

Joppke, C. (2004), 'The retreat of multiculturalism in the liberal state: theory and policy', *The British Journal of Sociology*, 55(2), 237–57.

Kahani-Hopkins, V. and Hopkins, N. (2002), '"Representing" British Muslims: the strategic dimension to identity construction', *Ethnic and Racial Studies*, 25(2), 288–309.

Klausen, J. (2005), *The Islamic Challenge: Politics and Religion in Western Europe*, Oxford: Oxford University Press.

Kunzman, R. (2005), 'Religion, politics and civic education', *Journal of Philosophy of Education*, 39(1), 159–68.

Kurien, P. (2001), 'Religion, ethnicity and politics: Hindu and Muslim Indian immigrants in the United States', *Ethnic and Racial Studies*, 24(2), 263–93.

Lewis, G. and Neal, S. (2005), 'Introduction: contemporary political contexts, changing terrains and revisited discourses', *Ethnic and Racial Studies*, 28(3), 423–44.

Lewis, P. (1994), *Islamic Britain: Religion, Politics and Identity among British Muslims*, London and New York: I. B. Tauris.

Lister, R. (1997), *Citizenship: Feminist Perspectives*. New York: New York University Press.

Macleod, A. L. (1991), *Accommodating Protest: Working Women, the New Veiling, and Change in Cairo*, New York: Columbia University Press.

Marston, S. (1990), 'Who are "the people"? Gender, citizenship and the making of the American nation', *Environment and Planning D: Society and Space*, 8, 449–58.

Mitchell, D. (1995), 'The end of public space? People's Park, definitions of the public and democracy', *Annals of the Association of American Geographers* 85, 108–33.

Mitchell, K. (2003), 'Educating the national citizen in neo-liberal times: from the multicultural self to the strategic cosmopolitan', *Transactions of the Institute of British Geographers*, 28, 387–403.

Modood, T. and May, S. (2001), 'Multiculturalism and education in Britain: an internally contested debate', *International Journal of Educational Research*, 35(3), 305–17.

Pateman, C. (1989), *The Disorder of Women: Democracy, Feminism and Political Theory*, Stanford, CA: Stanford University Press.

Phillips, D. (2006), 'Parallel lives? Challenging discourses of British Muslim self-segregation', *Environment and Planning D: Society and Space*, 24(1), 25–40.

Said, E. (1978), *Orientalism*, New York: Vintage Books.

Salvatore, A. (2004), 'Making public space: opportunities and limits of collective action among Muslims in Europe', *Journal of Ethnic and Migration Studies*, 30(5), 1013–31.

Sassen, S (1999), *Guests and Aliens*, New York: The New Press.

Soysal, Y. (1997), 'Changing parameters of citizenship and claims-making: organized Islam in European public spheres', *Theory and Society*, 26, 509–27.

Staeheli, L. (1996), 'Publicity, privacy, and women's political action', *Environment and Planning D: Society and Space*, 14, 601–19.

Staeheli, L. and Cope, M. (1994), 'Empowering women's citizenship', *Political Geography*, 13, 443–60.

Thomas, E. R. (2006), 'Keeping identity at a distance: explaining France's new legal restrictions on the Islamic headscarf', *Ethnic and Racial Studies*, 29(2), 237–59.

Turner, B. (2002), 'Religion and politics: the elementary forms of citizenship', in E. Isin and B. Turner (eds), *Handbook of Citizenship Studies*, London: Sage, pp. 259–76.

Walby, S. (1994), 'Is citizenship gendered?' *Sociology*, 28(2), 379–95.

Werbner, P. (2000), 'Divided loyalties, empowered citizenship? Muslims in Britain', *Citizenship Studies*, 4(3), 307–24.

Woltering, R. (2002), 'The roots of Islamist popularity', *Third World Quarterly*, 23(6), 1133–43.

Young, I. M. (1990), *Justice and the Politics of Difference*, Princeton, NJ: Princeton University Press.

Yuval-Davis, N., Anthias, F. and Kofman, E. (2005), 'Secure borders and safe haven and the gendered politics of belonging: beyond social cohesion', *Ethnic and Racial Studies*, 28(3), 513–35.

THE MULTICULTURAL CITY AND THE POLITICS OF RELIGIOUS ARCHITECTURE: URBAN PLANNING, MOSQUES AND MEANING-MAKING IN BRITAIN

Richard Gale

Introduction

Mosque buildings constitute an increasingly important feature of British urban landscapes. This is confirmed by the statistics on officially registered places of worship, which indicate that while in 1964 there were only nine officially registered mosques in England and Wales, by 1998 the number had increased to 614 (Peach and Gale 2003). Many of these mosques are in converted buildings, such as houses, factories and warehouses, but others have been purposely constructed, incorporating architectural features that draw upon conceptions of tradition in Islamic architecture. Such designs have often been publicly contested, in terms that construct them as symbols of 'alien' cultural presences (see for example Naylor and Ryan 2002). There is now a growing literature documenting contestation over sites of worship, in which the semiotic role played by such buildings in the articulation of opposing social identities constitutes a central theme (see for example, Eade 1993, 1996; Gale and Naylor 2002; Naylor and Ryan 2002). The contribution of this chapter is to explore the place of urban planning procedures in setting the parameters for such contestation, an issue that is receiving increasing academic attention (see for example, Gale 1999; Dunn 2001; Nye 2001; Gale and Naylor 2002; Isin and Siemiatycki 2002). It moves beyond the concern with aesthetic contestation per se to show how urban planning mediates processes of social boundary construction that coalesce around mosque designs, becoming in turn a nexus in which some of the meanings and associations that accrue to such sites are articulated.

There are two reasons that make this focus on the interface between planning and religious organisations a fruitful avenue for enquiry. First, it enables empirical investigation of the ways in which social relations and institutionalised forms of power interact to produce changes within the built environment.

Concomitantly, it enables research into how opposing symbolic constructions of (religious) space are contested and shaped within the deliberative processes of urban planning. The second reason, following on closely from the first, is that this approach allows one to examine the agency of religious groups who, through their engagement with planning procedures, have influenced the processes through which the built environment is materially (re)configured.

Taking three mosques in Birmingham as case studies, the chapter shows how Muslim groups have been important agents of institutional as well as urban change. The chapter is divided into three sections, each based on a case study of a specific purpose-built mosque in Birmingham. These case studies are ordered historically, to facilitate a discussion of the changing emphases of the City Council's planning policies relating to places of worship. Throughout the chapter, use is made of conceptual terminology derived from Henri Lefebvre's work, *The Production of Space* (1991). Specifically, the chapter employs Lefebvre's concepts of 'representation of space', referring to institutionalised conceptions of space inscribed within urban planning procedure; and 'representational space', which denotes physical spaces that have become imbued with social meanings and which, in this context, have been contested by Muslim and non-Muslim urban residents (Lefebvre 1991: 38–46 and *passim*). The chapter thus explores the ways in which urban planning's 'representations of space' intersect with the meanings ascribed to physical space by different social groups. The first case study is that of the Birmingham Central Mosque (Figure 7.1), which was planned during the late 1950s and opened in 1975, making it the oldest purpose-built mosque in the city.

A landmark for the city: the Birmingham Central Mosque

Referring to the relationship maintained between Birmingham City Council and the committee of the Birmingham Central Mosque, the President of the mosque commented in an interview upon the role the building fulfilled as a visible symbol of the city's multicultural composition (see Figure 7.2). He remarked that:

> The City Council was very cooperative. It gave them [the local Muslim community] a prime piece of land, and the idea was to build a landmark for the city. That is why it is on the route from the city centre to the airport [see Figure 7.2], so there's a lot of traffic, and that was the intention, that everybody have a look at the multicultural status of this city.

That the mosque performs an important symbolic role for the city, and that the City Council has actively promoted this role, is partially confirmed by planning documentation. In 1991, an application to develop a Muslim girls' school

Figure 7.1 A landmark for the city: the Birmingham Central Mosque

attached to the mosque was approved on the grounds that the development would not only 'enhance the facilities available for the Muslim community', but also 'further promote the significance of the Central Mosque'. In addition, it was argued that 'High quality design in such a prominent location will enhance the role of the mosque as a landmark and provide a gateway approach to the city core from the Middle Ring Road.'[1] Similar priorities were reflected in a proposal during the same year to grant the Central Mosque £46,000 in inner city aid, to assist with repairs to the fabric of the building and to provide additional parking space. While these proposals met with strong opposition from Conservative members of the City Council, they were defended by a spokesman for the Council's urban renewal team, who claimed that they were 'enhancing the city's image'. This was also cited as the 'grounds on which the Central Mosque has already been given quite a lot of money for floodlighting' (*Evening Mail*, 15 January 1991, no page). It is also apparent from the above statement of the President of the mosque that the promotion of the iconic role of the building not only extends from the priorities of the local authority, but is endorsed by representatives of the mosque itself. However, the aesthetic appropriation of the mosque as a symbol of Birmingham's social diversity is a recent phenomenon. It has occurred subsequent to a series of planning disputes in which attitudes towards the mosque have been more ambivalent.

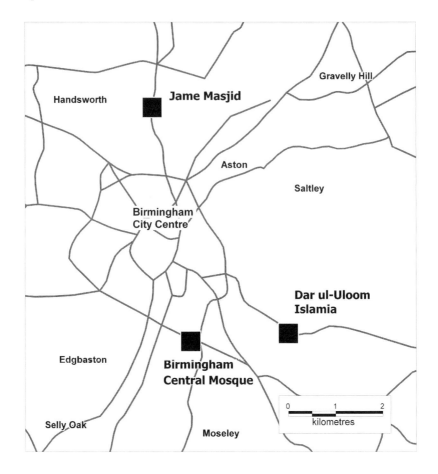

Figure 7.2 Map showing proximity of the three mosques to major arterial routes in Birmingham

The plan to construct the Central Mosque emerged in the late 1950s, a time when Highgate, the area in which the building stands, was a key focus for the settlement of migrants from South Asia, including Muslims from Pakistan and subsequently Bangladesh (Dahya 1974). The then City Council was approached in 1956 by a group known as the Muslim Association (*Jamiat ul-Muslimin*), with a view to establishing a mosque that would 'serve not merely this area but the city as a whole' (quoted from a report submitted to the Public Works Committee, entitled 'Gooch Street Redevelopment Area – zoning layout', 2 February 1956). However, the area was also the subject of a major redevelopment scheme of the City Council, involving the compulsory purchase and demolition of approximately 4,000 houses, consisting mostly of nineteenth-century terraces. The objectives of the scheme, as stated in the same planning report, were to construct lower-density housing – including several high-rise apartment blocks – a shopping precinct and a section of the city's inner ring road. Accordingly, the scheme was to have important consequences for the mosque. First, when put into practice, it resulted in the displacement of Muslim and other post-migration settlers in the area to other parts of the city. As a former treasurer of the Central Mosque recalled during an interview:

> At that time in the 1960s the majority of the Muslims were in the Balsall Heath area, and so the people who . . . were thinking to build up the mosque were thinking of that area. But they did not know – the planners should have told them – that after about ten, fifteen years, we, the Muslim population won't be living near there, because the houses would be demolished and rebuilt and the Council would not necessarily give them back to those who were living there.

This change in the composition of the population became a significant factor in the symbolic construction of the mosque in subsequent planning debates, in that a majority of those who took up residence in the area following the redevelopment were non-Muslims. The second consequence was that the plan to construct the Central Mosque became integral to the City Council's deliberations concerning the redevelopment of the area.

Thus, from its inception, the design of the mosque was subject to the Council's 'representation of space', in terms of what it conceived to be integrated urban regeneration. In records of the original planning of the site in the 1950s and 1960s, one does not find references to the symbolism of the building, but expressions of concern by planning officers over the size and ambitiousness of the proposal, and its perceived conflict with other elements of the Council's redevelopment scheme. The original proposal for the mosque also included eighteen shops, a lecture hall, residential accommodation and a library.

In a report submitted to the Public Works Committee, entitled 'Highgate site, Belgrave Road for Moslem Mosque' (15 June 1961), it was noted by the agents acting on behalf of the Muslim Association that it was 'of some importance to the scheme that some portion of the building should be available to produce an income which would enable the proper maintenance of the structure'. However, with regard to the shops, the Council argued that these would not be sustainable in view of the thirty to forty shops it had already proposed as part of the redevelopment. Moreover, the report noted that the shops associated with the mosque would have 'direct access to the principal traffic route, whereas the proposed neighbourhood centre is in the form of a pedestrian precinct at right angles to the road'. It was accordingly resolved by the Committee 'that the Muslim authorities be informed that this Committee are unable to agree to the proposals submitted for the development of the site in Belgrave Road . . . and that the City Surveyor be authorized to negotiate with them in respect of a smaller site to be developed by the erection of a mosque only'. No mention was made of the intrinsic importance of these other features of the mosque proposal to the sustainability of the building.

Owing to financial constraints upon the mosque committee, much of the surrounding area was redeveloped before work on the mosque commenced. As a result, when construction finally got under way in 1970, the mosque was made subject to a condition by the City Council concerning the building materials that should be used, in order that it should harmonise with the surrounding landscape. Whereas the original design had envisaged the building being finished in white stucco, the planning authority now requested that the major part of the building be finished in brick, 'to match the new development in the vicinity'. It was argued by the Council that 'this will be more satisfactory than the original proposal as the building will now blend in with the adjoining development of the Gooch Street shopping centre and adjoining flats'. Accordingly, on its completion in 1975, the building became a stylistic hybrid, signifying simultaneously its relation both to its local context and to traditions of mosque architecture. Moreover, there is an apparent tension here between the requirement that the mosque should 'blend in' with nearby development and the statement of the President of the mosque that it was consciously sited and designed to form a 'landmark' for the city. The financial difficulties experienced by the mosque committee strained relations with the City Council, to the extent that it was intimated in 1969 that the offer of land for the building would be retracted if progress had not been made by the beginning of the following year. Accordingly, when some time later the mosque committee applied for permission to establish an 'Islamic evening school' (*madrasa*) in association with the mosque, the application was initially refused, with one planning officer commenting upon what he termed 'the deplorable history of the construction of the mosque'. Importantly, the mosque committee persisted in the face of this perception of the mosque's history, and in June 1980 succeeded in gaining approval for the application.

The first explicit planning reference to the aesthetic contribution of the mosque to its surroundings emerged in the early 1980s, as a result of an application to surmount the building with a minaret. The application was approved with the encomium that the design was 'elegant and well proportioned', that it formed 'a good foil/contrast with the main domed building', and that it was 'visible over [a] wide area along Belgrave Road/Lee Bank Middleway and across Balsall Heath'. However, this approval was subject to a condition that 'no sound reproduction or amplification equipment shall be installed or used on any part of the said minaret at any time'. The comment of a planning officer at the time reveals how this condition abstracted the form of the minaret from its religious associations. He stated that in his understanding, 'such minarets were symbolic and that planning consents usually carried a condition to prevent such equipment being installed'. Thus, while the minaret was assimilated into public space as an 'interesting addition to the skyline', its customary use for the call to prayer (*azan*) was explicitly proscribed.

As with the application to establish a madrasa, the committee of the mosque challenged this restriction on broadcasting the azan, submitting planning applications on two separate occasions. On the first of these, in 1982/83, the mosque committee withdrew the application when it was perceived that it was to be refused by the City Council. However, it resubmitted it in 1986, resulting in the City Council's agreement to a trial period of one month, during which the midday (*sal'at al-zuhr*) and afternoon (*sal'at al-'asr*) prayers were called from the minaret. Bearing in mind the observation above that a large proportion of the population surrounding the mosque were non-Muslims, reactions to the application were frequently hostile, with respondents opposing the application by asserting the 'alien-ness' of the Muslim religion to the English national context. One opponent, in a letter that was fairly typical in content and tone, enquired of the City Council, 'since when has a foreign language and culture been allowed to override the wishes of the indigenous people of this country?'. However, the application was ultimately approved, with the calls being limited in terms of their number and duration (see Gale (2005) for a detailed discussion of the azan case).

The conclusion of the public debate over the use of the minaret to broadcast the azan in 1986 brings us to approximately the time of the planning and funding decisions with which this case study began, which showed that, by the 1990s, the mosque had been reinterpreted as a landmark. We thus observe a change in the perception of the mosque, considered initially as a controversial element of a regeneration scheme, and subsequently as a celebrated landscape 'icon'. At a general level, these shifts in the representation of the Central Mosque within planning discourse have coincided with the changing priorities of Birmingham City Council, which increasingly recognise the social and civic contributions of different sectors of the local population. Two further observations can be made regarding this history of interactions between the planning authority and the mosque. The first is that planning decisions are related reciprocally to the way in which space is represented within planning discourse. Thus, the signification of the mosque did not simply emerge at the time of the building's completion, but was also played out within the deliberative framework of urban planning, with observable consequences for the configuration of the mosque as an architectural space. The second point is the converse of the first, in the sense that the mosque was able to pass through the various vicissitudes that have marked its history because of the commitments that have been made to it by its committee, and by Muslims throughout Birmingham. This is exemplified by the fact that the financial difficulties experienced by the mosque during the 1960s and 1970s were overcome through the collection of donations from Birmingham's Muslim residents, identified by using the local electoral roll. Subsequently, as we have seen, the interactions of the mosque committee with the planning authority tested and redefined the limits to tolerance imposed upon the development and use of the site by the operations of planning

Figure 7.3 The Jame Masjid in Handsworth, incorporating domes and arched windows that signify mosque architectural traditions

procedure. Hence, the extent to which the mosque now forms a symbol for the city has been made possible by the practical commitment to (and investment of meaning in) the building by the committee of the mosque and the city's Muslim population.

Sign and context: the Jame Masjid in Handsworth

There are various points of comparison that can be made between the Central Mosque and the Jame Masjid (formerly known as the President Saddam Hussein Mosque) in Handsworth, lying to the north of Birmingham's central district. The first is that both mosques incorporate stylistic features that are intended to signify mosque architectural traditions (see Figure 7.3). Second, both buildings stand on sites that were allocated by the City Council. Third, the Jame Masjid is also immediately juxtaposed to a major arterial route, which – from the main road at least – makes the building visually prominent (see map in Figure 7.2).

With regard to the first and third of these points, in an interview with the author, a senior planning officer of Birmingham City Council made a comparison between the two mosques, indicating that if a place of worship is to be sited

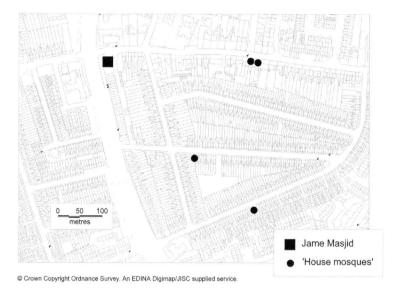

© Crown Copyright Ordnance Survey. An EDINA Digimap/JISC supplied service.

Figure 7.4 'Illegal' prayer houses in the residential area surrounding the Jame Masjid, Handsworth

near a major thoroughfare, it was appropriate that its style should signify its religious associations:

> If you are developing a site on the ring road, on one of the main radial routes, so the Central Mosque, Saddam Hussein, then why shouldn't its architecture reflect its use?

Although this statement reflects a personal view, it also gives rise to a fourth point of comparison between these buildings, which is that both have had assigned to them sets of contemporary meanings and associations that were not prevalent at the time of their planning and construction. The planning process surrounding the Jame Masjid began in 1976, and received the active support of the City Council. However, planning records suggest that part of the reason for their support was their wish to impose a particular spatial order upon an area of the city that was undergoing social change. As noted by Rex and Tomlinson (1979: 74–5), while the area to the south and south-east of the city centre had provided the primary areas of South Asian settlement, throughout the 1960s and 1970s an increasing number began to settle on the north side of the city, including Handsworth, Soho and Aston. While many were Sikhs and Hindus, sizable numbers were Muslims. Correspondingly, in the residential area surrounding the site allocated for the Jame Masjid, several mosques had been established in houses, without having been granted planning permission (Figure 7.4).

As Henry Hodgins (1981) has shown, the use of houses as mosques and *madrasas* was of concern to the City Council at this time, giving rise to concerns over 'noise' and 'disturbance' caused to neighbouring residents. The construction of a purpose-built mosque in this area was conceived as a way of counteracting the diffusion of smaller mosques across the residential area, as it was believed this would concentrate the activities associated with such 'unofficial' sites into a single designated facility. As was stated in the original planning reports:[2]

> At the present time, the group are meeting in a private house in Arden Road, and it is hoped that, should alternative premises become available, there would be a certain amount of amalgamation of other prayer-house groups in the area.

And:

> [T]here are a number of dwelling houses in this area for which enforcement action is in force, and it is felt that this development would overcome the problem of unlawful uses.

At this stage, therefore, a part of the significance attached to the mosque by the local authority was that it would provide a functional means to overcome a 'problem'. A further factor that made the location of the site favourable to the City Council was its proximity to the main road. However, as in the case of the Central Mosque, there is no historical evidence that this resulted from a determination to accord the building aesthetic prominence. Indeed, while the planning report cited above remarked that the building would be 'a traditional mosque design', it also noted that:

> There is a traffic fly-over immediately opposite the Birchfield Road frontage, which *effectively screens the site* from the opposite side of the road. [Emphasis added]

As such, the decision to juxtapose the mosque with the road was made with knowledge of the fact that the existing morphology of the location would mask the building from view (Figure 7.5). This location was also considered favourable by the planning authority on account of specific functional criteria. Thus, it was commented in the planning report that:

> Although many objections have been received from local residents, it is considered that the use of this site as a mosque would be appropriate. Birchfield Road is heavily trafficked and any disturbance caused by the religious activity should be considered in this context.

This statement has a positive connotation in revealing the exaggeration of claims that the site would cause 'noise' and 'disturbance'. However, it is still the

Figure 7.5 The Jame Masjid 'screened' by an adjacent flyover

case that the heavy traffic of the main road was offered as a reason why the use of the site to construct a mosque would be 'appropriate'.

While the initial planning reports were largely silent over the design of the mosque, contestation over the aesthetics of the building became pronounced as the detailed plans were negotiated. These negotiations indicate again the extent to which meanings invested in (religious) architectural designs can be relational to the interactions between individuals and groups, constituted and managed in this context within the institutional framework of urban planning.

The detailed plans of the building, which included a dome and a minaret, were due to be reviewed by the planning committee in December 1978. However, despite outline permission having been granted for the mosque, the proposal met with strong resistance from the owners of the adjacent property, who alleged that the land for the mosque had already been pledged to them by the City Council. Although this claim was made at an advanced stage in the planning process and without corroborating evidence, the planning committee deferred its decision on the plans for the building to allow an investigation.

The claim was subsequently shown to be spurious. Nevertheless, it set in train a series of departures within the planning process, which led to the dome and minaret becoming contested features of the mosque's design. Of interest here is the reaction of the Muslim group, who sought to resolve the tension surrounding the application by emphasising that the group's requirements were concordant with the City Council's priorities. In a letter addressed to the chairman of the planning committee, a representative of the group stated as follows:

Following the deferment of the decision on the mosque, I would ask you to put forward [to the planning committee] the following observations in support of the application. 1) We wish to point out that a minaret and a dome are not an obligatory condition for building a mosque at the corner of Birchfield Road and Trinity Road. 2) We must point out that this mosque will have the effect of reducing the number of prayer houses in the Fentham Road and Trinity Road areas. 3) All calls to prayer will not be on a loudspeaker system from outside, but will be given from inside the mosque.

As these comments suggest, the Muslim group expressed their support for the scheme in terms of the City Council's own criteria for curtailing the impact of mosques upon urban space. However, if the intention had been to propitiate the Council in relation to the proposal, the suggestion that the dome and minaret could be omitted from the design had quite the reverse effect. At the subsequent meeting of the planning committee, in January 1979, the letter from the mosque committee formed the principal subject of discussion. A summary of the committee meeting is given in the planning file:

The chairman opened the discussion by drawing attention to the fact that he had received a letter from the mosque authorities to the effect that they were prepared to delete from their proposals both the minaret and the dome. The chairman suggested that this would make the proposal *more sympathetic* to the design and architecture of the adjoining shops . . . After further discussion, and with the knowledge that representatives of the mosque authorities were present at the meeting, the committee deferred consideration until further plans [i.e. ones omitting the dome and minaret] were submitted. [Emphasis added]

It will be recalled that a similar concern to encourage the architecture of mosques to reflect that of neighbouring buildings had formed part of the deliberations over the Central Mosque. However, the pronouncement in this case reveals more starkly that the 'representations of space' made by urban planning can interleave with the subjective preferences of those in positions of power. Ironically therefore, rather than reinvigorating the planning process, the letter of the mosque committee led to a series of opportunistic deliberations over the building's design on the part of the planning authority.

However, the stance of the planning committee met with resistance from a number of quarters, all of them restating the importance of the dome and minaret to the mosque's design. These included the now defunct Council of Birmingham Mosques, who expressed their 'strong support' for the application 'to erect a mosque with dome and minaret'. Similarly, a representative of the mosque committee attempted to retract the contents of the original letter, stating that 'the Muslim community have been very distressed at the [planning] committee's ruling that the dome and minaret were not to be allowed'. In addition, a local Councillor, who was also employed by the Community Relations Council, expressed his 'concern' about the matter, stating his view that 'it could be construed as racial prejudice'. Subsequently, the Chief Planning Officer himself appeared to dissent from the planning committee's position, arguing that, in his view:

> A building should postulate the function it performs, and the removal of the minaret and the dome on this Temple [*sic*] is analogous to removing the church spire of a traditional Church of England building. The resulting building would be characterless in this location.

While also expounding a subjective view, this comment constitutes an attempt to reach beyond the vexed relations between the various actors involved in the planning process, appealing to the (modernist) notion of architectural form following a building's function. The statement constitutes a significant step forward in terms of the symbolic construction of purpose-built mosques in Birmingham, resonating strongly with the view of the planning officer cited at the beginning of this case study. Under the weight of opposition to its decision, the planning committee's position gave way, and the group was invited to submit further plans including the dome, though not the minaret.

These contestations over the mosque's design came full circle when the Muslim group received a substantial grant towards the construction costs from the Iraqi government. According to the architect's submission to the planning committee, this funding was subject to two conditions, one of which was that the mosque should bear the name of the Iraqi president. The other was that the design should be modified to incorporate a minaret. Yet another set of designs was produced, this time including both the dome and minaret (the dome was included on completion but the minaret in Figure 7.3 was not added until later). The application was finally approved in January 1981, some five years after the original land allocation, and the mosque was completed and opened in 1988. Allowing for the differences in social and architectural contexts, this analysis of the planning and construction of the Jame Masjid is germane to Mazumdar and Mazumdar's (1997) discussion of the domestic spaces of Zoroastrians in Iran: it has likewise shown that architecture can embody the interactions between individuals and groups in a given society, particularly when these interactions occur under sustained relations of power and resistance. As we have seen, the very location of the Jame Masjid reflects the power of urban planning institutions to represent, and thereafter govern, the configuration of urban space. However, as we have also seen, this power is relational to the capacities of different social groups to resist the 'representations of space' made by urban planning. Moreover, the exchanges between the planning authority and the Muslim group with regard to the dome and minaret indicate that these architectural features were invested with

Figure 7.6 The Dar ul-Uloom Islamia in Small Heath

considerable social meaning and value – perhaps all the more so for having been contested within the planning process. Examining these interactions thus deepens our perception of the mosque as a meaningful or 'representational space' for the respective Muslim group.

A new landmark for the city: the Dar ul-Uloom Islamia in Small Health

Both the Central Mosque and the Jame Masjid were developed some time ago, while the Dar ul-Uloom Islamia in Small Heath was planned and completed in the late 1990s (Figure 7.6). It thus illustrates how the City Council's representation of Birmingham as a 'multicultural city' has conjoined with observable changes in planning practice. In common with the buildings in the preceding case studies, the Dar ul-Uloom Islamia is located adjacent to a major road, on a site that was allocated by the City Council (see Figure 7.2). However, the Dar ul-Uloom Islamia is much larger than the other sites, and is also associated with a series of social and cultural facilities, housed in buildings that line both sides of a short road behind the mosque. In further contrast to the preceding buildings, the planning records for this mosque reveal clearly that, from its inception, the location was chosen by the City Council with the intention of making the building visually prominent. Reports that date to the initial planning stages in the late 1980s and early 1990s comment as follows:[3]

> Because the site also fronts the roundabout junction of Golden Hillock Road and Small Heath By-pass, a prominent building is required.

And:

> The proposed building is of considerable scale and mass and has been deliberately sited at the south eastern corner of the site to form a landmark adjacent to the Small Heath by-pass.

In addition, the City Council contributed to the scheme by selling the land to the group at a third of its market value. This is not to suggest that tensions were entirely absent from the planning process in relation to this site. For instance, when asked to describe its relationship with the planning authority during the development of the mosque, a member of the mosque committee replied that it was 'very good'. There had been an extended period during the early construction stages, in which the planning authority held up further progress on the mosque to consider what was perceived by the group to be a minor alteration in the design, while design conditions were strictly applied. As commented by the respondent:

> We were actually told what colours to use by the planners to blend in, socially, in the surrounding area . . . In our original drawings . . . we sort of had light bricks at the bottom and dark at the top, but they [the City Council] actually said, you know, we've got to do it this way or we don't do it at all!

There was also tension in terms of how the building was construed by non-Muslim residents responding to the planning application. One letter provides a chilling illustration of the theme, addressed throughout this chapter, that architectural aesthetics mediate the relations between social groups. It enquired of planners when they were 'going to stop allowing Birmingham being turned into England's own version of Baghdad?', exhorting that mosques should be 'built in modern style so that they fit in with other buildings, instead of sticking out like a sore thumb'. The letter went on:

> All of the people I have spoken to can't stand the sight of these buildings, which start to make them resent the people who are responsible for them, and if that's your idea of improving race relations then carry on, and watch the resentment grow.

However, unlike the planning of the Jame Masjid, the opposition of neighbouring residents in this case did not unduly influence the planning process. There was thus an explicit connection between the City Council's initial support for the scheme and the semiotic role the building performs for the local authority. In the words of the representative of the mosque committee cited above, the mosque is a 'stop' for members of the City Council when diplomats visit Birmingham from other countries:

> They use this as a model . . . showing other people the way it's integrated within the society . . . you know, [a] multicultural society. They're showing that this is the model, this is how we do it . . .

In a sense, the process of meaning making discussed in relation to the Central Mosque has been inverted. Whereas the Central Mosque's role as a landmark has developed subsequent to its construction, in the case of the Dar ul-Uloom Islamia, a concern with the symbolism of the site was woven into the planning process itself.

While noting the role of planning procedure in setting the parameters within which this change in the symbolism of purpose-built mosques has occurred, it is again important to acknowledge that this change has emerged through the investment of meaning in such buildings and the wider built environment by local Muslims. In this regard, the respondent cited above made the following observation:

> If you had known the place, especially this patch from roundabout to roundabout . . . about twenty-odd years ago, it was a dump . . . and that has changed. And the people that have changed it is [*sic*] the Muslim community within the area itself, so that's how it's been changed, the needs, trying to fulfil the needs of the communities.

Viewed from this perspective, the Council's commitment to the mosque constitutes recognition of the changes in the urban fabric that have emerged through the interactions of local Muslims with their surroundings, as well as with the planning process.

Conclusion

In tracing the planning histories of three purpose-built mosques in Birmingham, this chapter has raised several issues of importance to our understanding of how post-migration religious groups have interacted with and changed the spaces in which they reside, as an expression of their religious and cultural needs. In particular, it has shown the necessity for such groups to engage with planning procedures, which continue to be hegemonic in their relation to the processes through which the urban environment is (re)produced. However, the chapter has also shown that this hegemony is not absolute but relative, and that the engagement of Muslim and other religious groups with planning procedures can be effective in redefining the constraints that urban planning imposes.

The chapter has also shown that urban planning can perform an important role in relation to the designs of purpose-built mosques, not only framing but also mediating aesthetic contestation. This was most notable in the case of the Jame Masjid, in which opposition from a local property owner provided a pre-condition for conflict over the mosque's design, which was articulated by the planning process. Similar forms of contestation were also woven into the planning process surrounding applications to broadcast the azan from the Central Mosque.

Finally, through a chronological arrangement of the case studies, the chapter has shown that the City Council's stance in relation to the construction of mosques alluding to Islamic architectural antecedents has changed over time. In this regard, the chapter has noted a transition from an initial ambivalence – and even hostility – towards such buildings, to more recent endorsement, as they have been increasingly celebrated as signifiers of 'cultural diversity' in Birmingham. In the case of the Birmingham Central Mosque, this change of emphasis has resulted in a gradual transformation of the meanings attached to the same building; in the case of the Dar ul-Uloom Islamia, on the other hand, the perception that the building could form a landmark for the city was integrated into the planning process.

Some salient problems can of course attend these symbolic processes. For instance, the emphasis given to the semiotics of 'place' may bear little relation (and may even mask) other material realities and spatial processes experienced by minority groups. Although lying beyond the scope of the present chapter, it can be observed here that the increasingly positive treatment of applications to develop purpose-built mosques does not necessarily entail that other types of applications – such as for madrasas in residential districts – will meet with a correspondingly greater degree of success. There is also the danger that, in being too closely identified with the buildings of 'minorities', such celebration of difference through architecture does not sufficiently alter the patterns of marginalisation that, in the past, led such buildings to be sited in peripheral areas or 'screened' by flyovers.

Nevertheless, these tensions should not be over-stated. As Jane M. Jacobs has observed (1998), these patterns of 'aestheticization' do not inevitably disempower diaspora or other minority groups, but can intersect in important ways with political processes in which such groups engage. As we have seen in the statements of the President of the Birmingham Central Mosque and the representative of the Dar ul-Uloom Islamia, the local discourse of multiculturalism is not only promoted by the City Council, but is also shared by the members of Muslim organisations. Moreover, it is not fanciful to suggest that changes in the stance of the City Council noted in this chapter have emerged, in large part, as a result of the engagement of Muslim groups with planning procedures. This was exemplified most clearly by the applications to broadcast the azan from the Central Mosque, and to (re)insert a dome and minaret into the design of the Jame

Masjid. It is for this reason that examining the interactions between Muslim groups and planning and other institutions of the state contributes to our understanding of mosques in British urban settings as contextually meaningful spaces.

Notes

1. Except where stated otherwise, citations of this case are taken from the planning files, PA 23328/1–8, kept by the Planning Department of Birmingham City Council.
2. Except where stated otherwise, citations of this case are taken from the planning file, PA 4689/41 RM.
3. Except where stated otherwise, citations of this case are taken from the planning file, E/01112/90/FUL, kept by the Planning Department of Birmingham City Council.

References

Dahya, B. (1974), 'The nature of Pakistani ethnicity in industrial cities in Britain', in Cohen, A. (ed.), *Urban Ethnicity*. London: Tavistock, pp. 77–118.

Dunn, K. (2001), 'Representations of Islam in the politics of mosque development in Sydney', *Tijdschrift voor Economische en Sociale Geografie*, 92, 291–308.

Eade, J. (1993), 'The political articulation of community and the Islamisation of space in London', in Barot, R. (ed.), *Religion and Ethnicity: Minorities and Social Change in the Metropolis*, Kampen: Kok Pharos Publishing House, pp. 29–42.

Eade, J. (1996), 'Nationalism, community and the Islamization of space in London', in Metcalf, B. (ed.), *Making Muslim Space in North America and Europe*, Berkeley: University of California Press, pp. 217–33.

Gale, R. (1999), 'Pride of place and places: South Asian religious groups and the city planning authority in Leicester', *Papers in Planning Research*, 172, Cardiff: Department of City and Regional Planning, Cardiff University.

Gale, R. (2005), 'Representing the city: mosques and the planning process in Birmingham, UK', in *Journal of Ethnic and Migration Studies*, 31(6), 1161–79.

Gale, R. and Naylor, S. (2002), 'Religion, the planning and the city: the spatial politics of ethnic minority expression in British cities and towns', *Ethnicities*, 2, 387–409.

Hodgins, H. (1981), 'Planning permission for mosques: the Birmingham experience', *Research Papers – Muslims in Europe*, 9, 11–27.

Isin, E. F. and Siemiatycki, M. (2002), 'Making space for mosques – struggles for urban citizenship in diasporic Toronto', in S. H. Razack (ed.), *Race, Space and Law: unMapping and White Settler Society*, Toronto: Between the Lines Press, pp. 185–209.

Jacobs, J. M. (1998), 'Staging difference: aetheticization and the politics of difference in contemporary cities', in R. Fincher and J. M. Jacobs (eds), *Cities of Difference*, New York: Guilford Press, pp. 252–78.

Lefebvre, H. (1991), *The Production of Space*, Oxford: Blackwell.

Mazumdar, S. and Mazumdar, S. (1997), 'Intergroup social relations and architecture: vernacular architecture and issues of status, power and conflict', *Environment and Behaviour*, 29, 374–421.

Naylor, S. and Ryan, J. (2002), 'The mosque in the suburbs: negotiating religion and ethnicity in south London', *Social and Cultural Geography*, 3, 39–59.

Nye, M. (2001), *Multiculturalism and Minority Religions in Britain – Krishna Consciousness, Religious Freedom and the Politics of Location*, Richmond: Curzon Press.

Peach, C. and Gale, R. (2003), 'Muslims, Hindus and Sikhs in the new religious landscape of England', *The Geographical Review*, 95(4), 469–90.

Rex, J. and Tomlinson, S. (1979), *Colonial Immigrants in a British City*, London: Routledge and Kegan Paul.

Acknowledgements

This chapter was originally published in *Built Environment*, 30 (1), as part of a special issue entitled 'The Cosmopolis: Emerging Multicultural Spaces in Europe and North America', edited by Dr Noha Nasser of Birmingham City University. I am grateful to the editors of *Built Environment* for their kind permission to reprint the paper here. Versions of this chapter were previously presented at the annual meeting of the British Sociological Association (BSA) Sociology of Religion study group, held at Birmingham University in April 2002; at the annual meeting of the British Association for the Study of Religions (BASR), held at the University of Surrey at Roehampton in September 2002; and at the Institute of Social and Cultural Anthropology, University of Oxford in February 2003. I am grateful to the participants of these gatherings for their useful commentary and insights. I am also grateful to Dr Noha Nasser of Birmingham City University and Professor Ceri Peach of the University of Oxford for their comments on the original drafts. The photographs for the chapter were taken as part of a Leverhulme-funded survey, 'Ethnicity and Cultural Landscapes' (grant F/773) directed by Professor Ceri Peach of the University of Oxford between 1998 and 2001. The research on which the chapter is based was made possible by a Studentship from the Economic and Social Research Council (ESRC) to whom I also express my sincere thanks.

HOLY PLACES, CONTESTED SPACES: BRITISH PAKISTANI ACCOUNTS OF PILGRIMAGE TO MAKKAH AND MADINAH

Seán McLoughlin

Introduction

Taking a cue from Eade and Sallnow's (1991) key work in the anthropology of Christian pilgrimage, the present chapter is a study of the normative and contested accounts of sacred journeys to the holy places of Makkah and Madinah reported by Pakistani heritage Muslims in the UK diaspora. Following the likes of Durkheim (1912) and Turner (1974a, 1974b) respectively, Eade and Sallnow accept that pilgrimage both promotes social integration and the more temporary, liminal and anti-structural feelings associated with communitas. However, they also maintain that the reinforcement of social difference during sacred journeys is of equal significance. Specifically, then, this account documents: 1) British Pakistanis' symbolic constructions and ritual embodiments of sacred time and place, community and identity, during the various rites of *hajj* and other forms of pilgrimage; and 2) the cross-cutting and competing narratives of class and race, religious devotionalism and puritanism, that persist during pilgrimage.

Over two years, between 1999 and 2001, eighteen in-depth, semi-structured, interviews were conducted with respondents settled in Lancashire mill towns such as Bolton, Bury, Oldham, Rochdale and Nelson. Most interviewees traced their roots to Mirpur district in Pakistani-administered Kashmir (see Saifullah Khan 1977; Ballard 1983; Kalra 2000), while the ages of respondents ranged in more or less equal numbers across the following groups: those in their teens and twenties; thirties and forties; fifties to seventies. Their occupations were as follows: sales and business (four); further or higher education (three); retired (two); teaching/teaching assistant (two); housewife (two); community leader (one); computer programmer (one); chemist (one); housing support worker (one); and spinner (one). Around a quarter were women. Most importantly, all had either been on hajj (half) or *'umra* (the minor pilgrimage) (a quarter) – and some (a quarter) on both – at least once since the 1970s.

As many as 25,000 British Muslims travel to Makkah and Madinah for Hajj every year (Foreign and Commonwealth Office 2006). Indeed, so long as they are physically fit and can afford to make the journey, it is incumbent upon the followers of Islam to undertake the pilgrimage at least once in their lives from the eighth to the thirteenth day of the final month of the Islamic lunar calendar, *Dhu'l hijja*.[1] In contrast, *'umra* is a voluntary rite, which involves the performance of abbreviated rituals outside Hajj season. During Hajj and *'umra* many Muslims will also seek to do *ziyara* (visitation) of the tombs of sacred personalities such as the Prophet Muhammad, his family and companions. This is certainly true of the majority of South Asian heritage Muslims and especially the British Pakistanis interviewed here. Insofar as they have been influenced by any particular tradition of Islam, whether through socialisation at home and the mosque or more active religiosity, the respondents tended to be associated with the devotional Islam of various transnational Sufi cults and/or the reforming Sunni *'ulama* (religious scholars) movement founded in British India, the Ahl-i Sunna or 'Barelwis' (see Lewis 1994; Sanyal 1996; Geaves 2000; Werbner 2003)[2].

My initial motivation for undertaking this research was very much driven by an interest in imaginings of a global *umma* (Islamic community) in Muslim diasporas, this at a time when the study of transnationalism was rising to the top of social-scientific agendas. While the impact of contemporary international crises in this regard can not be ignored (see Werbner 2002, on '9/11' and the Gulf War, and McLoughlin 1996, on Bosnia), the pilgrimage to Makkah and Madinah is perhaps the most emblematic expression of a universal Muslim community, for both Muslims and non-Muslims alike. As one of the five pillars (*arkan*) of Islam, it is the Hajj that brings believers together at the site of their faith's genesis. The rites of this sacred journey are said not only to purify the individual believer of his or her sins, but also attest to, and reaffirm, the diachronic and synchronic continuity of the umma. So while pilgrims follow symbolically in the footsteps of the Prophet Muhammad – who is believed to have established the rituals prescribed by the Qur'an (2: 124ff) before his death – with more than 2.5 million pilgrims annually, the Hajj is now 'the largest and most culturally diverse assembly of humanity to gather in one place at one time' (Bianchi 1995: 88).

In the pre-modern period, the time, effort and even danger involved in travelling to Makkah and Madinah generally meant that numbers attending for pilgrimage were relatively small (Pearson 1994). However, in an age of globalised modernity, when the orthodox discursive tradition, or what Gellner (1992) calls 'High' Islam, has become more decisively and uniformly universalised at the expense of 'Folk' Islam, pilgrimage has become accessible and affordable to ordinary believers worldwide (Antoun 1989).[3] A tendency towards ideological coherence (Asad 1986) has undoubtedly been effected in modern Islam through state education and mass literacy, as well as the media, Islamic *da'wa* (propagation) organisations and international migration. Indeed, in her study of Sylhet in Bangladesh, Gardner (1995) argues that, among successful economic migrants, the performance of Hajj is part of a modern, more rationalised and textualised, 'Protestant' Islamic consciousness that is the product of working in Britain and especially in Saudi Arabia (1995: 243–5).

My argument here, however, is that the argument that Muslim identities are increasingly standardised and homogenised in the global postmodern requires significant qualification. As Lehman (2001) and Beckford (2003) suggest, and my ethnography of British Pakistanis shows, time-space compression sees religious actors make and remake boundaries of the sacred and profane, creating multiple, criss-crossing webs of friction and conflict, ambiguity and resistance, within and across competing communities and traditions. Indeed, for all the movement of so-called 'fundamentalism' from the margins of classical Islam towards the centre of modern Muslim discourse (Calder 1993), Islam remains 'polycentric . . . lacking any central global power' (Lehman 2001: 308). Moreover, as Eickelman and Piscatori insist in their study of mobility and the Islamicate imagination, 'a causal relationship between the act of travel and a heightened sense of being Muslim' cannot necessarily be assumed (1990: 16). Hajj is increasingly nationalised, with national delegations often limiting cosmopolitan interactions (1990: xvi) and travellers exhibiting a 'consciousness of locality and difference' (1990: xv). As Fischer and Abedi (1990) maintain elsewhere, even while the pilgrimage is performed within the boundaries of the authoritarian nation-state of Saudi Arabia, contested social, economic, cultural and political inferences from various local-global contexts are always in evidence.[4] At the same time, and paradoxically, the very processes which enable powerful attempts to regulate universalised Muslim identities also integrate the Muslim masses (and especially the new middle classes) into new public spheres and cultures of everyday consumerism, organic hybridisation and reflexive self-identities (Turner 1994: 202; Appadurai 1996; Featherstone 2002).

The sacred and profane: normative and improvised authenticities of 'being there'

The ritual mechanisms of British Pakistani pilgrims' symbolic separation from *dunya* (this worldliness) and liminal transition to the sacred are performed when, having made their ablutions and stated their intention to complete the pilgrimage, they don the *ihram*.[5] Depending on their route to Saudi Arabia, whether they come via a port of entry at Jeddah or Madinah, British Pakistanis may change into their ritual attire in the UK, where they make stopovers (for example, in Egypt, Jordan, the United Arab Emirates), on the aeroplane itself or at one of the *miqat* (boundary stations) outside Makkah.[6] Two female respondents spoke of ihram in terms of both physical separation from the familiar and a greater consciousness of Allah, what Fischer and Abedi describe evocatively as 'reawakening from the oblivion of ordinary life' (1990: 150):

> [Y]ou forget everything, your children, your families. I thought England was everything, my lifestyle was everything, but once I got there all I thought about was me as a Muslim. (Maryam, 26, teaching assistant)

> It prepares you as you're approaching the House of God that you're becoming more God-conscious, reciting the *talbiya* [invocation]: 'O God, I am here, what is your command?' at every part of the journey. (Shazia, 56, housewife)

Highlighting the sacred journey of pilgrims from sin and death to purity and rebirth as they repent and ask for God's forgiveness and mercy (Werbner, 1998: 97), Habib (45, spinner) explained that the ihram also anticipates how all humankind will appear before God on the Day of Judgement:

> When you're in the divine presence that's how you will be. A Muslim dies with only two sheets of cloth [their shroud]. Likewise, performing Hajj. No matter if he is a king or beggar, there is no difference between them in the sight of God.

However, another pilgrim cautioned that spiritual introversion and self-consciousness is not at all an automatic outcome of ritual separation: 'you need to be in touch with yourself or you can feel anything' ('Ali, 30, housing support worker). Certainly for Zafar (74, retired spinner) the prospect of coming so close to the House of Allah, the centre of the Islamic universe, made him feel excited but also humble and nervous because of his sins and a perceived need to keep to the elevated (and idealised) *adab* (good manners) he associated with the holy places. However, this was not true of everyone. He complained: 'In the past every moment of the journey was sacred and cherished but I see people with their mobile phones even when they are putting on their ihram – their mind is still on dunya, their business and football.'

Many pilgrims' incorporation into sacred time and space is confirmed when they are confronted with Masjid al-Haram, the Great Mosque of Makkah. Here they perform the first set of rituals which re-enact, in reverse order, the faith-testing ordeals of the founder of monotheism, Prophet Ibrahim, his son, Ismail, and the latter's mother and former's concubine, Hajar (Fischer and Abedi 1990: 150f; Werbner 1998: 97–100). When Ibrahim is forced by his wife Sarah to abandon Ismail and Hajar in the desert, the latter searches frantically for water to save her baby son from death, only for God to create a miraculous spring from the ground. Pilgrims commemorate these events by drinking water from the Well of Zamzam, this after the *sa'y* (hurrying seven times) between two small hillocks, al-Safa and al-Marwa, adjacent to the precincts of the Great

Mosque. Of course, it is the *ka'ba*, the large, cube-shaped stone structure, covered by a black silk *kiswa* or curtain embroidered with golden calligraphy, that recalls the most iconic and totemic images of the pilgrimage. This is the House of God (re)built later in life by Ibrahim and Ismail to mark their covenant with God when He tested a father by asking him to sacrifice his son.[7] Here pilgrims must complete the *tawaf* (seven circumambulations).[8]

In underlining the importance of 'being there' pilgrims reinforced the idea of the holy places as a spiritual homeland and 'one of the primal scenes of Islam' (Fischer and Abedi 1990: 150). As Tariq (53, retired factory shop steward) reflected: 'I had seen the large photographs in people's houses, but nothing prepares you for the splendour and immense size of the mosque'. In a similar vein, Amjad (55, chemist) discussed the contrast between assuming that one is facing the ka'ba when praying towards Makkah and then actually 'looking at it'.[9] He, like many pilgrims, was overwhelmed with awe and emotion:

> When I just walked into the Great Mosque, *al-hamdu-li-llah* [praise be to God] and I saw the ka'ba there, the only thing I could do was to cry. You just grab the wall and cry for forgiveness, all the sins and misdemeanours you've done . . . It is as though you have come back home. That the ka'ba is the very source of our beginning – this is the feeling I had. And checking with 'ulama, some say the reason why it is there is because in the beginning of the world, the ka'ba is the place where Ira'il [the Angel of Death] took the piece of earth that Allah used to make Adam. I returned and the whole of humanity needs to return. It was a great blessing.

Such narratives of sacred place and belonging are also inflected with more individualised and particularistic feelings of closeness to family and kin, especially the dead. Maryam (26, teaching assistant) reported the impact on her mother, who was recently bereaved by the death of a son:

> I remember my mother saying to me, 'My son's gone to a place like this and we're all going to go here'. As soon as she got there she was just consoled completely.

As they circumambulate the House of God most pilgrims salute the *hajar al-aswad* (black stone) lodged in one corner of the ka'ba and said by Muslim tradition to be a meteorite brought from Paradise by the Prophet Adam. However, others struggle through the crowds to kiss it (Bianchi 1995: 89). Ikram (25, teacher), a young man who went on Hajj primarily to accompany his elderly mother, told of how he improvised when he was unable to secure a clear path to the ka'ba: 'I just thought in my heart, I've got the black stone in my hand and this is everything to me, my ka'ba. It just came to me, I thought I should kiss her hand and that was good enough for me.'

As well as such novel and deeply personalised interpretations, Sajid (37, computer programmer) described another experience that was characteristic for many British Pakistanis. He underlined the continuing textual domination of an Islamic discursive tradition (Asad 1986; Messick 1993), one that has socialised generations of Muslims, directly or indirectly: 'the whole history of Islam actually goes round in your head, what you've read . . . it's like walking in the footsteps of the Prophet and the Companions'. However, in this regard, the influence of popular culture on the religious imagination is also apparent: 'I have a video called *The Message* and in it, it shows what the ka'ba would probably have looked like. This was how I pictured it when I closed my eyes' (Tariq, 53, retired factory shop steward).[10] Such popular texts are invoked to simulate authenticity, in part because contemporary Makkah has cheated them of the unadulterated tradition of their imaginations. Many appreciate the air conditioning at the Great Mosque: 'Asian Englandi are *nazak* [soft/spoilt] so Allah has made the Hajj much easier for our sake' (Munira, 69, widow). However, Suleyman (16, student) was not impressed with some of the many modern 'improvements' made by the oil-rich Saudi Arabian government since the 1950s and 1960s especially: 'I could not but help feel that I was not experiencing the true sa'y which generations in the past have done running on marble rather than rock'.[11]

Moreover, in a context where Makkah receives more visitors than any other city in the world for one month in the year, and in so doing provides Saudi Arabia with an income second only in importance to that from oil (Park 1994: 263), 'Ali (30, housing support worker) underlined the constant presence of the secular and profane worlds, cheek by jowl, with the sacred:

> You've got a big Arndale[12] centre sitting in front of Haram Sharif and in front of Masjid al-Nabi [the Prophet's mosque in Madinah] you see shops that have Nike trainers and even white wedding dresses. It makes you think, 'Who buys these? How much are they [the Saudis] influenced [by the West]?'[13]

Some welcome the supermarkets, with branded goods, or enjoy looking for bargains, while others are disappointed by the Saudi and UK agents who promise the world and deliver the bare minimum.[14] However, as a sage-like young pilgrim, Hamid (20, undergraduate) advised, underlining again that the sacred is constructed in the imagination and so very much concerned with consciousness and perception: 'If you want to look for tradition you will find tradition. If you don't look you will not find tradition. So it's a matter of where you look rather than being traditional or not.'

The height of the Hajj is the procession several miles east – via an overnight camp in the Mina Valley – to the plain of 'Arafat, where Adam is said to have met again with Eve after the Fall (Wolfe, 1997: xxiii). Here they repented of their sin and were taught to pray on the Mount of Mercy, where later Muhammad, in his time, gave his farewell sermon. Some pilgrims shelter from the heat of the day in tents while others participate more directly in the solemn congregational standing (*wuquf*) in supplication from noon until sunset:

> Us ladies just stayed in the tents, we made *du'a* [supplication] and prayed for every-thing we could think of. I was especially praying for my son, so that he becomes good and doesn't get into trouble, all these kinds of things . . . making du'a, asking for-giveness and doing *tasbih* [using prayer beads] and *zikr* [virtual rememberence of god]. (Shazia, 56, housewife)

Many hold that it is at this time and place that God is closest to the world, 'making it easier for human prayers to attract his attention' (Bianchi, 1995: 89), and pilgrims try to spend at least a short period on the Mount of Mercy making du'a. However, it was the sheer size, scale and openness of 'a vast plain of people all dressed in the same clothes as far as you can see on the horizon' (Majid, 23, petrol station manager) that made most impact on pilgrims. At 'Arafat they described an oceanic feeling of oneness and collective effervescence which again evoked the end as well as the beginning of time:

> You see the whole of humanity all around you and say 'al-hamdu-li-llah, I am actu-ally part and parcel of this sea that is before me, the sea of humanity', the oneness that it represents, our one Lord, Allah . . . The system, it just goes into a state of shock really, just looking at the size of the situation. (Amjad, 55, chemist)

If pilgrimage involves separation from dunya and the seeking of forgiveness, it also involves sacrifice 'without losing faith in God' (Werbner 1998: 98). Once the pilgrims have left the hotels and shops of Makkah behind and moved out into the desert, the stoning of three tall pillars (*jamrat*) back at Mina and then the sacrifice that follows commemorate the binding of Ismail and the repudia-tion of the Devil's temptations. Amjad (55, chemist), one of the theologically more literate pilgrims, once again explained his understanding of the symbolic significance of the rituals:

> You're getting people here [in Britain, Europe and the West] nowadays that say that the Devil is just a figment of the imagination but, with respect . . . a Muslim has to always be prepared for what a powerful adversary the Devil is. He's as real as anything and always tries to make sure you are never saved.

Trying to follow the example of exemplary persons such as Ibrahim and Ismail, who resisted the temptations of Satan and showed commitment and perseverance or *sabr* in their faith (Fischer and Abedi, 1990: 165), some pil-grims emphasised that: 'You have to be patient here, then in the rest of your life you're patient, it's good for you' (Farzana, 20, student). While there was only implicit criticism here, others were more explicit in their criticisms of fellow pilgrims, arguing that, given the vast expansion of numbers in the modern age, many had lost respect and required instruction on proper adab. This was all grist to the mill of older pilgrims like Zafar (74, retired spinner): 'Unless you suffer, hunger, thirst and feel discomfort, you have really not done Hajj . . . Have they been on Hajj or some holiday?'.

Nevertheless, some do find that the reality of completing this part of the Hajj really does test them to their limits, despite the buses and other modern conveniences. While many are extremely well prepared and organised, the heat combined with the sheer numbers can take its toll on others in terms of getting lost, dehydration, sunburn, exhaustion, injury and even the threat of death. It also impacts on the ability (and desire) of some pilgrims – and not just the elderly or infirm, who are excused – to complete their rites in the prescribed manner, again with some unusual improvisations. Most problems arise at the stoning of the pillars after the tiredness of a night meditating and collecting the requisite pebbles at Muzdalifa. The crush of people at the *jamrat* makes the act extremely hazardous, with some experiencing the stampedes that regularly make international news:[15]

> A stampede broke loose with people just crushed with each other, women without their scarves, screaming. A helicopter was monitoring on top of us and doing nothing. There wasn't even room for an ambulance to get through. I think on that day fifty to sixty people died. (Sajid, 37, computer programmer)

> He said, 'Oh, I've had enough, I put all six people's pebbles in one cloth and threw the big "football" at the Devil'. They were shouting at him, 'Stupid, you're supposed to throw them one by one'. He said, 'Oh, please don't say nothing to me, I've just about made it back myself. (Majid, 23, petrol station manager)

The pilgrim relating this last story, while completing his 'return' tawaf (Wolfe 1997: xxiii) having arrived back in Makkah from Mina, actually collapsed and had to be taken to the hospital inside the Great Mosque's precincts:

> That day was the longest and most painful of all the Hajj, the day when you really get purified . . . I realised that if someone had told me the pilgrimage was going to be so difficult I probably wouldn't have come but al-hamdu-li-llah I didn't know that.

Multiple locations, competing imaginaries: class and race, puritanism and devotionalism

The sacrifice of *'id al-'adha*, sometimes known as *'id al-kabir* (the 'big' festival), is the normative culmination of the Hajj. According to Werbner, the commemoration of Ibrahim's covenant with God is 'a moment of ordeal and release' (1998: 99). Celebrated by Muslims worldwide, it is also a symbolic reminder to pilgrims to share their blessings as the sacrificial meat is given to the poor. However, given the modern, depersonalised mechanisation and bureaucratisation of the Hajj, British Pakistanis now buy vouchers for the animal sacrifice before leaving the UK.[16] Neither do they participate in the ʿid celebrations, because of the demanding schedule of rituals. Nevertheless, reflecting back on the rites of pilgrimage, there are many accounts of the sacred unity and emotional bonding of Muslims as a community, with reference to the suspension of racial, class and national hierarchies described by Turner (1969). There is a strong sense of egalitarianism, anti-structure and communitas, that 'humanity is one single community . . . not different and separate nations' (Amjad, 55, chemist):

> Even all the barbers [who cut or shave pilgrims' hair as a sign of release from ihram] shook my hand. It really was a humbling experience. I really felt Islamic brotherhood and I'm just used to being with Pakistanis. (Abid, 30, sales assistant)

> Everyone tries to communicate with one another, even smiles or letting one person pass before you, letting them go in front or apologising, even sharing dates that you've got, or fruit, with the next person. I couldn't speak their language, they couldn't speak mine, but the smiles on each other's faces made you feel really, really happy. (Ikram, 25, teacher)

   The integrative function of ritual does not of course impose simple uniformity of meaning upon pilgrims. Rather, the pilgrimage is perhaps better seen as providing a common symbolic form which enables the aggregation of a sacred community, while at the same time allowing for the expression of multi-vocal interpretations and individual experiences (Turner 1974a; Turner 1974b; Cohen 1985). Moreover, while it is still possible to be treated as *dauyuf al-rahman* (Guests of the Merciful), perhaps especially in Madinah, which is described as more relaxed than Makkah, British Pakistanis complained about the harshness and harassment of those marshalling pilgrims at the key sites in Saudi Arabia and the fact that, although most shops are run by Pakistani immigrants, the latter cannot own property in their own right (Hamid, 20, undergraduate). They did not escape racism as easily as did Malcolm X (1968) during his somewhat privileged Hajj.
   Nevertheless, while in the holy places, many British Pakistanis were also confronted with experiences that prompted a deep realisation of the economic privileges and political freedoms that they benefit from by living in the West. Some members of the umma are undoubtedly more exposed than others to the stark inequalities and injustices that remain within a divided world. As members of a diasporic community, British Pakistanis were caught between a sense of connection and disconnection with pilgrims from South Asia, especially:

It's far too easy for us. Although we're going to Hajj, we still pick and choose. We'll travel on the coaches and things like that but those people, they'll sleep rough, they'll eat little and they'll walk from one place to another. Yeah, so I value those people's Hajj more than ours and I think it is more valuable to Allah. ('Ali, 30, housing support worker)

At the same time, British Pakistanis also revealed stereotypes and prejudices of their own in terms of race, culture and class: 'pilgrims from Africa [were] . . . seen as the cause of stampedes' (Zafar, 74, retired spinner) and Shi'as were criticised because they 'dress all in black, are always chanting something, behaving in odd ways and determined not to fit in' (Ikram, 25, teacher). Given her own affluence, Shazia (56, housewife) felt threatened by rumours about the alleged criminality of the poor:

I had a lot of jewellery on and the women started telling me these horror stories saying, 'If you go down there on your own, there are these black women who'll cut your hand off and slit your throat or they'll cut your stomach open and they'll take away your gold'.

As Suleyman (16, student) suggested, 'Some people give a bad name to their culture and because of this the rest of their people are looked down upon even on pilgrimage.'

Having completed the Meccan rites, many pilgrims travel north to Madinah to pay their respects to Muhammad, whose tomb is to be found at the Prophet's Mosque with its green dome, tall minarets and ornate calligraphic carvings. South Asian-heritage Muslims are among the most devoted to the Prophet, with those influenced by Sufi and Barelwi movements emphasising the concept of the 'light of Muhammad' (*nur-i Muhammadi*). This is said to have existed from creation and is derived from God's own light (*nur-i khuda*). According to Barelwi scholars, Muhammad is no mere mortal. Alive, not dead, he possesses *'ilm al-ghayb* (knowledge of the unknown) and is the primary focus for Muslims' *tawassul* (intercession) with God (Sanyal 1996: 255–9):

Our belief is that our *nabi* [prophet], like all the *anbiya'* [prophets] is living and if we are sincere our nabi is going to sort all our problems. Our 'ulama say there is a saying of our nabi that whoever comes and visits me in my mosque, *insha'Allah* [God willing], come the Day of Judgement, I will not let that person down. (Amjad, 55, chemist)

Other pilgrims described queuing in single file and then having a few seconds to give their *salams* (greetings) to the Prophet's tomb and make du's, with some believing that 'the carpets are meant to be part of *janna* ["the Garden", Paradise]' (Farzana, 20, student). For some British Pakistanis, time in Madinah was seen as the most profound and emotional of all their pilgrimage experiences, despite not being a part of the formal rituals:

> I felt a strong emotion thinking that just the other side of that gate, which was only a matter of a few feet away, lay the most beautiful person who has ever lived and I started to cry. It was totally involuntary and I cried until I left the mosque. (Tariq, 53, retired factory shop steward)

Even a young respondent who was sceptical about 'spiritual powers' still 'felt very strongly "There is something here"' (Maryam, 26, teaching assistant).

The British Pakistanis interviewed found that their visit to Madinah underlined their theological differences from other Muslims, differences already familiar from Pakistan and the UK. They described meeting 'different types of people who practise Islam according to their area of *fiqh* [jurisprudence, schools of law]', sometimes encountering annoying zealots who sought to 'correct' their practice on various matters: 'You get young people coming up to you and telling you, "Uncle, you should know better. It is *bid'a* [innovation] to make supplication in front of the Prophet"' (Zafar, 74, retired spinner). Indeed, familiar sectarian debates occasionally broke out, something that a majority found unacceptable in the holy places:

> When we were leaving 'Arafat riding on top of a bus, there were these two guys who came from Britain arguing about the Barelwi-Deobandi debate.[17] I was getting really cheesed off but remained quiet as they were quite old. I thought to myself, 'What a place to bring theses silly debates!' (Habib, 45, spinner).

Despite such disapproval, one young British-Pakistani admitted that he had found it difficult to be quite so pragmatic, given the backing that the Saudi Arabian state gives to the puritanical and anti-Sufi Wahhabi sect of Islam.[18] As a 'lover' of the Prophet, he decided that he must take drastic steps:

> Because I knew the differences between 'us' and 'them', their *'aqida* [creed] and our *'aqida*, one of my problems was reading *namaz* [obligatory prayers] behind them [Wahhabi imams]. The first day I read behind them but I felt very uneasy. Some were telling me, 'If you don't know the imam, it's ok' but I brushed it aside because we think they are *gustakh-i rasul* [blasphemers of the Prophet]. ('Ali, 30, housing support worker)

'Ali also complained that the Saudis 'try to push their beliefs onto others' through the publication of books and pamphlets given to all pilgrims, observing that: 'there are some simple brothers and sisters who aren't very educated and they get these leaflets and they think, "Oh, this must be wrong"'.

Boosted by its oil wealth, Saudi Arabia has pumped huge budgets into the global, multimedia export and propagation of Wahhabi ideas through pan-

Islamising international missionary projects and organisations such as the Muslim World League (Rabitat al-ʿAlam al-Islami, founded 1962) (Nasr 1994; Zaman 2002).[19] Other pilgrims also felt that their belief and practice of Islam was policed and disciplined while in Saudi Arabia in a way that was not true of Britain or Pakistan. They reported the 'paranoid' prohibition on carrying anything while paying respects to the Prophet and the 'bad looks' from security guards ensuring that no one touch the grilles of his tomb.[20] There were stories, too, of guards challenging (sometimes in a threatening manner) public behaviour which was judged to constitute *shirk* (polytheism) or bidʿa, from the kissing of a living saint's hand to carrying prayer beads for zikr. Pilgrims also spoke of papers vetted at the airport, one having a page removed from a book of devotions (Habib, 45, spinner). In the same way that some pilgrims were critical of Saudi Arabian organisation of the pilgrimage – 'and how organised people are back in Britain . . . if this was run by the British authorities how smoothly things would run' (Shazia, 56, housewife) – so too another compared the Saudis unfavourably to Britain in terms of freedom of speech:[21]

> I think it was a year before I went to Hajj when the Iranians did a demonstration and were shot down [1987] . . . about three hundred people got massacred.[22] In the West it doesn't matter how bad the demonstration is they never open fire on their own people. I think this is a problem, not maybe just with the Saudis. The majority of Muslim countries are 'trigger happy'. (Sajid, 37, computer programmer)

Pilgrims complained too that, in their drive to erase bidʿa – and despite many 'innovations' of their own – the Saudi authorities have left unmarked, unsigned or even destroyed many places of ziyara. While not part of the formal Hajj or ʿumra rituals, sites of pilgrimage such as al-Baqi Cemetery are still sought out by many pious Muslims from across the world as places that offer great continuity with their salvation history and certain *baraka* (blessing) in the present:

> There are so many thousand *sahabis* [Companions of the Prophet] in that graveyard, but you don't know where their graves are. There are no names, no tombs or anything like that. So one just keeps walking and doing *fatiha* [reading the opening chapter of the Qur'an] at various places. (ʿAli, 30, housing support worker)

And yet there were always minor victories that subverted such attempts at the discipline and regulation of religious belief and practice. Shazia (56, housewife) reported the success of a friend who wanted to smuggle religious souvenirs back to Britain:

> At each graveyard and other ziyara you go to they have these massive posters or signs saying, 'It's forbidden in Islam to touch the graves or to believe that there's any

blessing or to take stones or dust'. But people have a long tradition of taking things from graves of holy people and this friend of mine was collecting stones from different graves and mosques. We had to hide them in such a way that they wouldn't be detected at the airport and luckily those stones were brought back to England and now they adorn the front room, where people come and do ziyara.

Conclusion

The increasing mobility and prosperity associated with international migration has meant that pilgrimage to Makkah and Madinah has become more affordable, convenient and democratised for Pakistanis in Britain than it was for their ancestors. In the subcontinent, fulfilling the duty of Hajj was once the privilege of small numbers of middle-aged Muslim males, whereas visits to the holy places from Britain are increasingly arranged by pilgrims of all ages at times of their need, desire and choosing. Nevertheless, despite the contemporary ease of actually travelling to the holy places, British Pakistanis still report experiencing a sense of liminal separation from the profanities of dunya when they arrive. Influenced by a sacred history increasingly transmitted via a consumer and an electronic Islamic culture, pilgrims also continue to articulate feelings of collective effervescence and communitas in terms of an intensified consciousness of Allah and the prioritisation of their Muslim identity. British Pakistanis describe pilgrimage not only as an emotional and testing personal journey from sinfulness to purification but also – in commemoration of the lives of the Prophets Adam, Ibrahim and Muhammad – as a collective return to the mythic homeland of the umma and, ultimately, all monotheistic humanity.

　　Against this background, however, the perceived 'inauthenticity' of Saudi modernisation, the lack of adab among touristic pilgrims and the prevalence of 'McWorld' (Barber 1995; Featherstone 2002) is disappointing for some. Indeed, in an age where time-space compression is especially intense, the fact of a Western-influenced dunya materialised in and around the holy places highlights the fragility of the boundary between the sacred and the profane suggested by Eade and Sallnow (1991). Rather than a once-and-for-all separation of one from the other, then, pilgrims would seem to imagine and re-imagine their liminality step by step and moment to moment. In the same way, pilgrims' multi-vocal narratives about similarity and difference attest to the fragility of idealised and hyper-real imaginings of a sacred community where, cheek-by-jowl, cosmopolitanism and racism, theological utopias and dystopias, are routinely juxtaposed. Strong feelings of communal empathy can be cross-cut by the rhetorical tropes of negatively experienced encounters with Muslim 'others' from other parts of the world, as Eickelman and Piscatori (1990) maintain.

　　British Pakistanis therefore articulate not only a 'double' (Gilroy 1993) but more properly a 'triadic' (Sheffer 1986; Safran 1991) consciousness, reflecting multiple, genuinely rooted and highly contextualised locations and attachments in terms of: the homeland of Pakistan; the diaspora of Britain; and the wider Muslim world. The particular efficacy of travelling to the holy places for British Pakistani religious identities can be mapped along a continuum from a readily accessible source of strength to a sense of fading ambiguity. Despite some of the elderly grumbling about the banal over-availability and under-appreciation of sacred time and place in the global postmodern, and while few pilgrims can now adhere to the traditional ideal and 'cut off from dunya' on their return, for many the possibility of travel to the holy places has become an important reference point for the imagination of their increasingly transnational and translated identities. Moreover, despite tendencies towards ideological coherence in the global postmodern, and for all the symbolic power of religious imaginaries, in the present moment, British Pakistanis' highly differentiated and contextualised narratives about their collective and individual identities resist any simple incorporation by narrow and homogenised formulations of Islam.

Notes

1. It is not incumbent on children, the disabled, the enslaved, those with a mental illness or those women who do not have a *mahram* (a male relative to whom marriage is forbidden and so can act as an escort). Exceptions are also made when conditions are dangerous for political or other reasons (von Grunebaum 1951: 15–16).

2. Followers reject the term 'Barelwi' in favour of Ahl-i Sunna (People of the Sunna), underlining their claim to be authentic representatives of traditional Sunni Islam. Ahmad Riza Khan (d. 1921) of Bareilly (hence Barelwi), founder of the movement, was first and foremost a Hanafi scholar and his scholarship was deployed to defend many of these more customary aspects of religious practice that were being criticised as un-Islamic innovations by reformist movements of the period. Unlike the Deobandis (see below), for example, he distinguished between 'good' and 'bad' innovations (bid'a). In the literature it is usual to see reference to Barelwism as drawing much of its support from the rural masses in South Asia for whom Sufi saints and shrines remained as important as ever in late nineteenth-century India. However, the leadership of the Ahl-i Sunna was drawn mainly from the prosperous and land-owning families of small agricultural towns and larger urban settlements. See Sanyal (1996).

3. As Fischer and Abedi (1990: 170) report, numbers participating have mushroomed in the modern period: 1850 (40,000); 1902 (200,000); 1964 (1,000,000); 1984 (2,500,000).

4. Moreover, at different points in Islamic history and in individual Muslim lifetimes, travel to Sufi shrines or the homelands of migrant workers has been as compelling as the Hajj (Eickelman and Piscatori 1990: xiv).

5. Before changing into ihram, body hair is removed, beards and nails trimmed, and full ablution made. Two white sheets must be worn by men, while women simply dress modestly (Roff 1985: 84). Sex and the taking of any life are forbidden.

Mukhtar (42, community leader) reports that before departing for pilgrimage British Pakistanis do gather with relatives, as is reported by Roff to be customary. The latter may bring a gift and old clothes to be distributed among the poor. However, these are brief affairs. To make a will before departing – another custom suggested by Roff – is rarer than in Islamic countries.

6. These mark a thirty-kilometre radius around Makkah, beyond which no non-Muslim should pass (Park 1994: 265).

7. Pilgrims can literally follow in the 'footstep' (*maqam*) of Ibrahim as a miraculous stone within Haram Sharif is said to contain its imprint (Fischer and Abedi 1990: 160). Ibrahim's steadfastness is replayed in the life of Muhammad, who rid the House of God of the polytheistic idols on his triumphant return to Makkah from Madinah.

8. Pilgrims perform the rite at least three times; upon arrival in Makkah, at the end of the pilgrimage rituals and once more before leaving Makkah (Wolfe 1997: xxii). In Muslim traditions the ka'ba is often described as an earthly counterpart of Allah's heavenly throne, while tawaf is said to imitate the angels' circling of Him in adoration (Bianchi 1995: 89).

9. The Prophet Muhammad originally followed Jewish tradition and prayed towards Jerusalem, until he received a revelation instructing him to make the *qibla* (direction of prayer) of the Muslim world Makkah instead (von Grunebaum 1951).

10. *The Message* (1975) is an epic filmic representation of Muslim salvation history starring Anthony Quinn. Drawing on the Qur'an, but especially the *sirah* (Muhammad's biography) and *hadith* literatures, it was given a seal of approval by the most important centre of traditional religious learning, al-Azhar, in Cairo.

11. By 1957 the Great Mosque was transformed (Peters 1994: 362), while there are now modern roads and air-conditioned transportation, watersprinklers, modern slaughterhouses, medical, fire-fighting and surveillance personnel, and a media centre (Fischer and Abedi 1990: 169).

12. The Arndale is a large shopping mall in Manchester, UK.

13. I have subsequently been informed by two Muslim academics at conferences that Ann Summers adult shops are also to be found close by the holy places.

14. British Pakistani pilgrims travel in groups from tens to hundreds of people, having purchased packages organised through officially recognised Saudi providers in consort with UK-based travel agents.

15. For example, 'There was a stampede at the 2006 Hajj which resulted in the death of over 400 pilgrims, including three British Nationals . . . There has [also] been an increase in the number of reported cases of pick-pocketing and other forms of theft in Mecca, particularly in the region of the Grand Mosque and in Medina . . . during Hajj and Ramadan, contagious diseases spread quickly, and pilgrims should take basic medicines with them and consume adequate liquids and salts.' See www.fco.gov.uk/servlet/Front?pagename=OpenMarket/Xcelerate/ShowPage&c=Page&cid=1007029390590&a=KCountryAdvice&aid=1013618387135.

16. Mukhtar (42, community leader) reports that some do go to the modern slaughter areas (or, alternatively, to local Bedouin), touch an animal and pay for it to be

slaughtered and butchered. The Saudi authorities then ship most of the meat over-seas to the needy.

17. The message of the Deobandis, another 'ulama-led movement originating in British India, is one of a disciplined adherence to the divinely ordained *shari'a* (Islamic law), cultivating a disciplined personal morality and restrained ritual practice. Optional rites and 'innovations', with disputed sanction in the hadith but defended by the Barelwis, were actively discouraged by the Deobandis. In British India controversies were played out very publicly during preaching tours, oral disputations and in an increasingly elaborate sectarian literature. Nevertheless, Barelwis and Deobandis both follow the Hanafi law school. See Metcalf (1982) for a history of the origins of the movement. These disputes have all been reproduced in diaspora and the new media.

18. The Saudis took control from the Hashimite Sharifs in 1925, ushering in a new order: 'the pious accretions of shrine and rites that had grown up around the Hajj over many centuries were stripped away' (Peters 1994: 362).

19. The League first emerged as part of Saudi Arabia's attempt to counteract communism and especially the pan-Arab nationalism and socialism of revolutionaries such as Nasser of Egypt.

20. Mukhtar (42, community leader) also spoke of Hajj applications being sent back to UK-based agents by the Saudi authorities because common family names including words with divine associations like 'Ullah' or 'Wahid' were interpreted as constituting shirk.

21. It would be interesting to re-interview respondents in the wake of '9/11' and '7/7', to explore any impact on their constructions of Britain as much as of Islam.

22. For a discussion of changing Iranian Shi'ite interpretations and experiences of Hajj, including those of Jalal Al-e Ahmad, 'Ali Shariati and others, see Fischer and Abedi (1990).

References

Antoun, R. (1989), *Muslim Preacher in the Modern World: A Jordanian Case Study in Comparative Perspective*, Princeton, NJ: Princeton Paperbacks.

Appadurai, A. (1996), *Modernity at Large: Cultural Dimensions of Globalization*, Minneapolis, MN: University of Minnesota Press.

Asad, T. (1986), *The Idea of an Anthropology of Islam*, Washington, DC: Georgetown University.

Ballard, R. (1983), 'The context and consequences of migration: Jullundur and Mirpur compared', *New Community*, 11(1/2), 117–36.

Barber, B. (1995), *Jihad versus McWorld*, New York: Times Books.

Beckford, J. (2003), *Social Theory and Religion*, Cambridge: Cambridge University Press.

Bianchi, R. (1995), 'Hajj' in Esposito, J. (ed.) *Oxford Encyclopaedia of the Modern Islamic World*, Oxford: Oxford University Press.

Calder, N. (1993), 'Tafsir from Tabari to Ibn Kathir: problems in the description of a genre', in G. Hawting and A. Shareef (eds), *Approaches to the Qur'an*, London: Routledge, 101–40.

Cohen, A. (1985), *The Symbolic Construction of Community*, London: Routledge.

Durkheim, E. ([1912] 1964), *The Elementary Forms of the Religious Life*, trans. J. W. Swain, London: Allen and Unwin.

Eade, J. and Sallnow, M. J. (eds) (1991), *Contesting the Sacred: The Anthropology of Christian Pilgrimage*, London: Routledge.

Eickelman, D. F. and Piscatori, J. (eds) (1990), *Muslim Travellers: Pilgrimage, Migration and the Religious Imagination*, Berkeley and Los Angeles, CA: University of California Press.

Featherstone, M. (2002), 'Islam encountering globalization: an introduction', in A. Mohammadi (ed.), *Islam Encountering Globalization*, London: Routledge, pp. 1–13.

Fischer, M. and Abedi, M. (1990), *Debating Muslims: Cultural Dialogues in Postmodernity and Tradition*, Wisconsin: University of Wisconsin Press.

Foreign and Commonwealth Office (2006), 'Advice to British Hajjis', London: FCO.

Gardner, K. (1995), *Global Migrants, Local Lives*, Oxford: Clarendon Press.

Gellner, E. (1992), *Postmodernism, Reason and Religion*, London: Routledge.

Gilroy, P. (1993), *The Black Atlantic: Modernity and Double-Consciousness*, London: Verso.

Kalra, V. (2000), *From Textile Mills to Taxi Ranks: Experiences of Migration, Labour and Social Change*, Aldershot: Ashgate.

Lehmann, D. (2001), 'Religion and globalization', in L. Woodhead, P. Fletcher, H. Kawanami and D. Smith (eds), *Religions in the Modern World*, London: Routledge, pp. 299–315.

Lewis, P. (1994), *Islamic Britain*, London: I. B. Tauris.

Malcolm X with A. Haley, (1968), *The Autobiography of Malcolm X*, London: Penguin.

McLoughlin, S. (1996), 'In the name of the Umma: globalisation, "race" relations and Muslim identity politics in Bradford', in W. Shadid and P. van Koningsveld (eds), *Political Participation and Identities of Muslims in Non-Muslim States*, Kampen: Kok Pharos, pp. 206–28.

Geaves, R. (2000), *The Sufis of Britain*, Cardiff: Cardiff Academic Press.

Messick, B. (1993). *The Calligraphic State: Textual Domination and History in a Muslim Society*, Berkeley, CA: University of California Press.

Metcalf, B. D. (1982), *Islamic Revival in British India: Deoband 1860–1900*, Princeton, NJ: Princeton University Press.

Nasr, S. V. R. (1994), *The Vanguard of the Islamic Revolution: The Jama'at-i Islami of Pakistan*, London: I. B. Tauris.

Park, C. (1994), *Sacred Worlds: An Introduction to Geography and Religion*, London: Routledge.

Pearson, M. N. (1994), *Pious Passengers: The Hajj in Earlier Times*, London: Hurst.

Peters, F. E. (1994), *The Hajj: The Muslim Pilgrimage to Mecca and the Holy Places*, Princeton, NJ: Princeton University Press.

Roff, W. R. (1985), 'Pilgrimage and the history of religions: theoretical approaches to the Hajj', in R. C. Martin (ed.), *Approaches to Islam in Religious Studies*, Oxford: Oneworld.

Safran, W. (1991), 'Diasporas in modern societies: myths of homeland and return', *Diaspora*, 1, 83–99.

Saifullah Khan, V. (1977), 'The Pakistanis', in J. L. Watson (ed.), *Between Two Cultures*, Oxford: Basil Blackwell.

Sanyal, U. (1996), *Devotional Islam and Politics in British India: Ahmed Riza Khan Barelwi and His Movement, 1870–1920*, Delhi: Oxford University Press.

Sheffer, G. (ed.), (1986), *Modern Diasporas in International Politics*, London: Croom Helm.

Turner, B. S. (1994), *Orientalism, Postmodernism and Globalism*, London: Routledge.

Turner, V. (1969), *The Ritual Process*, Chicago: Aldine.

Turner, V. (1974a), *Dramas, Fields, and Metaphors: Symbolic Action in Human Society*, Ithaca/London: Cornell University Press.

Turner, V. (1974b), 'Pilgrimage and communitas', *Studia Missionalia*, 23, 305–27.

Von Grunebaum, G. E. (1951), *Muhammadan Festivals*, New York: Henry Schuman.

Werbner, P. (1998), 'Langar: pilgrimage, sacred exchange and perpetual sacrifice in a Sufi saint's lodge', in P. Werbner and H. Basu (eds), *Embodying Charisma: Modernity, Locality, and Performance of Emotion in Sufi Cults*, London: Routledge.

Werbner, P. (2002), *Imagined Diasporas Among Manchester Muslims*, Oxford: James Currey.

Werbner, P. (2003), *Pilgrims of Love: The Anthropology of a Global Sufi Cult*, London: Hurst.

Wolfe, M. (ed.), (1997), *One Thousand Roads to Mecca: Ten Centuries of Travelers Writing about the Muslim pilgrimage*, New York: Grove Press.

Zaman, M. Q. (2002), *The Ulama in Contemporary Islam*, Princeton, NJ and Oxford: Princeton University Press.

Acknowledgements

The interviews forming the data for this article were funded by a small research grant awarded to me by my employers at the time, Liverpool Hope University College. The interviews were conducted by the research assistant to the project, Dr Muzamil Khan, then a part-time doctoral research student under my supervision at Hope. Transcription of the interviews was undertaken by Mr Sirajuddin Holland. The contribution of Muzamil and Sirajuddin is acknowledged here with sincere thanks.

EXCESS BAGGAGE OR PRECIOUS GEMS? THE MIGRATION OF CULTURAL COMMODITIES

Anjoom Mukadam and Sharmina Mawani

Introduction

In writing a chapter on the processes of social and spatial transition in relation to those who follow the faith of Islam, it is necessary to understand that the Muslim *umma* (community) is a global one and is by its very nature diverse, embracing varying histories, ethnicities, languages and economic conditions. Therefore, sweeping generalisations cannot be made in relation to a 'community of communities' that falls within this broad category labelled Islam.

At a time when British Muslim identity has come to the fore and there is increased discussion around the issue of integration, the Nizari Ismaili Muslims, a minority Shia Muslim community that has successfully integrated, has been largely overlooked. Furthermore, most of the previous research on the identities of Muslims in Britain has focused on disadvantaged and less-well integrated groups (Modood et al. 1997; Ahmed et al. 2001; Begum and Eade 2005). Our aim is to provide a detailed analysis of the way in which cultural commodities of the Nizari Ismaili Muslims of Gujarati ancestry have changed as a result of the migration process from India to East Africa and subsequently to the United Kingdom.

This research is based on empirical findings from three qualitative/ethnographic studies (Mawani 2002, 2006; Mukadam 2003) and is interdisciplinary, as it focuses on language, identity, culture and religion. The interviews were semi-structured in nature and ranged from forty-five minutes to an hour in length, with a focus on respondents' personal accounts and perspectives in relation to the migratory processes, adaptation, integration and settlement. The respondents were drawn from both first- and second-generation Nizari Ismailis of Gujarati ancestry and for many this was an emotional experience which brought back memories of their migration from India, exodus from Africa, racism on their arrival in the West and the scars of life in a new land. For others it was a time of reflection, one of achievement and pride. Within the academic community there has been increasing debate as to the advantages and disadvantages of 'insider' research (Brah 1996; Hussain 2000; Mukadam 2003; Mawani 2006). We 'posit that there are in fact benefits to this type of insider research owing to the insiders' own first-hand knowledge through direct experience' (Mukadam and Mawani 2006b: 106). This gives 'insider' researchers the advantage when positioned on Neuman's (2003) 'Access Ladder', as 'the highest rung of access is in most cases almost immediately attainable due to their long-standing social networks with members of the community being researched' (Mukadam and Mawani, 2006b: 106).

> As interviewers from within the community, we were privileged to be allowed access to the most private thoughts of those who had been kind enough to share their experiences with us. The respondents' honesty and tenacity was moving and it would appear that our position as 'insiders' had positioned us so that we were trusted with information that is normally kept within the individual's private sphere. This is the qualitative dimension of the study that focuses on lives lived through a period of uncertainty, a time of conflict and racism, a time of change leading to a new vision of pluralism, diversity, and acceptance. These are their stories, and their comments do matter because they helped shape and bring about changes to the societies in which they reside. (Mukadam and Mawani 2006a: 191)

Although it appears that issues of integration and social cohesion are contemporary phenomena, these processes are synonymous with the process of migration and long-term settlement. Berry (1992) suggests that groups do not acculturate en masse and that the rate of acculturation differs from individual to individual. He proposes that the two primary elements of acculturation are contact and change, involving a majority culture and acculturating minority culture. Mawani (2006: 265) has summarised Berry's (1992) acculturation framework:

> This acculturation framework illustrates two cultures (A and B) in contact, and while in theory each can influence the other equally, in practice there is usually a dominant group (Culture A) and an acculturating group (Culture B). Due to contact and influence a transformation occurs to the cultural features of group B thus producing an acculturated group (B[1]). A parallel phenomenon takes place amongst individuals in group B who undergo psychological changes and become acculturated individuals (B[1]).

One of the first visible signs of acculturation is a change in the cultural patterns and behaviours of those from the minority group. This chapter will illustrate this in further detail after providing a brief outline of the position of the Nizari Ismailis within the broader Islamic context.

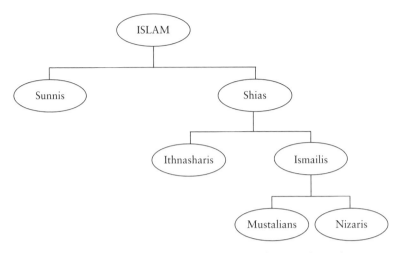

Figure 9.1 The position of Nizari Ismailism within Islam

The Nizari Ismailis, otherwise known as the Shia Imami Ismaili Muslims, are a small minority within the global Muslim faith who recognise His Highness Prince Karim Aga Khan IV as their imam (spiritual leader). This global community is estimated at numbering approximately twenty million, with 80,000 adherents in Canada and 10,000 in the United Kingdom.[1] The imam's presence is crucial in contextualising Islam for his followers during changing times and circumstances (Picklay nd; Mamiya 1996; Nanji 1996; Israel 1999; Daftary 1998). More specifically, 'the imam, while caring for the spiritual well-being of the community was also to be continuously concerned with its safety and material progress' (Nanji 1983:150). The Ithna'ashariyya (Twelvers) are the largest Shia group, followed by the Ismailis, who are to be found in more than twenty-five countries spanning Asia (including India, Pakistan, Iran, Afghanistan, Syria, the former Soviet Union and China), Eastern Africa, Europe and North America (Nanji 1986; Daftary 1998). The historical framework above (Figure 9.1) situates the position of the Nizari Ismailis within the wider Islamic context. Following the death of the Prophet Muhammad in 632 CE, his followers were divided into two branches, the majority being Sunnis and the minority 'Shi'at 'Ali' or more commonly referred to as Shia (Dahya 1996).

This chapter focuses on two distinct periods in the history of the Nizari Ismailis of Gujarati ancestry,[2] namely, the East African era and the Western settlement and the way in which cultural commodities have been transported, adapted and remoulded as a result of these migratory processes.

East African era

Ismaili trading families began settling in Zanzibar from the early sixteenth century; by the end of the eighteenth century there were 450 families in Zanzibar and this number had increased to 750 by 1876 (Nanji 1974; Vellani 1989; Daftary 1990). South Asians began migrating in larger numbers to East Africa in the early nineteenth century, with the earliest settlers arriving in Zanzibar and other coastal towns, such as Lamu and Mombasa. Due to harsh economic conditions, famine and drought in Gujarat, migration to East Africa was seen as an economic opportunity. Furthermore, the move of the Omani Sultanate in the 1840s from Muscat to Zanzibar resulted in an increase in the numbers leaving India for more prosperous plains. This migration process took place gradually and kinship ties were paramount in encouraging family members to become reunited in their new homeland. Between 1880 and 1920 the South Asian community in East Africa increased from approximately 6,000 to 54,000 and despite their different religious backgrounds they developed stronger social and economic bonds (Mawani 2006; Oonk 2004; Mukadam 2003; Walji 1995).

The first *jamaatkhana* (house of assembly) in Zanzibar was built in 1838, and 1905 saw the establishment of the Ismailia Council and the first Aga Khan school in Zanzibar. By the First World War, Ismaili migrants from India were concentrated in Zanzibar, Mombasa, Dar-es-Salaam, Nairobi, Kampala and Tanga. Schools were opened on the mainland in the 1920s and it was at this time that Aga Khan III began encouraging the importance of educating girls, thus emphasising the role that women play in imparting core values and traditions to future generations. During a visit to Mombasa in 1945 he advised:

> If a man has two children – one boy and the other girl, and if he could only afford to give education to one, I would say that he must give preference to the girl. Her influence in the family circle is enormous and the future of the generations depends upon her ability to lead the young along the right path and instruct them on the rudiment of culture and civilization. (Walji 1995: 5)

Soon after the Second World War, Ismailis from Zanzibar began migrating to the mainland in greater numbers. Today only a small number of Ismaili families continue to reside in Zanzibar and Ismaili institutions continue to serve the community (Walji 1974; Nanji 1974, 1986; Vellani 1989; Daftary 1990).

Gulbanu and Kassamali, two first-generation Ismailis, relate their experiences of leaving India for East Africa. Gulbanu, a 74-year-old first-generation Ismaili, explains how, after her marriage at the age of 16, she eventually moved to East Africa, due to a job offer:

Gulbanu: If there was a need of teachers in Africa they would advertise in a newspaper, Ismaili. And couples were given the first preference . . .

I think it was published in Mumbai. But if there was any news they wanted to convey it would be published in this. So, Altaf's father read the Ismaili. He immediately said that this was an opportunity for us that there was a need for teachers in Africa and they were giving couples the first preference. And it was for a position in our religious school. Then we got the forms and we filled them out, signed them and sent them in. And our application was accepted. And we came to Dar-es-Salaam . . . In 1945 I took my oldest son, who was 10 months old, and we went to Africa.

Mawani: So, you must have travelled by ship?

Gulbanu: We went by ship.

Mawani: How long did it take?

Gulbanu: It took three weeks. We got there in 21 days. (Mawani 2006: 73)

Kassamali, an 86-year-old first-generation Ismaili, narrates how leaving Karachi for Mumbai, due to family strife, eventually led him to East Africa at a young age:

Mawani: Where did you migrate from?

Kassamali: From Karachi, 1936.

Mawani: You came to Moshi in '36?

Kassamali: I came to Moshi in '36 . . . you see, I was so frustrated by my grandmother (paternal) who was forcing me to marry the girl whom I never liked. So that was my point of leaving Karachi . . . I left Karachi with the help of my maternal uncle . . . So I came to Mumbai . . . to find if I can get a place . . . in Mumbai as a . . . musician. So, I went to see a friend, he was the secretary of the Recreation Club [now known as the Ismaili Tariqah and Religious Education Board] . . . He showed me a list, 'there is a need for teachers in Africa and you have taken the diploma in teachers' training. I'm strongly recommending you to take this job. I want you to accept this job.' You believe it or not, within two hours I accepted the offer . . . My intention was to stay in Mumbai for about a year or so . . . But when this offer came, it was a tempting offer naturally . . . So I said, ok, I accept.

Mawani: How old were you?

Kassamali: Twenty . . . I took a ship from Mumbai to Africa in the month of July and the ocean was fierce. On the first day, I went to eat the food and when I was coming back I vomited. And I was in bed for 7 days, I couldn't eat anything . . . At that time in Mombasa, volunteers used to come to help Ismailis that were arriving in Mombasa. Somebody in the steamer told me Moshi is a very beautiful town. So I left in the evening . . . There was a two-storey house near jamaatkhana in which I was given a room. It was pitch dark. It was dark and the watchman was calling out, I was very scared. (Mawani 2006: 74)

Gulbanu describes the conditions she was faced with when she arrived in Dar-es-Salaam with her husband and ten-month-old son.

. . . we didn't know the language here, they spoke Swahili here . . . we had no relatives . . . it was a completely new place and we didn't know Swahili . . . they took us to a block of flats that they had rented for all the teachers that were coming from out of town to teach. There were Hindu teachers, Sikh teachers, teachers from all religions and communities. There was a common washroom out in the back. And it was of such a kind that today's children wouldn't even stand there! They hadn't organised what kind of work they were going to give us. So the first period was religion in every class. All the Ismaili teachers taught for 40 minutes . . . when the first period was over they were free to go home. So I would teach for 30–45 minutes and go home . . . they gave us a boy [servant] and wrote down some Swahili terms for us. So we slowly picked up the language . . . they asked me to go to our maternity home, Lady Alisha Maternity Home, it was here in Dar-es-Salaam. So they told me to go there so I would meet people, learn the language, I would learn the ways of African living . . . I would go there and do whatever had to be done. (Mawani 2006: 74–5)

While the newly arrived Ismailis attempted to integrate into African society, racial apartheid was the primary British colonial policy, which divided East Africa into three groups: the Africans, the Asians and the Europeans. Everything, including 'access to education, health, land and economic resources, professions and occupations' (Asani 2001: 163) was systematically planned along racial lines. The Asians were sandwiched between the ruling Europeans at the top and local African community at the bottom (Brah 1979). In an attempt to establish cordial relations between the Muslims in East Africa and the Ismaili community, the East Africa Muslim Welfare Society was formed in 1945 with the aim to enhance the education and social welfare of the indigenous African Muslims. In addition, schools and hospitals run by Ismailis were the first to open their doors to all Africans (Nanji 1974; Asani 2001). In a speech made during his installation ceremony in Nairobi, Kenya on 22 October 1957, prior to independence, Aga Khan IV encouraged his followers to remain loyal to their chosen country in East Africa:

As true Ismailis, you must remember that you will always have two principal obligations. The first and paramount of these is your religious obligation to Islam and to your Imam. Your second obligation is a secular one. You must always be loyal to the country of your adoption and whatever Government is responsible for your security and well-being. This is advice which My beloved Grandfather often gave to you. I believe it is as wise and true today as it was when He was alive. It constitutes the surest guarantee by which you can maintain your faith and your civic identity. (*Kalam*, vol. 3, n.d.: 2)

Due to the limited success of breaking down the racial barrier, the Ismailis of East Africa 'have continued to think of themselves as Indian or Asian' (Asani 2001: 164).

One of the main factors influencing change in a culture is the infiltration of new elements from an outside, often dominant, culture that leads to the process of acculturation. It is important to mention that all individuals do not acculturate as a collective, rather, the rate of acculturation of individuals differs from person to person (Berry 1992). The two key elements of acculturation are contact – that is, continuous first-hand interaction between cultures – and change amongst the people in contact, which is often passed on to subsequent generations. The situation in East Africa for the Ismailis was slightly more complicated in that there were two main cultural influences, that of the dominant coloniser (British) and that of the local East African culture. Prior to independence the South Asians, including the Ismailis, made up the middle layer and were known as the 'colonial sandwich', as they were in a favourable position compared to the native African population, but secondary to the British rulers (Brah, 1979). Figure 9.2 illustrates the way in which the Ismailis, who predominantly arrived from Gujarat with their Gujarati culture, adapted and incorporated aspects of both British and African culture, thereby creating a new identity that constituted a hybrid culture which put them in a position to benefit from both. In the process of adapting to the ways and customs of mainstream African society, the Ismailis did not discard their own cultural and religious practices, rather they maintained symbolic links with Gujarat by retaining Gujarati cuisine, dress and language, as well as fully participating in the Ismaili *tariqa* (path), by attending congregational worship at *jamaatkhana* and singing *ginans* (devotional songs).

In East Africa, major social welfare and economic development institutions were organised by the Ismaili community. Schools, *jamaatkhanas* and hospitals were established alongside economic development institutions such as the Diamond Jubilee Investment Trust (now known as the Diamond Trust of Kenya) and the Jubilee Insurance Company (Dahya 1996). Having resettled in new lands, the Ismailis, like other South Asians, continued to practise their traditional customs of dress, food preparation, ritual and language. Apart from religious differentiation, which perhaps was not so clearly visible, the Ismailis appeared as any other South Asian community (Nanji 1974; Mohamed 1992). In order to distinguish them from other South Asian groups and allow them to integrate with the indigenous population, for economic, political and perhaps even social reasons, Aga Khan III took significant steps in an attempt to modernise the community (Williams 1988). He felt that, 'To have retained an Asiatic

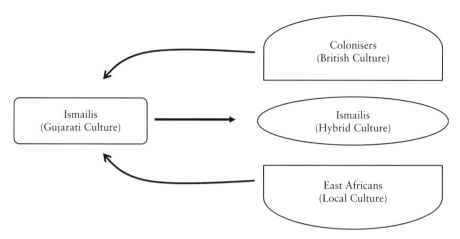

Figure 9.2 Acculturation patterns in 'colonial sandwich' as applied to the Nizari Ismaili Muslims of Gujarati ancestry

outlook in matters of language, habit, and clothing would have been for them a complication and in society an archaic dead weight for the Africa of the future' (Aga Khan III, 1954: 30). The 1952 Evian conference in France, held to discuss economic and social matters of the Ismailis in East Africa, saw two noteworthy outcomes. First was the replacement of Gujarati with English as the language of instruction, with Swahili as a second language, in all Aga Khan schools. However, Gujarati/Kacchi were maintained in the home and in the majority of religious rituals. Second was the change in dress for women. Traditionally women wore 'a long frock, with matching three yards of material called pachedi hung on the shoulders, or in many cases a saree' (Walji 1995: 7). Aga Khan III encouraged women to discard this traditional method of dress and adopt 'Western' dress (i.e. short dress), the style worn by European women in colonial East Africa. As an incentive, women who followed this advice received a signed photograph featuring Aga Khan III and Her Highness the Begum Aga Khan, who also adopted the 'Western' dress, and the change in dress was taken up successfully by Ismaili women (Walji 1995; Ruthven 1998). In 1956, under the direction and guidance of Aga Khan III, the language of the daily prayer was changed from Gujarati to Arabic (Nanji 1974). An article in *East Africa Today* describes the Ismaili community in East Africa as one which 'made this country their home and from the beginning had ceased looking backwards to the country of their origin. Due to this outlook, Ismailis had their marriages – most of them – in this country unlike other Indian communities. They seldom went to India for marriages' (*Africa Today* 1959: 79).

It is apparent that Aga Khan III was aware that in order to progress as a successful community it was necessary for the Ismailis to integrate with the colonial and indigenous cultures while maintaining their own religious and cultural identities. In his *Memoirs* he states, 'Ismailism has survived because it has always been fluid. Rigidity is contrary to our way of life and outlook' (Aga Khan III, 1954: 185). Adatia and King (1969: 191) reiterate this point when they state that 'the Ismailis in East Africa [are] the most prosperous, healthy, and go-ahead of the communities which originally came from outside Africa—the one with the best hope of survival into the long future as fully accepted African citizens'. Due to their resettlement in East Africa the

> Ismailis evolved a culture which reflected their Indian heritage, their British colonial experience, and their African environment. What evolved was a completely new culture, different from their original Asian culture which the immigrants had brought with them from their homeland. (Walji 1995: 11)

The creation of this new culture saw the adoption of the safari suit by Ismaili men, alongside the incorporation of East African cuisine, such as kuku paaka (chicken in coconut cream), mogo paaka (cassava in coconut cream), vitumbua (fried rice bread), mandazi (fried doughnut-like bread), mkate mimina (rice bread), ugali (porridge made from corn flour) and tangawizi (ginger tea) (*A Taste of Our Cooking*, 2002). In addition, Swahili words, such as machungwa (an orange), sufuria (a pot), fagio (a broom), mboga (vegetables), mwiko (wooden cooking spoon), mto (pillow), ndizi (bananas), njugu (peanuts), jikoni (kitchen), fujo (disorder, chaos, unrest) and kelele (noise) were incorporated into the Gujarati and Kacchi spoken by East African Ismailis.

   In a message sent to the East African Ismaili community in 1951, Aga Khan III foresaw that the Ismailis in East Africa, numbering over 50,000 by the 1960s (Nanji 1983), were to face another period of change and transition: 'Your grandfathers crossed India to come to Africa. You have to cross right up to the Atlantic' (Ismailia Associations 1955: 20). Aga Khan III had a vision for his community in East Africa, that it would eventually migrate westwards; however, nobody could have predicted the traumatic and devastating manner in which this transition would take place. After a period of almost a century, the Ismailis were to face an immense upheaval as adverse political policies and anti-Asian riots became regular features of life in East Africa. The decades after the Second World War saw the end of British rule in East Africa triggering a series of events that caused a significant deterioration in the position of the South Asians (Buchignani et al. 1985; Israel 1999). Kassamali outlines the situation in Tanzania after it gained independence in 1961:

> After a couple of years in power [Julius] Nyerere [President of Tanzania] thought that 'we have an obstacle and they are the Asians'. So he tried to . . . frighten us. First, he took away all our properties. Number one blow. We didn't move an inch. Second blow, he took away all our businesses. The Asians didn't move. Very few, who had a lot of money, they thought, 'we better go to a safer place'. But the rest of the people

remained there. And Nyerere thought these people are not moving. So the third . . .
tactic he applied was to arrest prominent people. (Mawani 2006: 82)

During a visit to Tanzania in 1966 Aga Khan IV urged the Ismailis to obtain
citizenship in the newly independent East African states of Kenya, Tanzania and
Uganda.

> Some spiritual children have been worried about their future. Some have been think-
> ing of moving out of Tanzania, but I do not recommend this . . . But what I am sure
> about is that each and everyone of you, everyday whenever possible, should in your
> daily habits and in your daily way of living show to the people of Tanzania that you
> are loyal citizens of this country . . . you must continue to work in Tanzania sincerely
> and loyally. (*Kalam*, vol. 3, n.d.: 173)

> . . . concerning the future of My Jamats [communities] also in Kenya and in Uganda
> . . . It is more important than ever before that you should try, each one of you, to
> make it quite clear, in your everyday contacts, that you are citizens, loyal citizens of
> Tanzania and that you intend to help citizens of Tanzania as you have done in the
> past. I say each one of you should make this effort . . . (*Kalam*, vol. 3, n.d.: 196)

The 15,000 Ismailis in Uganda, as well as many in Kenya and Tanzania, followed this advice. In the late 1960s non-citizens were faced with employment
and trade restrictions, which resulted in South Asians leaving East Africa for
Britain. Due to racism, unfavourable economic conditions and strict immigration laws in Britain, many South Asians fled instead to Canada (Thakkar 1999;
Crewe and Kothari 1998). In 1972, Idi Amin, the President of Uganda, expelled
40,000–80,000 South Asians from Uganda. It is said that he received a message
from God during a dream, at which point he was determined to make Uganda
'a black man's country'; he stated: 'I am going to ask Britain to take responsibility for all Asians in Uganda who are holding British passports, because they
are sabotaging the economy of the country' (Keatley 1972). The South Asians,
most of whom were third-generation descendants of workers brought to
Uganda by the British colonial administration, were given ninety days to leave
the country and were allowed to take only what they could carry. The businesses, homes and possessions they left behind were distributed without compensation to Amin's military favourites. Almost overnight, Uganda saw a mass
outflow of South Asians, including Ismailis, primarily to Britain, Canada and
the United States. For the second time in their history, the Ismaili community
had left behind homes, businesses and other possessions, this time in search of
safety, and were faced with the challenge of integrating into an alien society and
re-creating new homes. In an interview with Mukadam (2003: 51) on 30
November 2001, Professor Azim Nanji, Director of the Institute of Ismaili
Studies in London, outlined three key factors that were, in his opinion, vital to

the success of the Ismaili community in Britain: '1. The community's skill at adapting to new environments; 2. Its history of enterprise; 3. The ability to develop support institutions.'

Western settlement

A large majority of those affected by the expulsion were in possession of British passports and over 28,000 entered the United Kingdom to fierce opposition and a very intimidating welcome (United Nations, 1973). The arrival of the East African Asians was to have a profound effect on the lives of both the white community and the Indian community already settled in Britain. Unlike the migrants who had arrived from India, many East African Asians had trans-ferred funds from Africa to Britain before nationalisation and their subsequent expulsion (Brah 1996; Hinnells 2000; Burholt 2004). This gave them the advantage of being able to move into the leafy suburbs, as opposed to deprived inner cities, thereby distinguishing them from many of the other minority ethnic groups settling in Britain at this time. Rashida, who came from a wealthy family background, conveys her view of life before the exodus: 'we had drivers picking us up, dropping us off to school . . .. [We] used to go to New Africa Hotel with an aunt for Sunday morning breakfast' (Mukadam 2003: 36). Iqbal was far more blunt about the financial position of those who came from the more afflu-ent families: 'you buy yourself into middle class. Problems that refugees have: discrimination on housing, discrimination on jobs, discrimination on educa-tion, we didn't encounter any of that. We bought our way' (ibid.). It must be stressed at this point that these experiences were not of the majority, but of a minority, whose business acumen had enabled them to capitalise on opportu-nities in East Africa. A large number, like the journalist Yasmin Alibhai-Brown, were put into reception camps. She describes life in this interim period: 'Resettlement camps, language lessons and other essential teaching were pro-vided for us by the State. People could choose not to go to the camps, but most decided to take up the offer' (Alibhai-Brown 2001). Despite this period being the height of Powellism[3] and racial discrimination, many, like Sabrina, recall the kindness they received from the British people at a stage in their life when they had lost everything:

> I didn't ever feel discriminated or anything like that which other people in built up areas like Leicester felt. We were told when we were leaving Uganda 'Please avoid those areas like Leicester' . . . We were taken care of the minute we got out of the plane . . . we were given a very warm welcome, it was just amazing. (Mukadam 2003: 37)

Government policy recommended that the East African refugees be placed in areas where there was not an existing high concentration of South Asians.

Brah (1996: 34), herself a former Ugandan citizen, records the forced dispersal of these individuals and families:

> In order to disperse them, Britain was divided into 'red' and 'green' zones. The 'red' zones were those where the size of the Asian populations was deemed to be already 'too high' and hence they were designated as out of bounds for Ugandan Asian refugees. The green zones, on the other hand, were defined as places where the Asian population was non-existent or so low that a slight rise in their numbers would be 'tolerated'.

Already expelled from their homeland, they were now thrown into rural Britain without community channels of support, be they cultural or religious. Isolated, dispirited and in many cases depressed, the refugees were faced with a challenge that was to make or break them. This is where the strength of the East African Ismailis lay: they had already experienced life in another country and had adapted strategies enabling them to maintain their distinct cultural, linguistic and religious identities. Together with the existing group of South Asians that had come directly from India, they began to assert their presence. Many had arrived in the country as family units, unlike the once-migrants (Vertovec 2000), and they began to intermingle with others belonging to the same community, be they once-migrants or, like themselves, twice-migrants. Ballard (1994: 23) questions the whole issue of difference between those who had come from East Africa and those already settled in Britain: 'Despite their greater affluence and more "westernised" material lifestyles, they [East African Asians] also have a strong commitment to religious and ethnic reconstruction, and are thus much less different from the other settlers than is commonly supposed'. This is a sentiment shared by Michaelson (1983) and Hahlo (1980), who state that one of the most noticeable characteristics of Gujarati communities residing in Britain is their inclination to be self-contained.

Communal networking in Britain was re-established by way of letter writing, telephone calls and other social activities. Once these links were forged, refugees stood their ground and defied government policy by moving into areas that were marked as 'red' zones, as kinship ties and friendship networks were crucial to these communities (Anwar 1979; Werbner 1979; Bhachu 1985). They had found a 'home' and gradually obtained a greater sense of belonging and familiarity; they were no longer sojourners but settlers, the first-generation. The long-associated stereotype of the Indian corner shop was attributed mainly to Gujaratis, who worked long hours and included their families in all aspects of the business (Janjuha-Jivraj and Woods 2002). This commitment to their families and ambition for them has led to this group's success. An article in the *Daily Mail* highlighted how corner shops were in danger of disappearing as the children of the owners are now highly educated professionals: 'They're the daughters of Asian corner shop owners who came to this country with nothing. But now they're all at the top of their professions' (Dam 2002). Ismailis of

Gujarati ancestry are heralded as being among the most affluent and successful of Britain's South Asian settlers. This community boasts a wide range of highly educated professionals, as well as entrepreneurs, some of whom find themselves on 'rich lists' published annually.

Cultural commodities

An area in which this community is steadfast is that of religious beliefs and practices (Mawani 2006). Initially the new ethnic minority communities had no choice but to congregate in school halls and converted warehouses for the purposes of religious worship. However, so vital were these centres to the lives of the Ismailis, for both religious purposes and communalism, that April 1985 saw the opening of the first purpose-built, high-profile *jamaatkhana* in London. Every high-profile *jamaatkhana* is officially known as 'The Ismaili Centre' and is designed to incorporate traditional and contemporary architecture. In a speech made at the foundation stone-laying ceremony of the Ismaili Centre in Lisbon on 18 December 1996 Aga Khan IV articulated the role of high-profile *jamaatkhanas*:

> Although Ismailis have lived in the West since the late 1950s, only two other Ismaili Centres of this importance and magnitude have been built in the Occident . . . Through lectures, presentations, conferences, recitals, and exhibits of art and architecture, and alone or joined by other national, international entities in the cultural field, these centres have become ambassadorial buildings which today reflect and illustrate much of what the Shia Ismaili community represents in terms of its attitude towards the Muslim faith, its organisation, its discipline, its social conscience, the effectiveness of its community organisations and, more generally, its attitude towards modern life and the society in which it lives. (Aga Khan Speeches, 20.2.03)

For the Ismailis, these centres are a source of pride and offer a sense of belonging. Today there is a total of forty-seven *jamaatkhanas* across the United Kingdom, with nine in the Greater London area (Heritage Society). The origin of *jamaatkhanas* can be traced back to the Ismaili community in Gujarat, before migration to East Africa and other cities in India. The Ismailis established *jamaatkhanas* in the new countries that they adopted as their homes and many *jamaatkhanas* evolved to meet the changing needs of the growing Ismaili community in the West, East Africa and other parts of India.

Where language is concerned, Martin-Jones (1984) indicates that South Asians from East Africa were brought up with a history of language maintenance and community-run schooling in the 'mother tongue' alongside mainstream English-medium schooling. The situation faced by many Ismaili children brought up in Britain is dominated by their need to understand and behave appropriately in two or more languages and cultures. The response of parents to these conflicting demands is usually to make one of two decisions:

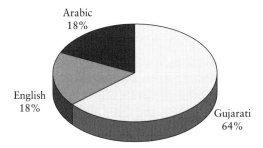

Figure 9.3 Language used on an average day in *jamaatkhana* during congregational worship

1. strictly insist that Gujarati/Kacchi be the medium of communication at home, and English at school, thereby making their offspring bilingual;
2. try desperately to maintain Gujarati/Kacchi, but fail due to the child's need to conform to the new social and educational environment.

Most frequently, parents are forced into accepting the dominance of English which results in the individual becoming monolingual, but with a passive knowledge of Gujarati/Kacchi (Mukadam 2003). Hawkes (1966: 13) comments on the parents' feelings in such a situation: 'children tend by a natural process of adaptation to conform increasingly to the British pattern as they grow up. This may upset the parents who are often strongly determined to maintain features of their traditional life.' For many second-generation Ismailis in Britain, their parents 'did not actively encourage . . . [them] to learn Gujarati, as they were afraid that it would interfere with their command of the English language. What they and others like them had overlooked was the relationship between language and culture/religion – a basic human right which forms the basis of one's own sense of identity' (Mukadam 1995: 65). In the case of many Ismaili families, while Gujarati/Kacchi was no longer the predominant language of the home, it still played a prominent role within the liturgy in the *jamaatkhana* (Figure 9.3), which includes the congregational singing of the ginans.

The recitation of *ginans* is an integral part of congregational worship amongst the Ismailis, in which all members of the community participate, by leading the congregation in singing a *ginan*, singing along with the congregation or by listening to the often familiar tune (Kassam 1995; Asani 2002). Individuals participate in the congregational singing of *ginans* because singing as a congregation is an act of shared values, represents a common goal, a collective identity and provides a sense of group solidarity. '*Ginans* establish continuity with the past and provide a basis for identity that securely bridges the space between the past and the present' (Mawani 2006: 459).

Conclusion

Relatively little research within the field of Nizari Ismaili migration has focused on the manner in which cultural commodities are transported and transformed as a result of such movements. In creating a new home in a new country the Ismailis, first in East Africa and then in Britain, mirrored the ways of life in their original homeland, Gujarat, while adapting aspects of the local majority culture and sometimes merged the two together to create new hybrid forms, many of which are still in existence today. Interestingly, it appears that some aspects, especially those that fall within the sacred sphere, such as the *jamaatkhana* and *ginans*, have been maintained almost in their original form, whereas mundane practices, involving cuisine, dress, music and language, are fluid and have been adapted according to the majority cultures and societies encountered. This process of differential adaptation is commonly referred to as hybridity and is seen by many as a form of cultural dilution (Hutnyk 2005). For the Ismailis, it appears that it was this very process of cultural creativity alongside the maintenance of certain relatively unchanged core elements that was paramount in their successful integration in their new homelands. The history of migration of the Ismaili community clearly shows their ability to discard aspects of traditional life that were seen as 'excess baggage' and to maintain, preserve and protect those aspects that have travelled with them and that remain to this day as their 'precious gems'.

> [N]o matter where you are, your responsibilities to your faith, to your Jamaat [community], to your traditions, remain identical; there is no difference, none whatsoever, in practicing your faith in London, or in Vancouver or in Montreal or in New York rather than in Karachi, Nairobi, Bombay or other parts of the world. (Aga Khan IV, (*Kalam*, vol. 1, n.d.: 102)

Notes

1. There are no official census figures for the Ismaili communities of North America and Britain. Estimates have been obtained from members of community institutions, who wish to remain anonymous.
2. From here on, the term 'Ismaili' will be used to refer to those of Gujarati ancestry.
3. Enoch Powell was a British politician (1950–74) who vocalised his controversial views in relation to immigration, as well as issues of national identity. On 20 April 1968 he infamously delivered what came to be known as the 'Rivers of Blood' speech, in which he warned the British public of the dangers of immigration from the Commonwealth.

References

A Taste of Our Cooking (2002), London: His Highness Prince Aga Khan Shia Imami Ismaili Council for the United Kingdom.

Adatia, A. K. and King, N. Q. (1969), 'Some East African firmans of H. H. Aga Khan III', *Journal of Religion in Africa*;2(3).

Africa Today (1959), 'The Ismailis in East Africa: small but progressive community', *East Africa Today*, quoted in R. M. Kadende-Kaiser, and P. J. Kaiser, (1998) 'Identity, citizenship, and transnationalism: Ismailis in Tanzania and Burundians in the diaspora', *Africa Today*, 45(3/4).

Aga Khan III (1954), *The Memoirs of Aga Khan*, London: Cassell.

Aga Khan Speeches – Timeline – (1996), Speech by Prince Karim Aga Khan: foundation stone-laying ceremony of the Centro Ismaili Lisbon, Portugal http://globale,net/~heritage/timeline/1996/961218.html accessed 20 February 2003.

Ahmed, N. M., Bodi, F., Kazim, K. and Shahdjerah, M. (2001), The Oldham Riots: Discrimination, Deprivation and Communal Tensions in the United Kingdom, London: Islamic Human Rights Commission.

Alibhai-Brown, Y. (2001), 'My time in a resettlement centre', *The Independent*, October 29.

Anwar, M. (1979), *The Myth of Return*, London: Heinemann.

Asani, A. (2001), 'The Khojahs of South Asia: Defining a Space of Their Own', *Cultural Dynamics*, 13(2).

Asani, A. (2002), *Ecstasy and Enlightenment: The Ismaili Devotional Literature of South Asia*, London: I. B. Tauris.

Ballard, R. (ed.) (1994), *Desh Pardesh: The South Asian Presence in Britain*, London: Hurst.

Begum, H. and Eade, J. (2005), 'All quiet on the eastern front? Bangladeshi reactions in Tower Hamlets', in T. Abbas (ed.), *Muslim Britain: Communities Under Pressure*, London: Zed Books.

Berry, J. W. (1992), 'Cultural Transformation and Psychological Acculturation', in J. Burnet et al., *Migration and the Transformation of Cultures*, Toronto: Multicultural History Society of Ontario.

Bhachu, P. (1985), *Twice Migrants: East African Settlers in Britain*, London: Tavistock.

Brah, A. (1979), 'Inter-generational and Inter-ethnic Perceptions: A Comparative Study of South Asian and English Adolescents and Their Parents in Southall,' unpublished PhD thesis, University of Bristol.

Brah, A. (1996), *Cartographies of Diaspora*, London: Routledge.

Buchignani, N., Indra, D. M. and Srivastava, R. (1985), *Continuous Journey: A Social History of South Asians in Canada*, Toronto: McClelland and Stewart.

Burholt, V. (2004), 'The settlement patterns and residential histories of older Gujaratis, Punjabis and Sylhetis in Birmingham, England', *Aging and Society*, 24, 383–409.

Crewe, E. and Kothari, U. (1998), 'Gujarati migrants' search for modernity in Britain', *Gender and Development*, 6(1), 13–19.

Daftary, F. (1990), *The Ismailis, Their History and Doctrine*, Cambridge: Cambridge University Press.

Daftary, F. (1998), *A Short History of the Ismailis: Traditions of a Muslim Community*, Edinburgh: Edinburgh University Press.

Dahya, B. (1996), 'Ethnicity and modernity: the case of Ismailis in Britain', in R. Barot (ed.), The Racism Problematic, New York: The Edwin Mellen Press.

Dam, R. (2002), 'From corner shop to high flyers', *The Daily Mail*, 7 February.

Hahlo, K. G. (1980), 'Profile of a Gujarati community in Bolton', New Community, 8.

Hawkes, N. (1966), *Immigrant Children in British Schools*, London: Pall Mall Press.

The Heritage Society, *Jamatkhanas in the United Kingdom* http://www.ismaili.net/jk/europe/jkaddress.html#J7 accessed 20 June 2002.

Hinnells, J. R. (2000), 'South Asian religions in migration: a comparative study of the British, Canadian, and U. S. Experiences', in H. Coward, J. R. Hinnells, and R. B. Williams (eds), *The South Asian Religious Diaspora in Britain, Canada, and the United States*, New York: State University of New York.

Hussain, Y. (2000), 'Identity and British South Asian women: gender, race and ethnicity – theoretical and imaginative perspectives', unpublished PhD dissertation, University of Bradford.

Hutnyk, J. (2005), 'Hybridity', *Ethnic and Racial Studies*, 28(1).

Ismailia Associations for Africa (1955), *Mubarak Talika and messages: Mowlana Hazir Imam's Guidance and Advice in Spiritual and Worldly Matters to Ismailis of Africa*, Mombasa: Shia Imami Ismailia Associations for Africa.

Israel, M. (1999), 'Ismailis', in P. R. Magocsi (ed.), *Encyclopedia of Canada's Peoples*, Toronto: University of Toronto Press.

Janjuha-Jivraj, S. and Woods, A. (2002), 'Successional issues within Asian family firms: learning from the Kenyan experience', *International Small Business Journal*, 20(1), 77–94.

Kalam-e Imam-e-Zaman: Farmans to the Western World (1957–1991), Volume 1 (n.p., n.d.).

Kalam-e Imam-e-Zaman: Farmans to Africa (1957–1993), Volume 3 (n.p., n.d.).

Kassam, T. R. (1995), *Songs of Wisdom and Circles of Dance: Hymns of the Satpanth Ismaili Muslim Saint, Pir Shams*, Albany: State University of New York Press.

Keatley, P. (1972), 'Britain could face influx of 80,000 Asians', *The Guardian*, 5 August.

Mamiya, L. H. (1996), 'Islam in the Americas', in A. A. Nanji (ed.), The Muslim Almanac: A Reference Work on the History, Faith, Culture, and Peoples of Islam, New York: Gale Research.

Martin-Jones, M. (1984), 'The new minority languages: literacy and educational issues', in P. Trudgill (ed.), Language in the British Isles, Cambridge: Cambridge University Press.

Mawani, S. (2002), 'Devotional songs of the South Asian Nizari Ismailis in Toronto: the attitudes of the older generation', unpublished MSc dissertation, London School of Economics and Political Science.

Mawani, S. (2006), 'The Construction of identities amongst young adult Nizari Ismaili Muslims in Toronto and Mumbai,' Unpublished PhD thesis, SOAS, University of London.

Michaelson, M. (1983), 'Caste, kinship and marriage: a study of two Gujarati trading castes in England', unpublished PhD thesis, SOAS, University of London.

Modood, T., Berthoud, R, Lakey, J., Nazroo, J., Smith, P., Virdee, S., and Reishon, S. (1997), *Ethnic Minorities in Britain: Diversity and Disadvantage*, London: Policy Studies Institute.

Mohamed, H. E. (1992), 'Our African legacy', *Hikmat*, 3(6).

Mukadam, A. (1995), 'Tug of war: Gujarati fights back', Modern English Teacher,(3)3.

Mukadam, A. (2003), 'Gujarati speakers in London: age, gender and religion in the construction of identity', unpublished PhD thesis, University of Reading.

Mukadam, A. and Mawani, S. (2006a), 'Nizari Ismailis in the West: negotiating national, religious and ethnic identities', in Y. Kalogeras, E. Arapoglou and L. Manney (eds), *Transcultural Localisms: Responding to Ethnicity in a Globalized World*, Heidelberg: Universitätsverlag Winter.

Mukadam, A. and Mawani, S. (2006b), 'Post diasporic indian communities: a new generation', in S. Coleman and P. Collins (eds), *Locating the Field: Space, Place and Context in Anthropology*, Oxford: Berg.

Nanji, A. (1974), 'Modernization and change in the Nizari Ismaili community in East Africa – a perspective', *Journal of Religion in Africa*, 6(2).

Nanji, A. (1983), 'The Nizari Ismaili Muslim community in North America: background and development', in E. H. Waugh, B. Abu-Laban, and R. B. Qureshi (eds), *The Muslim Community in North America*, Edmonton: The University of Alberta Press.

Nanji, A. (1986), 'The Ismaili Muslim identity and changing contexts', in V. C. Hayes (ed.), *Identity Issues and World Religions*, Bedford Park: Australian Association for Study of Religions.

Nanji, A. (1996), 'The ethical tradition in Islam', in A. Nanji (ed.), *The Muslim Almanac*, Detroit, MI: Gale Research Inc.

Neuman, W. L. (2003), Social Research Methods: Qualitative and Quantitative Approaches, Boston: Allyn and Bacon.

Oonk, G. (2004), 'The changing culture of the Hindu Lohana community in East Africa', *Contemporary South Asia*, 13(1).

Picklay, A. S. (n.d.), *History of the Ismaili*, Bombay: Popular Printing Press.

Ruthven, M. (1998), 'Aga Khan III and the Isma'ili renaissance' in P. B. Clarke (ed.), *New Trends and Developments in the World of Islam*, London: Luzac Oriental.

Thakkar, R. (1999), 'Gujaratis', in P. R. Magocsi (ed.), *Encyclopedia of Canada's Peoples*, Toronto: University of Toronto Press.

United Nations (1973), 'Asians from Uganda in European transit camps', *New Community*, 2(3).

Vellani, M. A. M. (1989), 'The Isma'ilis and Zanzibar', *Hikmat*, 3(3).

Vertovec, S. (2000), *The Hindu Diaspora: Comparative Patterns*, London: Routledge.

Walji, S. R. (1974), 'A History of the Ismaili community in Tanzania,' unpublished PhD thesis, University of Wisconsin.

Walji, S. R. (1995), 'Ismailis in Kenya: some perspectives on continuity and change', in M. Bakari and S. S. Yahya (eds), *Islam in Kenya: Proceedings of the National Seminar on Contemporary Islam in Kenya*, Kenya: Mewa Publications.

Werbner, P. (1979), 'Ritual and social networks: a study of Pakistani immigrants in Manchester', unpublished PhD thesis, University of Manchester.

Williams, R. B. (1988), *Religions of Immigrants from India and Pakistan: New Threads in the American Tapestry*, Cambridge: Cambridge University Press.

SECTION 3

• • •

RELIGION, RACE AND DIFFERENCE

SITUATING MUSLIM GEOGRAPHIES

Lily Kong

Introduction: (re-)emergent geographies of religion

Since the beginning of this century, two collections of essays in important and well-regarded journals of geography gave dedicated attention to the phenomenon of religion. In 2002, Julian Holloway and Oliver Valins led a themed section in *Social and Cultural Geography* on 'placing religion and spirituality in geography', while in 2006, James Proctor (2006) organised a forum in the *Annals of the Association of American Geographers* on 'theorizing and studying religion'. The AAG's study group on Geographies of Religion and Belief Systems has started a new online journal of the same name. A new book on the *Geographies of Muslim Women* (Falah and Nagel 2005) brings together a range of essays focusing on different parts of the globe, while a new edited collection on *Geographies of Muslim Identities* has just hit the bookstands (Aitchison et al. 2007). In the mean time, a host of papers examining various aspects of religion and geography has been produced in the last decade, more so than in the preceding 20 to 30 years (just some examples are: Chivallon 2001; Dunn 2001; Dwyer 1999a, 1999b; Graham 1998; Graham and Murray 1997; Henkel 2005; Hervieu-Leger 2002; Knippenberg 1998; Kong 2002, 2005a and b, 2006; Tong and Kong 2000; Livingstone et al. 1998; Nagar 1997; Numrich 1997; Pacione 2005; Prorok 2003; Raivo 1997, 2002; Sidorov 2000a, 2000b; Slater 2004; Valins 2003; Vincent and Warf 2002; Zelinsky 2001). Definite attention is being given to religion by geographers, even if some still believe that there is yet to be a distinctive geography of religion (Proctor 2006).

Amid this growth of geographical research interest in religion, a noticeable proportion of work in the post 1990s is focused on Muslim geographies, that is, the geographical analysis of Muslim populations – their places, identities, communities and societies – at various local, national and transnational scales.

Often, research has focused on Islam as a minority religion within multireligious or largely Christian societies. In fact, much of this research has focused on European Muslim populations, and indeed, British Muslim geographies, while there is a stark dearth of research on Muslim geographies in the United States. Little has also been written by geographers on Muslims in majority Islamic societies, though this work is beginning to emerge (see, however, Falah and Nagel 2005; van Wichelen 2007). Further, much of the work has addressed relationships of tension and conflict, focusing, for example, on negotiated meanings and resources between Muslim and non-Muslim communities, and within Muslim communities. In other words, Muslim geographies have principally been geographies of contestation and conflict.

Islamic geographies of the 'golden age': historical contingencies and knowledge production

This understanding of 'Muslim geographies' as the geographical analysis of Muslim populations must be understood as a sort of intellectual latecomer to a much earlier 'Islamic geography' that was often much less focused on contentious circumstances. This earlier 'Islamic' geography reaches back to a time when Islamic scholars (including geographers) contributed greatly to an understanding of the world, through the documentation of new places and practices (in the manner of early voyagers) and the development of social thought. Whereas present-day Muslim geographies are largely occupied with issues of conflict and negotiation, the early Islamic geographies that emerged between the ninth and thirteenth centuries were far from motivated by conditions of discord.

Islamic geographers were great travellers, given the Qur'anic injunction for able-bodied male adherents to undertake a pilgrimage to Mecca at least once in their lifetime, which often led to exploration beyond the Arabian peninsula, and good records of their travels. Among the well-known Islamic geographers were: Al-Idrisi (1099–1166 or 1180), who worked for the King of Sicily and wrote for him a book quaintly entitled *Amusement for Him Who Desires to Travel Around the World*; Ibn-Batuta (1304–1369 or 1377), who was the Muslim world's Marco Polo, travelled in Africa, India, China and Russia, and documented Islamic practices around the world; and Ibn-Khaldun (1332–1406), who wrote a comprehensive history and geography of the world. Ibn-Khaldun was an environmental determinist, believing that the northern and southern extremes of the earth produced those least civilised. Indeed, in the eleventh century, Islamic scholarship reflected the great civilisation that the Muslim world was, in contrast to the Dark Ages that engulfed Europe, while fourteenth-century Ibn-Khaldun has sometimes been acknowledged as the first scholar to observe human-ecology relations (James and Martin 1972: 53), and to define the 'true scope and nature of geographical inquiry' (Kimble 1938:

180) (see Alatas, 1995). In brief, scholars and scholarship such as these meant that Islamic geographers contributed significantly to an understanding of the world before the discovery of the New World.

The different Muslim/Islamic geographies of two vastly different periods reflect the historical contingencies and divergent conditions of the times. The early (pre-New World) contributions of Islamic geographies were part of an Islamic 'golden age,' a period when Muslim thinkers, travellers, traders, poets, philosophers, artists, scientists and engineers introduced new ideas, new technologies and new ways of understanding. The geographies written by Muslim scholars were not exclusively about Muslim geographies. Indeed, they were often about other peoples and other places. The great Muslim civilisations were thus the hearths from where others were observed and documented. In contrast, in the contemporary world, they have become the 'other' and the subject of Muslim geographies has precisely become the scrutiny of Muslims as 'other'.

New World and Christian ambitions: dominant European geographies of religion

With the discovery of the New World and the spread of Christian beliefs, the sixteenth and seventeenth centuries saw the development of a geographical scholarship on religion that was influenced by Christian ambitions, and the submergence of Islamic geographies. The emerging Christian-inspired geographies constituted what Isaac (1965: 10) called 'ecclesiastical geography', which primarily involved mapping the spatial advance of Christianity in the world. Such work was propelled by the desire to disseminate the Christian faith and gained much impetus from the support of Christian churches. During the mid seventeenth century, a related form of ecclesiastical geography emerged, with attempts to describe the spheres of influence of other religions. Ostensibly this appeared to have liberated geography from purely Christian influence and given it a more neutral position through paying attention for the first time to other religions as well (Büttner 1980: 92). In reality, however, the underlying aim was to determine which religions Christian missionaries found in what part of the world and how missions progressed among them. The underlying impetus for geographical work still stemmed largely from Christian interests, and relatedly from colonial advances. These European colonising and Christian missionary interests of the period thus eclipsed the earlier significant contributions of Muslim geographers, coinciding with the decline of the Islamic 'golden age,' again an exemplification of the historical contingencies of knowledge production. The further development of a 'biblical geography' which developed in the sixteenth and seventeenth centuries, involving attempts to identify places and names in the Bible and to determine their locations, further illustrates the powerful influence of the Christian church at that time (Isaac 1965: 8).

As the European Enlightenment of the eighteenth century overshadowed the former Islamic 'golden age', the dominance of European thinking in understanding the relationship between geography (environment) and religion emerged, and while the shape of European thought has changed over time, the dominance has persisted even since. In the eighteenth and nineteenth centuries, under the influence of Montesquieu and Voltaire, ideas of environmental determinism developed and, for a time, dominated thinking about religion so that explanation was sought for the essential nature of religions in terms of their geographical environments. In fact, this resonates with the earlier work of Ibn-Khaldun and illustrates the pioneering but forgotten (at best, and unacknowledged, at worst) contributions of early Islamic geographers. During this time, Islam, as with other religions, became understood in environmentally deterministic terms.

Following the nineteenth-century fascination with environmental determinism came the reverse philosophy from the 1920s onwards, where the idea came to be accepted that religion was not only acted upon, but could in turn assert influence on social and economic structures as well as landscapes. The emphasis turned to the ways in which landscapes could be altered by human hands – akin to the more possibilistic stance of the Vidalian school of geography and particularly, Sauer's school of cultural geography, in which the landscape is the primary object of research. The geographer begins with the landscape and its related anthropo-geographical facts (such as settlement, transportation routes and population) and seeks to understand the underlying forces. Geographers interested in religion would seek out landscapes which were both the medium and the outcome of religious beliefs and practices, and offer description and explanatory analysis. Much of the work within geography focused on antiquarian landscapes and, reflecting the Euro-American bias of the discipline, focused on Christian landscapes. Where there was some attention paid to Islamic societies and landscapes, it was pilgrimages, and particularly the *hajj* to Mecca, that received most research attention, with analysis of the patterns and volumes of flow, and landscape changes arising from pilgrim movements (King 1972; Shair 1981a, 1981b).

Secularisation and the geography of relics?

The 1960s were a period that Bryan Wilson (1966) and others identified as the start of secularisation of the world in which religious thinking, institutions and practices were observed to have lost their social significance. This shaped the ways in which geographers approached the study of religion. Büttner (1980: 100, 104) called for the incorporation of this widespread process of secularisation into the geography of religion to prevent it from becoming a 'geography of relics', 'restricted to the study of those ever-shrinking areas in which religion still has a formative effect on the environment'. Instead, the geography of religion may develop into a 'geography of spiritual attitudes' instead. Like Büttner, Isaac (1959–60: 17) too recognised that, with increasing secularisation, religion's impact on the landscape would become minimal when compared to the historic past, where it played an important role in the patterning of the landscape. However, instead of calling for the study of this very secularisation process, he appeared content to study the past landscapes and to see the geography of religion as an essentially 'ethnological and historical study'. Islam rarely featured in this retreating geography of religion, though in reality, the revival of religion in many places, including the then communist USSR and Eastern Europe, and the growth of religious fundamentalism put paid to any misconception that secularisation was here to stay. It is in this climate that 'new' geographies of religion have emerged (Kong 2001).

'New' geographies of religion

The 1990s and even more so the 2000s have become a growth period for the geographies of religion, including Muslim geographies. The somewhat moribund state of geographical research on Islam and Muslims (and religion more generally) of the middle twentieth century has changed somewhat, largely as a response to the new empirical realities of an increasingly interconnected world with growing social and cultural pluralities and complexities. That an emergent Islamic influence and impact has to be addressed is increasingly apparent, especially with the flashpoint of the 11 September 2001 attacks on New York's World Trade Center, and continuing through the subsequent 2002 Bali, 2004 Madrid and 2005 London bombings.

Geographers researching religion during this period have contributed most significantly to an understanding of how places are not only implicated in meaning making for religious groups and individuals, but also constitute a way through which states manage religions, and a site where religious groups and individuals intersect with one another, sometimes in violent conflict. Conflicts surrounding places are therefore a barometer of state-religion relationships, inter-religious relationships and intra-religious relationships.

The politics of space

Geographical research on the politics of religious space has focused primarily on those places of worship belonging to religious groups that have minority status in their respective countries. In this regard, research on Muslims and their mosques has particularly helped to shape the analytical frame. Here, geographers have trained their gaze on two key sites – mosques and schools – to examine and explain the place of Islam in society. The research issues and approaches have situated Muslim geographies within the reorientations of cultural geography of the late 1980s and early 1990s (see Kong 1997), adopting the analytical frames of cultural politics and the politics of space. The earliest works, as well as the majority of research since then, have focused on mosques, beginning with Kong's (1993a, 1993b) analysis of the politics surrounding establishment, relocation and demolition of religious buildings in Singapore. On account of its indigenous status, the special place of the Malay Muslim population in Singapore (despite their minority status) translates into cheaper land for the establishment of places of worship in a regime where allocation of space for religious use is carefully controlled by the state. However, state rhetoric of equality and its translation into other forms of space management are real. For example, the state points out that the relocation and demolition of religious buildings to accommodate secular developmental needs applies to all religions (whether Buddhist, Taoist, Christian, Sikh, Hindu, Muslim or any other). Conversely, it also heralds the occasional establishment of different religious buildings side by side as evidence of freedom of worship and multiculturalism, a reality which is not completely bereft of difficulties for religious adherents in practical terms. Religious place (including mosques) is thus part of a state strategy that simultaneously emphasises affirmative action for the indigenous population, equality of all religions, freedom of worship and multiculturalism, with both embedded consistencies and contradictions.

This acknowledgement of the role of religious place in the analysis of the interplay between social and political conditions and religious considerations, and between state objectives, policies and practice and everyday experience, has become somewhat of a pioneering approach in 1990s geographies of religion. Examination of the politics of urban space as a way of examining social relations and religion-state relations has since developed into an established frame of analysis, with a growing body of works that examine the spatial politics of ethnic and religious minority expression. Particularly, some excellent research on minority Hindu and Muslim communities, primarily in the 'western' world, has been carried out, of which the study of Muslims in Britain and Australia have especially illuminated the negotiation of inter-ethnic and inter-religious relationships. Without attempting to be comprehensive, the elaborations below demonstrate the manner in which this early 1990s approach of examining places of worship as sites of negotiation and contestation has since been adopted.

While much of the geographical study of religion in North America has primarily been influenced by the traditional Sauerian school of cultural geography (see Kong 1990), US-based geographers Prorok and Hemmasi (1993) take on board issues of cultural politics in their paper on Trinidadian mosques, reflecting some of the arguments that have thus far been outlined within anthropology and British cultural geography about the politics of community and the dialectical relationship with place. The authors analyse Muslim politicisation through a historical geography of mosque development, arguing that mosques reflect and help resolve the tension between political assimilation and maintenance of ethnic identity among members of the East Indian Muslim community. Mosques disclose the strength of their identity, and the intensity of Muslim participation and assimilation in Trinidad's political history. This is because to (re)build a mosque, the community must organise itself, have good leadership and accumulate resources. To be able to build a mosque, then, means there is likely to be a strong sense of community spirit. At the same time, mosque building also reflects external political impetuses. Fervent mosque building usually coincided with peak periods when Trinidad's Muslim population was organised for socio-political purposes – for example, just before Trinidad gained independence and leading up to the first elections. Mosque-building activity was particularly strong in a heavily contested area involving one party dominated by conservative Hindus with no real secular agenda and another, an Afro-Creole party. By this means, Prorok and Hemmasi (1993) illustrate that mosques contribute to the consolidation and reproduction of communities.

In Australia, Dunn (2001) turned attention to the land-use disputes surrounding mosque applications in 1980s and 1990s Sydney, and particularly the refusal of development consent for the construction of mosques. Dunn illustrated how the constructions of fanaticism and intolerance associated with Islam were difficult to use as grounds for opposing mosque development but did succeed in intensifying public unease and widening opposition. In the end, local authorities refused development consent because 'the proposals were "out of character" with surrounding development, drawing on the construction of Muslims as alien and ultimately out of place' (Dunn 2001: 291). Thus, apart from the stereotypes of Islam, opposition to mosque construction also relied on constructions of 'local citizen' and 'local community', while those who supported the construction of mosques called on counter-constructions of Muslims as 'moderate, tolerant, peaceful, clean living, family-orientated, ordinary local citizens' (Dunn 2001: 291). This points to the politicisation of planning decisions in relation to religious buildings, and problematises ideas of multiculturalism and nationalism (Dunn 2005).

In Britain, Gale and Naylor's (2002: 387) work on the spatial politics of religious minority expression in British cities and towns examined how the buildings of non-Christian communities had previously been portrayed as 'alien', but were witnessing a changing geography in which they had come to be held up as symbols of multicultural cities. With local planning authorities approaching the establishment of such religious sites more positively than hitherto had been the case, Gale and Naylor (2002: 389) suggested that 'a set of more hopeful urban multicultural geographies' had been developing (see the case of a Buddhist temple in predominantly white Wollongong in Australia, where Waitt (2003) argues that the temple is held up as a symbol of multiculturalism and accepted as a tourist site). This is in contrast to earlier geographies, as explained by Naylor and Ryan (2002), who had examined how London's first mosque held different meanings for different religious, ethnic and social groups from the time it was first established in the 1920s to its late twentieth-century unsuccessful attempt to expand its premises. Such meanings range from exotic curiosity in the earlier period to conflict and tension in the latter period, with residents 'scuppering' mosque expansion plans.

Mosques aside, religious schools have been another site of contention and negotiation. Dwyer and Meyer (1995) conducted pioneering work, comparing the institutionalisation of Islam in the Netherlands and the UK by examining the manner in which debates evolved and decisions were made about whether to establish state-funded Islamic schools. The issue drew attention to questions about integration and segregation. For example, would state-funded Islamic schools detract from integration by not facilitating a greater mixing of children from different cultural-religious backgrounds, or would they help to bolster a strong sense of identity, only after which integration might occur? Some argue that Islamic schools detract from integration as they will be populated largely, if not exclusively, by immigrant children. Without the mixing of children of different cultural-religious backgrounds, integration was thought to be impossible. The multicultural school, in this view, is the 'site of the creation of a multicultural society'. On the other hand, others argued that Islamic schools provided the grounds for the development of a strong sense of identity, only after which integration might occur. What Dwyer and Meyer (1995) drew attention to the ways in which 'Muslim' and 'integration' were ideologically constructed, and how these ideological constructions intersect with the political decision-making process. They illustrated how these negotiated notions of 'integration' inform decision making (see also Dwyer and Meyer 1996).

Kong's (2005a) analysis of Islamic religious schools in Singapore again demonstrates how secular schools and *madrasahs* can become sites of negotiation. In the case of Singapore, the state plays a significant role in the social construction of 'schools', as sites of multiculturalism, multiracialism, multireligiosity and modernity. However, these constructions are sometimes opposed by religious groups who see their schools as sites where religious life is maintained and enhanced. Madrasahs are a good case in point. Through an analysis of the Muslim community's response to debates about the place of madrasahs in secular Singapore, it is apparent that the Muslim community is multiple rather than monolithic, and that debates about what constitutes legitimate and important knowledge systems which deserve to be perpetuated are anchored in deeply ideological positions. Perhaps signifying the importance of both mosques and schools in the making of Muslim identity, one of the most recent additions to the literature focuses on how France seeks to regulate Muslim communities by particularly exercising state control over religious places (mosques and schools) (Bertrand 2006).

The politics of urban religious space, particularly Muslim spaces in the form of mosques and schools, has thus received a fair amount of research attention since the early 1990s. Indeed, it would be fair to say that such studies constitute a significant part of the geographical literature on religion. Muslim geographies have thus been influential in shaping an important part of geographical enquiry more generally.

The politics of identity and community

While studies on the politics of religious space constitute a significant body of geographical research on religion in general, and Muslim geographies in particular, a second approach that geographers have contributed much to since the early 2000s is the 'decenter[ing] of the homogenizing assumptions about [religious] community' (Olson and Silvey 2006: 807). Through analysis of various communities, geographers have illustrated that religious community is fractured rather than monolithic. It is constituted through constant struggles and negotiations, and needs to be understood as always constructed or imagined, the outcome of political processes. This is the 'politics of identity and community' that Kong (2001) has referred to, and several important geographical studies have analysed these dynamics. It must be noted, though, that geographers have not been alone in making these observations and analyses, and must share the credit with anthropologists, sociologists and others (see, for example, Eade 1991 and Baumann 1996).

Be that as it may, research on Muslim identities has been important in advancing our understanding of the constructedness of religious identity and community, and has been pioneering within geographical studies of religion. Here, several strands of research have emerged: a focus on gendered youth identities, a concern with residential segregation (which has drawn attention implicitly or explicitly to ethnic and religious intersections in community construction) and an acknowledgement of the complexities of interconnected transnational, national and local forces in the construction of identities.

Dwyer's and Hopkins' work on young Muslim women and men in Britain respectively has made significant contributions to the geographical study of religious identities (see Cooper 1995, for earlier work on young Christians). Dwyer's (1999a) work on young Muslim women in a small town near London examines the ways in which different constructions of community – both 'local' and 'globalised' – are used by young British Muslim women, which are simultaneously empowering and constraining. Participants in Dwyer's study spoke about a local 'Asian community', evoked by the availability of specialised services such as *halal* meat shops, which signals for them a sense of security and acceptance (hence no racism) in the town. This is a construction of an 'Asian community' that corresponds to the ethnic community discourse of conventional multiculturalism in which the 'Asian community' is imagined in opposition to 'British society'. While this was positive, it came at a cost: living in an 'Asian community' meant all sorts of surveillance by other members of the 'community' over one's actions and behaviour. This is the contradiction of community that confronts young British Muslim women. 'Community' is a source of security and strength, but also of constraint and oppression.

Because the boundaries of 'community' are fluid, different imaginations of Muslim community can be evoked or denied. Dwyer (1999b) explores contradictions within a 'community', with those who construct and those who deny the existence of a 'Muslim community'. While some insist that divergences within the 'community' must be recognised, such consciousness of diversities is countered by those who seek to define an inclusive collectivity of Muslims, rejecting the salience of sectarian divisions such as Sunni, Shia and Ismaili Islam in their own 'community'. For them, banding together is important because Muslims the world over are oppressed. Calling upon the global sense of a Muslim community (the *umma*') thus becomes a source of empowerment (see also Samad 1998; Eade 1993, 1994; Lewis 1994; and Back 1996).

While Dwyer worked with young Muslim women, Hopkins (2006, 2007a, 2007b) has focused on young Muslim men's identities. Hopkins (2006) demonstrates from his study of young Muslim men in Glasgow and Edinburgh that their masculinities are multiple and fluid, shaped by social difference and locality. This runs counter to two dominant discourses about the masculinities of young Muslim men, which are divergent but coexistent: either about patriarchy and aggression, or effeminacy and academicism. On the contrary, Hopkins argues that the masculine identities of young Muslim men are racialised, ethnicised, gendered and sexualised, as well as influenced by class positions, young men's relationships with their fathers, and their specific locations in urban Scotland.

A second strand of geographical research on the politics of identities and communities has drawn attention either implicitly or explicitly to the nexus between ethnicity and religion, through analysis of residential segregation. Like the work on young Muslims, this work has focused on Britain, although analysis of residential segregation drawing on ethnic data may be found elsewhere (see, for example, Poulsen et al. 2001 on Australia, New Zealand and the US; Musterd 2005 on American and European cities). In part, the research attention that has gathered around Muslims in Britain has grown as a response to public debates around urban disturbances in Bradford, Oldham and Burnley in 2001 and the London bombings in 2005, and the general anxiety about 'extremist' Muslims in Britain. Concerns about the extent to which Muslims have failed to spatially and socially integrate into British society have thus prompted scholarly analyses (Gale 2007).

In this regard, Phillips' work on British Muslims in the northern cities of Bradford, Oldham and Burnley is an example of how analysis of 'minority ethnic residential segregation' in Britain has been carried out. Phillips (2006) highlights how official reports contend that British Asian and white people are living a 'series of parallel lives'. In particular, British Muslims are thought to be

withdrawing from interactions with wider British society and displaying negative isolationist and self-segregationist behaviours. Phillips draws on her
research to counter this view and to show how segregation is not self-imposed
or desired, but that a racialisation of space is occurring. Here, the conflation of
race and religion, or at best, the lack of acknowledgement of the confluence of
the two (if confluence it is) draws attention to how 'British Asians' are basically
assumed to be Muslims, a problem serious enough in its own right, even if we
do not begin to address the reductionism of 'Asian' to those from South Asia
or, even more specifically, Pakistan or India.

In contrast, Munoz (2006) examines ethnic minority segregation in the
Scottish cities of Dundee and Glasgow with an awareness of the internal religious composition of ethnic populations. She thus assesses whether Indian residents of different faiths (Hindu, Muslim and Sikh) have divergent experiences
of segregation, and indeed concludes that 'incorporating religious affiliation
into the calculation of a segregation index reveals more about ethnic segregation than when ethnicity alone is considered' (Munoz 2006: 97). Similarly,
Peach (2006) points out how British Muslims are often refered to as if they were
a single community when in fact they are ethnically heterogeneous. For the first
time, in 2001, when ethno-religious ward-level data became available in
Britain, it became apparent from Peach's analysis that there is a high level of
intra-Muslim ethnic segregation in London, and that intra-South Asian
mixing irrespective of religion is greater than intra-Muslim mixing, irrespective
of ethnicity.

The cross-cutting influences of gender, age and ethnicity in specific localities
aside, religious identities are also shaped by transnational and national forces,
and local, national and global scales intersect in complex ways. Muslim geographies have focused attention on issues such as the role of the state, the role
of transnational connections, including familial ties, and the role of global
events in (re)shaping religious identities and communities.

Kong (2006) analyses how state policies regarding religious broadcasting in
Singapore have implications for the construction of identities that simultaneously fold the local and national 'into' and 'against' the transnational.
Specifically, Singapore's broadcasting policy has resulted in the relative absence
of local Islamic radio and television broadcasting, but permits access to free-to-
air broadcasts from Malaysia. This transnational access, however, does not
simply contribute in a straightforward, linear way of perpetuating transnational identities and communities. Instead, there is evidence of an assertion of
the national in the face of transnational influences, though simultaneously,
there is also an enabling and challenging of the transnational. Such state interventions which shape identities and communities is evident also in Samers's
(2003) study of Maghrebin (North African) migrants in France during the
1980s and 1990s. Samers demonstrates how identity among Muslims of
Maghrebin origin in France is shaped not only by the policies and actions of

the French state but by those in Algeria as well, illustrating the transnational influences on identity formation.

Apart from the role of the state, transnational connections through familial ties may also shape identities. For example, Hopkins (2007a) examines how young Muslim men identify as Scottish Muslims in his study context, but are also connected with a global network of identifications that are anchored in family ties in Africa and Asia.

While the public media certainly assume or imply that global events impact on local identities, Hopkins (2007b) examines systematically how global events do in fact impact on the lives and experiences of a specific group of people – young Muslim men living in urban Scotland – and shows how global events shape these young people's political actions locally (such as tactical voting, protesting in marches, or writing letters and petitions to politicians).

The above literature about the intersections of the global and transnational with the local is clearly an area to which geographers are uniquely placed to contribute. As the geographical literature on Muslim identities demonstrates, a hallmark of geographic interventions in globalisation research is the emphasis on how transnational processes must be understood as rooted in local contexts (Olson and Silvey 2006: 807). Thus, 'place and place-based notions of community have not been made obsolete in the face of transnationalism' (Olson and Silvey 2006: 807). Rather, as the various interventions discussed above demonstrate, using the experience of Muslim communities, the local and transnational intersect in complex, non-linear ways. Indeed, Muslim communities and identities provide an excellent site of analysis, given the Islamic notion of a transnational community, the umma, on the one hand, and the knowledge that religious experience is surely mediated by historical and geographical contingencies.

Taking stock of Muslim geographies

The dominance of research about Muslim place, identity and community by British geographers and on British geographies should be glaring by now. In part, this must be because of the reality of public anxieties centring on Islam in Britain. Yet, while these anxieties exist too in Australia and in the US, for example, the same research attention by geographers has not been accorded. In part, this may be because of the global dominance of British geography (especially social and cultural geography) anyway.

The various Muslim geographies, principally emanating from Britain (with key exceptions from Singapore by Kong and Australia by Dunn), have contributed various pioneering perspectives and approaches. For example, Muslim geographies have served as a primary impetus for the body to become a significant site and scale of analysis for geographers of religion, on account of study of the hijab. So too have the analyses of building sites (whether mosques or schools) become the key foci for the study of urban spatial politics. And extending further outwards, the diasporic community that Muslims constitute and the abiding notion of an idealised transnational community in the form of the umma have prompted analysis of transnational connections and their interplay with national and local conditions. In short, some of these Muslim geographies have made important innovative contributions and brought to bear original geographical perspectives in understanding religion.

Other faiths, other places, other scales: expanded geographies of the sacred

The positive contributions of Muslim geographies notwithstanding, to understand more fully the contributions of Muslim geographies and to situate this work within larger disciplinary, discursive fields and global developments necessitates that we ask the following questions: what other kinds of work characterise contemporary geographies of religion, what kinds of questions are being asked, which religions are being studied and which specific geographies are researchers examining? Relatedly, and perhaps most importantly, what are the gaps? In what follows, I selectively highlight some excellent work that has been done on Hindu populations, which has also focused on similar diasporic conditions to those of Muslim populations. Some interesting work on Christianity and Judaism is foregrounded, but the absences are what I will give particular attention to.

Just as the politics of space, identity and community have constituted a focus for the study of Muslim geographies, so too with work on Hinduism. Nagar's (1997) analysis of post-colonial Dar es Salaam, Tanzania, for example, focused on communal (religious) organisations and how the struggles between castes were played out in communal places in terms of who used those places for what purposes and eliciting what kinds of counterpublic discourses. Focused on the *mandir* (Hindu temple), Naylor and Ryan's (1998) study of how local residents perceive the mandir to be a threat to their homes, public areas and community turned attention to inter-religious relations. The ways in which new senses of territoriality were developed are reminiscent of Dunn's observations of community reactions to the establishment of mosques in Sydney. For the Orthodox Jews, the construction of their symbolic and material space in the form of the *eruv* in public space similarly elicits conflict and contestation, exposing 'some of the limits of living with difference and normative versions of multiculturalism in the city' (Watson 2005: 597; see also Valins 2000; Vincent and Warf 2002).

But geographical research on other religions is not confined only to the politics of space, identity and community, even if that forms a significant proportion of recent work. Bailey et al. (2007), for example, focused on the disciplining of youthful bodies (via temperance) and analysed how that was used to achieve Methodist institutional goals in Cornwall, England in the nineteenth century, engaging with issues of citizenship and public performance. On the other hand, McNeill (2003) tackled the question of what makes a global city and how religion is implicated in its making. His study of the Jubilee 2000 examined intersections between the political and the religious. Whereas the Pope used the Jubilee to enhance the Vatican's place in the world, the mayor of Rome used the same event to pursue national goals while adopting a global or 'universal' discourse.

These short reviews can but offer a brief sense of the other kinds of work that are being pursued as part of a rejuvenated geography of religion. But, despite the growth in the number, range and sophistication of research, there are several absences. First, the dearth of geographical research on the syncretic Chinese religions that characterise much of the Chinese population around the world, and also on Buddhism, Taoism and other belief systems, is marked.

Second, religion is an influential aspect of public and private lives in many different parts of the world. Yet there are many absent geographies just as there are absent religions. In just too many parts of the world, religious differences have reshaped national and local social formations, too often posing a barrier to social integration and constituting a common source of strife. Nigeria and Indonesia both witness internecine strife between Christians and Muslims; in India, conflicts between Hindus and Muslims have taken thousands of lives; Sri Lanka has witnessed a prolonged and violent confrontation between Hindus and Buddhists; Thailand and the Philippines both have Muslim insurgencies; in Iraq, tensions between Sunnis and Shias threaten an already fragile situation; and much of Africa today is an arena of intense competition between Islam and Christianity (see Steenbrink 1998). Yet geographers have been largely silent.

Contributions such as that by Jones (2007) show what is possible. In attempting to understand the origins of communal violence in South Asia, Jones disputes received wisdom which relies on the discursive creation of 'distinct and adversarial Hindu and Muslim identity categories at the beginning of the twentieth century'. Instead, he argues, social differences have to be understood in terms of 'performative place-making practices', where 'religious or cultural practices are reified into official tradition'. He illustrates this using the example of how the cow-protection movement campaigned to ban the playing of music as Hindu processions passed in front of mosques. Zones of tradition were established as practices developed (but were also contested). This, he argued, began the symbolic and actual division of British India even before it was officially partitioned. Studies such as Jones's, however, remain rare.

Third, many of our geographical contributions are focused on the micro scale. These are important, but a more multi-scalar analysis is warranted, one that (a) pays greater attention than has hitherto been the case to macro-scale issues and phenomena; and (b) recognises more explicitly the links between phenomena occurring across multiple scales.

Consider the works of geographers post-11 September, post-Bali/

Madrid/London bombings. The focus of works has remained on the body, the neighbourhood and places of worship. While these are important and contribute to an understanding of various relationships that religions are implicated in, the connections to major events of the day that confront the world are not always made more explicitly, so that the geography of religion is also in the public discourse. Ironically, when news reports night after night featured Osama bin Laden and the 'war against terror', those occasions when geography was called to service were focused on how the geological rock formations in the video images of Bin Laden might reveal from where, in Afghanistan, he was wielding influence.

Consider also the massive problems of underdevelopment in Latin American and African countries and the role of religion in simultaneously reinforcing and alleviating poverty, the rise of religion in post-communist China and Russia, the growth of new religious movements in the advanced, developed world, the religious strifes that continue in Sri Lanka, the southern Philippines and southern Thailand, and the rapidly growing influence of the internet on every dimension of life, including the religious. It is fair to say that geographers (of religion) have yet to help bring understanding to these various phenomena, let alone help to find solutions in specific context-sensitive ways. Of course, there have been some sterling efforts – witness, for example, Elizabeth Olson's (2006) work on development in the High Provinces of Peru, where she studies the ways in which transnational religious organisations contribute to the construction of 'development epistemologies' or the 'socioeconomics of development truths', analysing the ways in which transnational religions are mapped onto local development processes in rural communities.

Other attempts to understand a major global threat – al-Qa'ida – adopt a discourse analysis approach. Hobbs's (2005) attempt at understanding the geographical ideology of al-Qa'ida centered on the extent to which 'al-Qa'ida terrorism is motivated by a desire to control geographical space, and how the organization defines that space as place in its communiqués'. By examining statements and interviews by and with al-Qa'ida leaders, an attempt is also made to decipher al-Qa'ida's geographical rhetoric to reveal the nature or locations of future attacks. Oza (2007) similarly uses discursive material as primary material, analysing discourses of threat and security deployed by the United States and India after 11 September. Oza shows how the Muslim male is discursively constructed as perpetually dangerous, and this is used in the justification of war in Afghanistan and in Iraq. India has similarly echoed the US in this construction of the Muslim male as dangerous, principally because it served to fulfil internal and regional supremacy agendas. This led, unfortunately, to the Hindu right orchestrating genocide against Muslims in Gujarat in 2002. Oza argues that the similarity in discourses between the US and India was born of two conditions: first, the similar distortion of history so that 'revenge for past atrocities and the threat of future ones are used to justify preemptive military action', and second, the demarcation of 'us' against 'them'.

But such studies are few and far between, and not sufficient for us as geographers to claim a collective body of works or a set of actions that we can point to as evidence of our contribution to a better world. This relative 'diffidence' may have roots in larger disciplinary and sub-disciplinary conditions, particularly critiques of early projects of geography and cultural geography, which have prompted geographers to eschew particular kinds of work. First, critique of the role that geography played in the imperialist projects of the eighteenth and nineteenth centuries has led to a retreat among geographers willing to talk on the global scale. As Bonnett (2003: 60) highlighted, 'aversion to the colonial paradigm' has meant that it is dangerous territory for 'Western scholars claiming to represent, claiming to know, "other societies"'. Bonnett (2003: 60) points to Rogers's (1991: 131) attack on those who attempt to 'talk at the global scale' as engaging in an 'imperial "claiming of the globe" by "the Patriarchs of Geography"'. Yet, as Bonnett (2003: 57) reminds us, addressing the global scale is neither necessarily determined by colonial intents nor reducible to them.

Second, the reaction against the focus on the rural and antiquarian in Sauerian 'traditional' cultural geography, which was exemplified by studies of exotic rural societies and places of the 'other', has had implications for the kinds of places that cultural geographers have researched. Anglo-American cultural geographers turned attention inwards, towards the study of predominantly white, urban 'western' settings. This has become limiting, given the urgency of issues in many other parts of the world.

Taken together, the effect has been a focus on the micro scale, and particularly a limiting tendency to study 'western' urban settings. As Murphy (2006: 5) argues about geography more generally: 'The push toward the individual and the unique has yielded important intellectual dividends, but unless that push is balanced by a concern with larger-scale issues and more generalized explanatory frameworks, the opportunities for geographers to intervene in public debate will necessarily be limited.' As he is quick to also point out, '[t]he point is not simply to undertake larger empirical studies; it is to pose topically bigger questions and to be willing to offer broader-scale ideas about how they might be addressed' (Murphy 2006: 6).

How might geographers of religion respond to Murphy's call? In what ways might the agenda expand, without jettisoning micro-scale analysis? Any temptation to throw the baby out with the bathwater must be resisted, for there is much value in understanding the micropolitics of religious expression, if this understanding is drawn back onto a larger canvas to help understand some of the larger conflicts and tensions in the contemporary world. The politics of mosque building, or conflicts arising from secular representations of religious community, or modifications to spaces of worship – as microgeographies and micropolitics – altogether can and do contribute to an understanding of the more macro-scale conflicts in the world, but there is clearly room for geographers of religion to expand beyond that, and for the focus to move beyond Muslim geographies.

Final remarks

This chapter began by situating 'Muslim geographies' as we know them today within the broader canvas of intellectual history, in which their recent shape and form is as much a reflection of the historical and geographical contingencies of knowledge production as the early 'Islamic geographies' were a reflection of a prior 'golden age' of Islamic civilisation. With the realities of public anxiety over Islamic fundamentalism, urban disorders and terrorist attacks, the Muslim geographies of the 1990s and 2000s have come to focus on conflict and politics. Much of this has come out of Britain, focused on British concerns. Some pioneering work has been done, offering innovative perspectives on the geographies of religion, including research on embodiment, transnationalism, the contestation of identity and community, and landscape politics. This is a conspicuous change from the state of research in much of the twentieth century, when geographical research on religion paid little attention to geographies of religion, including Muslim geographies.

Yet, even while British Muslim geographies have contributed significantly to an understanding of contemporary British social dynamics, there remain many absent religions and absent geographies. Geographical analysis of other faiths, other geographies, and other scales is needed to yield new understanding, new geographies of religion which acknowledge and examine multiplicities while jettisoning assumptions of uniformity among non-western societies (Taylor 1993; Bell 1994). With such study will come possibilities for the development of indigenous knowledges and engagement in indigenous theorising (Alatas 2006) that the dominance of British Muslim geographies has not made possible. Inasmuch as the Islamic geographies of the ninth to thirteenth centuries remind us of the need to decentre the hegemony of New World anglophone and European geographies, there remains promise and prospect for new/alternative geographies of the sacred.

References

Aitchison, C., Hopkins, P. and Kwan, M. P., (eds) (2007), *Geographies of Muslim Identities: Representation of Diaspora, Gender and Belonging*, Aldershot: Ashgate.

Alatas, S. F. (1995), 'The theme of "relevance" in Third World human sciences', *Singapore Journal of Tropical Geography*, 16(2), 123–40.

Alatas, S. F. (2006), *Alternative Discourses in Asian Social Science: Responses to Eurocentrism*, New Delhi: Sage Publications.

Back, L. (1996), *New Ethnicities and Urban Culture: Racisms and Multiculture in Young Lives*, London: UCL Press.

Bailey, A. R., Harvey, D. C. and Brace, C. (2007), 'Disciplining youthful Methodist bodies in nineteenth-century Cornwall', *Annals of the Association of American Geographers*, 97(1), 142–57.

Baumann, G. (1996), *Contesting Culture: Discourses of Identity in Multi-ethnic London*, Cambridge and New York: Cambridge University Press.

Bell, M. (1994), 'Images, myths and alternative geographies of the Third World', in D. Gregory, R. Martin and G. Smith (eds), *Human Geography: Society, Space and Social Science*, London: Macmillan, pp. 174–99.

Bertrand, J. R. (2006), 'State and church in France: regulation and negotiation', *GeoJournal*, 67(4), 295–306.

Bonnett, A. (2003), 'Geography as the world discipline: connecting popular and academic geographical imaginations', *Area*, 35(1), 55–63.

Büttner, M. (1980), 'Survey article on the history and philosophy of the geography of religion in Germany', *Religion*, 10(2), 86–119.

Chivallon, C. (2001), 'Religion as space for the expression of Caribbean identity in the United Kingdom', *Environment and Planning D: Society and Space*, 19(4), 461–83.

Cooper, A. (1995), 'Adolescent dilemmas of landscape, place and religious experience in a Suffolk parish', *Environment and Planning D*, 13, 349–63.

Dunn, K. (2001), 'Representations of Islam in the politics of mosque development in Sydney', *Tijdschrift voor Economische en Sociale Geografie*, 92(3), 291–308.

Dunn, K. (2005), 'Repetitive and troubling discourses of nationalism in the local politics of mosque development in Sydney, Australia', *Environment and Planning D*, 23(1), 29–50.

Dwyer, C. (1999a), 'Veiled meanings: young British Muslim women and the negotiation of differences', *Gender, Place & Culture*, 6(1), 5–26.

Dwyer, C. (1999b), 'Contradictions of community: questions of identity for young British Muslim women', *Environment and Planning A*, 31(1), 53–68.

Dwyer, C. and Meyer, A. (1995), 'The institutionalisation of Islam in the Netherlands and in the UK: the case of Islamic schools', *New Community*, 21(1), 37–54.

Dwyer, C. and Meyer, A. (1996), 'The establishment of Islamic schools – a controversial phenomenon in three European countries', in W. A. R. Shadid and P. S. Van Koningsveld (eds), *Muslims in the Margin: Political Responses to the Presence of Islam in Western Europe*, Kampen, The Netherlands: Kok Pharos, pp. 218–42.

Eade, J. (1991), 'Nationalism and the quest for authenticity: the Bangladeshis in Tower Hamlets', *New Community*, 16, 493–503.

Eade, J. (1993), 'The political articulation of community and the Islamisation of space in London', in R. Barot (ed.), *Religion and ethnicity: minorities and social change in the metropolis*, Kampen, The Netherlands: Kok Pharos, pp. 27–42.

Eade, J. (1994), 'Identity, nation and religion: educated young Bangladeshi Muslims in London's East End', *International Sociology*, 9, 377–94.

Falah, G. and Nagel, C. (2005), *Geographies of Muslim Women: Gender, Religion, and Space*, New York and London: Guilford Press.

Gale, R. (2007), 'The place of Islam in the geography of religion: trends and intersections', *Geography Compass*, 10, 15–36.

Gale, R. and Naylor, S. (2002), 'Religion, planning and the city: the spatial politics of ethnic minority expression in British cities and towns', *Ethnicities*, 2(3), 387–409.

Graham, B. (1998), 'Contested images of place among Protestants in Northern Ireland', *Political Geography*, 17(2), 129–44.

Graham, B. and Murray, M. (1997), 'The spiritual and the profane: the pilgrimage to Santiago de Compostela', *Ecumene*, 4, 389–409.

Henkel, R. (2005), 'Geography of religion – rediscovering a subdiscipline', *Hrvatski Geografski Glasnik*, 67(1), 5–25.

Hervieu-Léger, D. (2002), 'Space and religion: new approaches to religious spatiality in modernity', *International Journal of Urban and Regional Research*, 26(1), 99–105.

Hobbs, J. J. (2005), 'The geographical dimensions of Al-Qa'ida rhetoric', *Geographical Review*, 95(3), 301–27.

Holloway, J. and Valins, O. (2002), 'Editorial: placing religion and spirituality in geography', *Social & Cultural Geography*, 3(1), 5–9.

Hopkins, P. E. (2006), 'Youthful Muslim masculinities: gender and generational relations', *Transactions of the Institute of British Geographers*, 31(3), 337–52.

Hopkins, P. E. (2007a), 'Global events, national politics, local lives: young Muslim men in Scotland', *Environment and Planning A*, 39(5), 1119–33.

Hopkins, P. E. (2007b), '"Blue Squares", "proper" Muslims and transnational networks', *Ethnicities*, 7(1), 61–81.

Isaac, E. (1959–60), Religion, landscape and space, *Landscape*, 9, 14–18.

Isaac, E. (1965), 'Religious geography and the geography of religion', in *Man and the Earth*, University of Colorado Studies, Series in Earth Sciences. Boulder, CO: University of Colorado Press, pp. 1–14.

James, P. E. and Martin, G. J. (1972), *All Possible Worlds*, New York: John Wiley & Sons.

Jones, R. (2007), 'Sacred cows and thumping drums: claiming territory as "Zones of Tradition" in British India', *Area*, 39(1), 55–65.

Kimble, G. H. T. (1938), *Geography in the Middle Ages*, London: Methuen & Co. Ltd.

King, R. (1972), 'The pilgrimage to Mecca – some geographical and historical aspects', *Erdkunde*, 26, 61–73.

Knippenberg, H. (1998), 'Secularization in the Netherlands in its historical and geographical dimensions', *GeoJournal*, 45(3), 209–20.

Kong, L. (1990), 'Geography and religion: trends and prospects', *Progress in Human Geography*, 14(3), 355–71.

Kong, L. (1993a), 'Ideological hegemony and the political symbolism of religious buildings in Singapore', *Environment and Planning D: Society and Space*, 11(1), 23–45.

Kong, L. (1993b), 'Negotiating conceptions of "sacred space": a case study of religious buildings in Singapore', *Transactions of the Institute of British Geographers*, 18(3), 342–58.

Kong, L. (1997), 'A "new" cultural geography? Debates about invention and reinvention', *Scottish Geographical Magazine*, 113(3), 177–85

Kong, L. (2001), 'Mapping "new" geographies of religion: politics and poetics in modernity', *Progress in Human Geography*, 25(2), 211–33.

Kong, L. (2002), 'In search of permanent homes: Singapore's house churches and the politics of space', *Urban Studies*, 39(9), 1573–86.

Kong, L. (2005a), 'Religious schools: for spirit, (f)or nation', *Environment and Planning D: Society and Space*, 23, 615–31.

Kong, L. (2005b), 'Re-presenting the religious: nation, community and identity in museums', *Social & Cultural Geography*, 6(4), 496–513.

Kong, L. (2006), 'Religion and spaces of technology: constructing and contesting nation, transnation and place', *Environment and Planning A*, Special issue on Geographies and Politics of Transnationalism, 38, 903–18.

Lewis, P. (1994), *Islamic Britain*, London: I. B. Tauris.

Livingstone D. N., Keane, M. C. and Boal, F. W. (1998), 'Space for religion: a Belfast case study', *Political Geography*, 17(2), 145–70.

McNeill, D. (2003), 'Rome, global city? Church, state and the Jubilee 2000', *Political Geography*, 22, 535–56.

Munoz, S. A. (2006), 'Divided by faith – the impact of religious affiliation on ethnic segregation', *Scottish Geographical Journal*, 122(2), 85–99.

Murphy, J. T. (2006), 'Building trust in economic space', *Progress in Human Geography*, 30(4), 427–50.

Musterd, S. (2005), 'Social and ethnic segregation in Europe: levels, causes, and effects', *Journal of Urban Affairs*, 27(3), 331–48.

Nagar, R. (1997), 'Exploring methodological borderlands through oral narratives', in H. J. Nast, J. P. Jones III and S. M. Roberts (eds), *Thresholds in Feminist Geography*, Lanham, MD: Rowman & Littlefield, pp. 203–24.

Naylor, S. K. and Ryan, J. R. (1998), 'Ethnicity and cultural landscapes: mosques, gurdwaras and mandirs in England and Wales', Religion and Locality Conference 8–10 September, University of Leeds.

Naylor, S. and Ryan, J. (2002), 'The mosque in the suburbs: negotiating religion and ethnicity in South London', *Social & Cultural Geography*, 3(1) 39–59.

Numrich, P. D. (1997), 'Recent immigrant religions in a restructuring metropolis: new religious landscapes in Chicago', *Journal of Cultural Geography*, 17, 55–76.

Olson, E. (2006), 'Development, transnational religion and the power of ideas in the High Provinces of Cusco, Peru', *Environment and Planning A*, 38(5), 885–902.

Olson, E. and Silvey, R. (2006), 'Transnational geographies: rescaling development, migration, and religion', *Environment and Planning A*, 38(5), 805–8.

Oza, R. (2007), 'Contrapuntal geographies of threat and security: the United States, India, and Israel', *Environment and Planning D: Society and Space*, 25(1), 9–32.

Pacione, M. (2005), 'The geography of religious affiliation in Scotland', *The Professional Geographer*, 57(2), 235–55.

Peach, C. (2006), 'Islam, Ethnicity and South Asian Religions in the London 2001 Census', *Transactions of the Institute of British Geographers*, 31(3), 353–70.

Phillips, D. (2006), 'Parallel lives? Challenging discourses of British Muslim self-segregation', *Environment and Planning D: Society and Space*, 24(1), 25–40.

Poulsen, M., Johnston, R. and Forrest, J. (2001), 'Intraurban ethnic enclaves: introducing a knowledge-based classification method', *Environment and Planning A*, 33(11), 2071–82.

Proctor, J. (2006), 'Introduction: theorizing and studying religion', *Annals of the Association of American Geographers*, 96(1), 165–8.

Prorok, C. (2003), 'Transplanting pilgrimage traditions in the Americas', *The Geographical Review*, 93(3), 283–307.

Prorok, C. M. and Hemmasi, (1993), 'East Indian Muslims and their mosques in Trinidad: a geography of religious structures and the politics of ethnic identity', *Caribbean Geography*, 4(1), 28–48.

Raivo, P. J. (1997), 'The limits of tolerance: the Orthodox milieu as an element in the Finnish cultural landscape, 1917–1939', *Journal of Historical Geography*, 23, 327–39.

Raivo, P. (2002), 'The peculiar touch of the East: reading the post-war landscapes of the Finnish Orthodox Church', *Social & Cultural Geography*, 3(1), 11–24.

Rogers, A. (1991), 'The boundaries of reason: social and cultural geography and the world', in C. Philo (ed.), *New Words, New Worlds: Reconceptualising Social and Cultural Geography*, Aberystwyth: Social and Cultural Geography Study Group of the Institute of British Geographers, pp. 131–43.

Samad, Y. (1998), 'Imagining a British Muslim identification', in S. Vertovec and A. Rogers (eds), *Muslim European Youth: Reproducing Ethnicity, Religion, Culturei*, Aldershot: Ashgate, pp. 59–76.

Samers, M. E. (2003), 'Diaspora unbound: Muslim identity and the erratic regulation of Islam in France', *International Journal of Population Geography*, 9(4), 351–64.

Shair, I. M. (1981a), 'Frequency of pilgrimage to Makkah and pilgrims' socio-economic attributes', *Journal, College of Arts*, University of Riyadh. 813–22.

Shair, I. M. (1981b), 'Volume of Muslim pilgrims in recent years, 1975–1980; source areas and ports of entry', *Journal, College of Arts*, King Saud University, 9, 293–320.

Sidorov, D. (2000a), 'National monumentalization and the politics of scale: the resurrection of the Cathedral of Christ the Savior in Moscow', *Annals of the Association of American Geographers*, 90, 548–72.

Sidorov, D. (2000b), 'Playing chess with churches: Russian Orthodoxy as re(li)gion', *Historical Geography*, 28, 208–33.

Slater, T. R. (2004), 'Encountering God: personal reflections on "geographer as pilgrim"', *Area*, 36(3), 245–53.

Steenbrink, K. (1998), 'Editorial', *Exchange*, 27(3), 193.

Taylor, P. J. (1993), 'Full circle or new meaning for global', in R. J. Johnston (ed.), *The Challenge for Geography: A Changing World, A Changing Discipline*, Oxford: Blackwell, pp. 181–97.

Tong, C. K. and Kong, L. (2000), 'Religion and modernity: ritual transformations and the reconstruction of space and time', *Social & Cultural Geography*, 1(1), 29–44.

Valins, O. (2000), 'Institutionalised religion: sacred texts and Jewish spatial practice', *Geoforum*, 31, 575–86.

Valins, O. (2003), 'Stubborn identities and the construction of socio-spatial boundaries: ultra-orthodox Jews living in contemporary Britain', *Transactions of the Institute of British Geographers*, 28(2), 158–75.

Van Wichelen, S. (2007), 'Gendering Muslimness: new bodies in urban Jakarta', in C. Aitchison, M. Kwan and P. Hopkins (eds), *Geographies of Muslim Identities: Representations of Diaspora, Gender and Belonging*, Aldershot: Ashgate, pp. 93–108.

Vincent, P. and Warf, B. (2002), 'Eruvim: Talmudic places in a postmodern world', *Transactions of the Institute of British Geographers*, 1, 30–51.

Waitt, G. (2003), 'A place for Buddha in Wollongong, New South Wales? Territorial rules in the place-making of sacred spaces', *Australian Geographer*, 34(2), 223–38.

Watson, S. (2005), 'Symbolic spaces of difference: contesting the eruv in Barnet, London and Tenafly, New Jersey', *Environment and Planning D*, 23(4), 597–613.

Wilson, B. (1966), *Religion in Secular Society: A Sociological Comment*, London: Watts.

Zelinsky, W. (2001), 'The uniqueness of the American religious landscape', *Geographical Review*, 91(3), 565–85.

MUSLIMS AND THE POLITICS OF DIFFERENCE

Tariq Modood

Introduction

There is an anti-Muslim wind blowing across the European continent. One factor is a perception that Muslims are making politically exceptional, culturally unreasonable or theologically alien demands upon European states. My contention is that the claims Muslims are making in fact parallel comparable arguments about gender or ethnic equality. Seeing the issue in that context shows how European and contemporary is the logic of mainstream Muslim identity politics.

Muslims in Europe

European anxieties and phobias in relation to immigration and cultural diversity focus on Muslims more than on any other group. This does, however, beg the question: in what way are Muslims a group and to whom are they being compared? Here I can do no more than note that there is no satisfactory way of conceptualising people of non-European descent, what Canadians call 'visible minorities', and therefore also of conceptualising the constituent groups that make up this category. Nevertheless, it is clear that the estimated 15 million people in the European Union (EU) who subjectively or objectively are Muslim, whatever additional identities they may have, form the single largest group of those who are the source of public anxieties.

Muslims are not, however, a homogeneous group. Some Muslims are devout but apolitical; some are political but do not see their politics as being 'Islamic' (indeed, they may even be anti-Islamic). Some identify more with a nationality of origin, such as Turkish; others with the nationality of settlement and perhaps citizenship, such as French. Some prioritise fundraising for mosques, others campaigns against discrimination, unemployment or Zionism. For some, the Ayatollah Khomeini is a hero and Osama bin Laden an inspiration; for others, the same may be said of Kemal Ataturk or Margaret Thatcher, who created a swathe of Asian millionaires in Britain, brought in Arab capital and was one of the first to call for NATO action to protect Muslims in Kosovo. The category 'Muslim', then, is as internally diverse as 'Christian' or 'Belgian' or 'middle-class', or any other category helpful in ordering our understanding of contemporary Europe; but just as diversity does not lead to an abandonment of social concepts in general, so with that of 'Muslim'.

My contention, then, within the limitations of all social categories, is that 'Muslim' is as useful a category for identifying 'visible minorities' as country of origin – the most typical basis for data collection and labelling. It points to people whose loyalties, enmities, networks, norms, debates, forms of authority, reactions to social circumstances and perception by others cannot all be explained without invoking some understanding of Muslims. Yet Muslims in Europe do not form a single political block or class formation, although they are disproportionately among the lowest paid, unemployed and underemployed. Muslims do have the most extensive and developed discourses of unity, common circumstance and common victimhood among non-EU origin peoples in the EU. This sense of community may be partial, may depend upon context and crisis, may coexist with other overlapping or competing commitments or aspirations; but it is an actual or latent 'us', partly dependent upon others seeing and partly causing others to see Muslims as a 'them'.

For many years Muslims have been the principal victims of the bloodshed that has produced Europe's asylum seekers (think of Palestine, Somalia, Iraq, Bosnia, Kosovo, Chechnya, Afghanistan) and so are vulnerable to the anti-refugee mood and policies in the EU today. This, of course, also affects Muslim residents and citizens, and the situation has been thrown into sharp relief by 11 September 2001 and its aftermath, including the Iraq war. There are many reports of harassment and attacks against Muslims;[1] and Muslims, who have expressed both vulnerability and defiance, have become a focus of national concern and debate in many countries. They have found themselves bearing the brunt of a new wave of suspicion and hostility, and strongly voiced if imprecise doubts are being cast on their loyalty as citizens.

There has been widespread questioning about whether Muslims can be and are willing to be integrated into European society and its political values. In particular, whether Muslims are committed to what are taken to be the core European values of freedom, tolerance, democracy, sexual equality and secularism. Across Europe, multiculturalism – a policy suitable where communities want to maintain some level of distinction – is on the defensive and 'integration' is once again the watchword.[2] These questions and doubts have been raised across the political spectrum, voiced by individuals ranging from Berlusconi in Italy and the Dutch politician Pim Fortuyn to eminent *Guardian* intellectuals such as Hugo Young and Polly Toynbee. In the UK, many politicians, columnists, and letter-writers and phone-callers to the media, again from across the political spectrum, have blamed these concerns on the perceived cultural separatism and self-imposed segregation of Muslim migrants and on a 'politically correct' multiculturalism that has fostered fragmentation rather than integration and 'Britishness'.

National contexts

The same wind is blowing across the Continent, yet the landscape is not uniform. Of the three most populous European countries, Germany, France and the UK, the first two have, in both absolute and relative terms, larger foreign-born populations and populations of non-European origin than has the UK. Yet issues of racial discrimination, ethnic identity and multiculturalism have less salience in those two countries than in the UK. One aspect of this is that national debates on these topics have a lesser salience, and that such debates are less frequently led by non-whites or non-Europeans, who are more the objects of, rather than participants in, the debates. Another aspect is the relative lack of data about ethnicity and religious communities, and consequently of research and literature. Yet this is not a simple matter of scale. Each of the countries in the EU has a very different conception of what the issues are, depending upon its history, political culture and legal system.[3]

The British experience of 'coloured immigration', in contrast to the case in Germany and France, has been seen as an Atlanto-centric legacy of the slave trade, and policy and legislation were formed in the 1960s in the shadow of the US civil rights movement, black power discourse and the inner-city riots in Detroit, Watts and elsewhere. It was, therefore, dominated by the idea of 'race', more specifically by the idea of a black-white dualism. It was also shaped by the imperial legacy, one aspect of which was that all colonials and citizens of the Commonwealth were 'subjects of the Crown'. As such, they had rights of entry into the UK and entitlement to all the benefits enjoyed by Britons, from NHS treatment to social security and the vote. (The right of entry was successively curtailed from 1962 so that, while in 1960 Britain was open to the Commonwealth but closed to Europe, twenty years later the position was fully reversed.)

Against the background of these distinctive national contexts and histories, it is quite mistaken to single out Muslims as a particularly intractable and uncooperative group characterised by extremist politics, religious obscurantism and an unwillingness to integrate. The case of Britain is the one I know in detail and can be illustrative.

The relation between Muslims and wider British society and the British state has to be seen in terms of the developing agendas of racial equality and multiculturalism. Muslims have become central to these agendas even while they have contested important aspects, especially the primacy of racial identities, narrow definitions of racism and equality, and the secular bias of the discourse and policies of multiculturalism. While there are now emergent Muslim discourses of equality, of difference and of, to use the title of the newsletter of the Muslim Council of Britain, 'the common good', they have to be understood as appropriations and modulations of contemporary discourses and initiatives whose provenance lies in anti-racism and feminism.

While one result of this is to throw advocates of multiculturalism into theoretical and practical disarray, another is to stimulate accusations of cultural separatism and revive a discourse of 'integration'. While we should not ignore the critics of Muslim activism, we need to recognise that at least some of the latter is a politics of 'catching up' with racial equality and feminism. In this way, religion in Britain is assuming a renewed political importance. After a long period of hegemony, political secularism can no longer be taken for granted but is having to answer its critics; there is a growing understanding that the incorporation of Muslims has become the most important challenge of egalitarian multiculturalism.

British equality movements

The presence of new population groups in Britain made manifest certain kinds of racism, and anti-discrimination laws and policies began to be put into place from the 1960s. These provisions, initially influenced by contemporary thinking and practice in relation to anti-black racism in the United States, assume that the grounds of discrimination are 'colour' and ethnicity. Muslim assertiveness became a feature of majority–minority relations only from around the early 1990s; and indeed, prior to this, racial-equality discourse and politics were dominated by the idea that the dominant post-immigration issue was 'colour racism'. One consequence of this is that the legal and policy framework still reflects the conceptualisation and priorities of racial dualism.

To date, it is lawful to discriminate against Muslims *qua* Muslims because the courts do not accept that Muslims are an ethnic group (though, oddly, Jews and Sikhs are recognised as ethnic groups within the meaning of the law). While initially unremarked upon, this exclusive focus on race and ethnicity, and the exclusion of Muslims but not Jews and Sikhs, has come to be a source of resentment. Muslims do enjoy some limited indirect legal protection *qua* members of ethnic groups such as Pakistanis or Arabs. Over time, groups like Pakistanis have become an active constituency within British 'race relations', whereas Middle Easterners tend to classify themselves as 'white', as in the 1991 Census, and on the whole have not been prominent in political activism of this sort, nor in domestic politics generally. One of the effects of this politics was to highlight race.

A key indicator of racial discrimination and inequality has been numerical under-representation, for instance in prestigious jobs and public office. Hence, people have had to be (self-) classified and counted; thus group labels, and arguments about which labels are authentic, have become a common feature of certain political discourses. Over the years, it has also become apparent through these inequality measures that it is Asian Muslims and not, as expected, Afro-Caribbeans, who have emerged as the most disadvantaged and poorest groups in the country.[4] To many Muslim activists, the misplacing of Muslims into 'race' categories and the belatedness with which the severe disadvantages of the Pakistanis and Bangladeshis have come to be recognised mean that race relations are perceived at best as an inappropriate policy niche for Muslims, and at worst as a conspiracy to prevent the emergence of a specifically Muslim socio-political formation. To see how such thinking has emerged we need briefly to consider the career of the concept of 'racial equality'.

The initial development of anti-racism in Britain followed the American pattern, and indeed was directly influenced by American personalities and events. Just as in the United States the colour-blind humanism of Martin Luther King Jr came to be mixed with an emphasis on black pride, black autonomy and black nationalism as typified by Malcolm X, so too the same process occurred in the UK (both of these inspirational leaders visited Britain). Indeed, it is best to see this development of racial explicitness and positive blackness as part of a wider socio-political climate which is not confined to race and culture or non-white minorities. Feminism, gay pride, Quebecois nationalism and the revival of a Scottish identity are some prominent examples of these new identity movements which have become an important feature in many countries, especially those in which class politics has declined in salience; the emphasis on non-territorial identities such as black, gay and women is particularly marked among anglophones.

In fact, it would be fair to say that what is often claimed today in the name of racial equality, again especially in the English-speaking world, goes beyond the claims that were made in the 1960s. Iris Young expresses well the new political climate when she describes the emergence of an ideal of equality based not just on allowing excluded groups to assimilate and live by the norms of dominant groups, but on the view that 'a positive self-definition of group difference is in fact more liberatory'.[5]

Equality and the erosion of the public–private distinction

This significant shift takes us from an understanding of 'equality' in terms of individualism and cultural assimilation to a politics of recognition; to 'equality' as encompassing public ethnicity. This perception of equality means not having to hide or apologise for one's origins, family or community, and requires others to show respect for these. Public attitudes and arrangements must adapt so that this heritage is encouraged, not contemptuously expected to wither away.

These two conceptions of equality may be stated as follows: the right to assimilate to the majority/dominant culture in the public sphere, with toleration of 'difference' in the private sphere; the right to have one's 'difference' (minority ethnicity, etc.) recognised and supported in both the public and the private spheres. While the former represents a liberal response to 'difference', the latter is the 'take' of the new identity politics. The two are not, however, alternative conceptions of equality in the sense that to hold one, the other must be rejected. Multiculturalism, properly construed, requires support for both conceptions. For the assumption behind the first is that participation in the public or national culture is necessary for the effective exercise of citizenship, the only obstacle to which is the exclusionary processes preventing gradual assimilation. The second conception, too, assumes that groups excluded from the national culture have their citizenship diminished as a result, and sees the remedy not in rejecting the right to assimilate, but in adding the right to widen and adapt the national culture, and the public and media symbols of national membership, to include the relevant minority ethnicities.

It can be seen, then, that the public–private distinction is crucial to the contemporary discussion of equal citizenship, and particularly to the challenge to an earlier liberal position. It was in this political and intellectual climate – namely, a climate in which what would earlier have been called 'private' matters had become sources of equality struggles – that Muslim assertiveness emerged as a domestic political phenomenon. In this respect, the advances achieved by anti-racism and feminism (with its slogan 'the personal is the political') acted as benchmarks for later political group entrants, such as Muslims. As I will show, while Muslims raise distinctive concerns, the logic of their demands often mirrors those of other equality-seeking groups.

Religious equality

So, one of the current conceptions of equality is a difference-affirming equality, with related notions of respect, recognition and identity – in short, what I understand by political multiculturalism. What kinds of specific policy demands, then, are being made by or on behalf of religious groups and Muslim identity politics in particular, when these terms are deployed? I suggest that these demands have three dimensions, which get progressively 'thicker'.

No religious discrimination

One Muslim organisation concerned with these issues is the Forum Against Islamophobia and Racism (FAIR). It was set up in 2000 'for the purpose of raising awareness of and combating Islamophobia and racism, monitoring specific incidents of Islamophobia and racism, working towards eliminating religious and racial discrimination, campaigning and lobbying on issues relevant

to Muslim and other multi-ethnic communities in Britain', and its mission statement sets out this first dimension of equality.

The very basic demand is that religious people, no less than people defined
by 'race' or gender, should not suffer discrimination in job and other opportunities. So, for example, a person who is trying to dress in accordance with their
religion or who projects a religious identity (such as a Muslim woman wearing
a headscarf, a *hijab*), should not be discriminated against in employment. At
the moment in Britain there is no legal ban on such discrimination, and the government said until recently that the case for it was not proven.

The legal system thus leaves Muslims particularly vulnerable because, while
discrimination against yarmulke-wearing Jews and turban-wearing Sikhs is
deemed to be unlawful racial discrimination, Muslims, unlike these other faith
communities, are not deemed to be a racial or ethnic group. Nor are they protected by the legislation against religious discrimination that does exist in one
part of the UK: being explicitly designed to protect Catholics, it covers only
Northern Ireland. The best that Muslims are able to achieve is to prove that the
discrimination against them was indirectly against their ethnic characteristics:
that they suffered discrimination by virtue of being, say, a Pakistani or an Iraqi.

While it is indeed the case that the discrimination against Muslims is mixed
up with forms of colour racism and cultural racism, the charge of race discrimination will provide no protection if it is clearly the individual's religion,
not their race, that has led to that discrimination. Moreover, some Muslims are
white and so do not enjoy this second-class protection; and many Muslim
activists argue that religious freedom, being a fundamental right, should not be
legally and politically dependent on dubious concepts of race and ethnicity. The
same argument applies to the demand for a law in Britain (as already exists in
Northern Ireland) making incitement to religious hatred unlawful, to parallel
the law against incitement to racial hatred. (The latter extends protection to
certain forms of anti-Jewish literature, but not anti-Muslim literature.)

After some years of arguing that there was insufficient evidence of religious
discrimination, the British government has had its hand forced by Article 13 of
the EU Amsterdam Treaty (1997), which includes religious discrimination in
the list of the forms of discrimination that all member states are expected to
eliminate. Accordingly, the government, following a European Commission
directive (that it played a key role in drafting and that many member states have
been slow to implement), outlawed religious discrimination in employment,
with effect from December 2003. This was, however, only a partial 'catching
up' with the existing anti-discrimination provisions in relation to race and
gender. For, unlike the Race Relations Acts, it did not extend to discrimination
in provision of goods and services but was confined to employment until April,
2007. Even so, it still does not create a duty upon employers to take steps to
promote equality of opportunity, as does the new Race Relations Act
(Amendment) 2000. This may, however, be remedied within a proposed Single

Equalities Act that the government is to table in the 2008/9 parliamentary session, which will bring together, and perhaps 'equalise', the various and differential anti-discrimination legislation that the recent Commission on Equalities and Human Rights has been created to implement.

Even-handedness in relation to native religions[6]

Many minority faith advocates interpret equality to mean that minority religions should get at least some of the support from the state that longer-established religions do. Muslims have led the way on this argument, and have made two particular issues politically contentious: the state funding of schools and the law of blasphemy. After some political battle, the government has agreed in recent years to fund a few (so far, seven) Muslim schools, as well as a Sikh and a Seventh Day Adventist school, on the same basis enjoyed by thousands of Anglican and Catholic schools and some Methodist and Jewish schools. (In England and Wales, over a third of state-maintained primary and a sixth of secondary schools are in fact run by a religious group – but all have to deliver a centrally determined national curriculum.)

Some secularists are unhappy about this. They accept the argument for parity but believe this should be achieved by the state withdrawing its funding from all religious schools. Most Muslims reject this form of equality in which the privileged lose something but the under-privileged gain nothing. More specifically, the issue between 'equalising upwards' and 'equalising downwards' here is about the legitimacy of religion as a public institutional presence.

Muslims have failed to get the courts to interpret the existing statute on blasphemy to cover offences beyond what Christians hold sacred, but some political support exists for an offence of incitement to religious hatred, mirroring the existing one of incitement to racial hatred. The government inserted such a clause in the post-11 September 2001 security legislation, in order to conciliate Muslims who, among others, were opposed to the new powers of surveillance, arrest and detention. As it happened, most of the latter was made law, but the provision on incitement to religious hatred was defeated in Parliament. The government continued to have difficulties getting support for such legislation, not least from its own supporters both inside Parliament and outside it, where it especially provoked resistance from comedians, intellectuals and secularists, who feared that satire and criticism of religion was at risk. Finally, Parliament passed a bill in early 2006 to protect against incitement to religious hatred. Yet the bill was only passed after members of both houses of Parliament, supported by much of the liberal intelligentsia, had lobbied the government to accept amendments that weakened its initial proposals. Unlike the incitement to religious hatred offence in Northern Ireland and the incitement to racial hatred offence in the UK, mere offensiveness was not an offence and, moreover, the incitement must require the intention to stir up hatred. Nevertheless, a controversy shortly after this bill was passed showed that the British media was coming to restrain itself voluntarily. This was the case of the Danish Muhammad Cartoons Affair. The cartoons, originally published in the Danish newspaper Jyllands Posten, were opposed by some Muslims who believed they were derogatory of the Prophet Muhammad and racist in implying that Muslims were terrorists. At the height of the controversy in early 2006 they were reprinted in several leading European newspapers but not by any major organ in Britain, suggesting there was a greater understanding in Britain than in some other European countries of anti-Muslim racism and of not giving gratuitous offence to Muslims.[7]

Positive inclusion of religious groups

The demand here is that religion in general, or at least the category of 'Muslim' in particular, should be a category by which the inclusiveness of social institutions may be judged, as they increasingly are in relation to race and gender. For example, employers should have to demonstrate that they do not discriminate against Muslims, by explicit monitoring of Muslims' position within the workforce, backed up by appropriate policies, targets, managerial responsibilities, work environments, staff training, advertisements, outreach and so on.[8] Similarly, public bodies should provide appropriately sensitive policies and staff in relation to the services they provide, especially in relation to (non-Muslim) schools, social and health services; Muslim community centres or Muslim youth workers should be funded in addition to existing Asian and Caribbean community centres and Asian and black youth workers.

To take another case: the BBC believes it is of political importance to review and improve its personnel practices and its output of programmes, including its on-screen 'representation' of the British population, by making provision for and winning the confidence of, say, women, ethnic groups and young people. Why should it not also use religious groups as a criterion of inclusivity and have to demonstrate that it is doing the same for viewers and staff defined by religious community membership?

In short, Muslims should be treated as a legitimate group in their own right (not because they are, say, Asians), whose presence in British society has to be explicitly reflected in all walks of life and in all institutions; and whether they are so included should become one of the criteria for judging Britain as an egalitarian, inclusive, multicultural society. There is no prospect at present of religious equality catching up with the importance that employers and other organisations give to sex or race. A potentially significant victory, however, was achieved when the government agreed to include a religion question in the 2001 Census. This was the first time this question had been included since 1851 and it was largely unpopular outside the politically active religionists, among whom Muslims were foremost. Nevertheless, it has the potential to pave the way for widespread 'religious monitoring' in the way that the inclusion of an ethnic question in 1991 had led to the more routine use of 'ethnic monitoring'.

These policy demands no doubt seem odd within the terms of, say, the French or US 'wall of separation' between the state and religion, and may make secularists uncomfortable in Britain too. But it is clear that they virtually mirror existing anti-discrimination policy provisions in the UK. In an analysis of some Muslim policy statements in the early 1990s, following the activism stimulated by the Rushdie affair,[9] I argued that the main lines of argument were captured by the following three positions: a 'colour-blind' human rights and human dignity approach; an approach based on extension of the concepts of racial discrimination and racial equality to include anti-Muslim racism; and a 'Muslim power' approach. I concluded that these 'reflect not so much obscurantist Islamic interventions into a modern secular discourse, but typical minority options in contemporary Anglo-American equality politics, and employ the rhetorical, conceptual and institutional resources available in that politics'.[10]

All three approaches are present today, though some high-profile radicals have made a Muslim power approach more prominent, in a manner not dissimilar to the rise of black power activism after the height of the civil rights period in the United States. This approach is mainly nourished by despair at the victimisation and humiliation of Muslims in places such as Palestine, Bosnia, Kashmir and Afghanistan. For many British Muslims, such military disasters and humanitarian horrors evoke a strong desire to express solidarity with oppressed Muslims through the political idea of the *umma*, the global community of Muslims, which must defend and restore itself as a global player. To take the analogy with US black power a bit further, one can say that as black nationalism and Afrocentrism developed as one ideological expression of black power, so, similarly, we can see political Islamism as a search for Muslim dignity and power.

Muslim assertiveness, then, though triggered and intensified by what are seen as attacks on Muslims, is primarily derived not from Islam or Islamism but from contemporary western ideas about equality and multiculturalism. While simultaneously reacting to the latter in its failure to distinguish Muslims from the rest of the 'black' population and its uncritical secular bias, Muslims positively use, adapt and extend these contemporary western ideas in order to join other equality-seeking movements. Political Muslims do, therefore, have an ambivalence in relation to multicultural discourses. On the one hand, as a result of previous misrecognition of their identity, and existing biases, there is distrust of 'the race relations industry' and of 'liberals'; on the other hand, the assertiveness is clearly a product of the positive climate created by liberals and egalitarians.

This ambivalence can tend towards antagonism, as the assertiveness is increasingly being joined by Islamic discourses and Islamists. Especially, as has been said, there is a sense that Muslim populations across the world are repeatedly suffering at the hands of their neighbours, aided and abetted by the United States and its allies, and that Muslims must come together to defend themselves. Politically active Muslims in Britain, however, are likely to be part of domestic multicultural and equality currents emphasising discrimination in educational and economic opportunities, political representation and the media, and 'Muslim-blindness' in the provision of health, care and social services; and arguing for remedies which mirror existing legislation and policies in relation to sexual and racial equality.

A panicky retreat to a liberal public–private distinction

If the emergence of a politics of difference out of and alongside a liberal assimilationist equality created a dissonance, as indeed it did, the emergence of a British Muslim identity out of and alongside ethno-racial identities has created an even greater dissonance. Philosophically speaking, it should create a lesser dissonance, for a move from the idea of equality as sameness to equality as difference is a more profound conceptual shift than the creation of a new identity in a field already crowded with minority identities. But to infer this is naively to ignore the hegemonic power of secularism in British political culture, especially on the centre-left. While black and related ethno-racial identities were welcomed by, indeed were intrinsic to, the rainbow coalition of identity politics, this coalition is deeply unhappy with Muslim consciousness.

While for some this rejection is specific to Islam, for many the ostensible reason is simply that it is a religious identity and, in virtue of that, should be confined to the private sphere. What is most interesting is that, if this latter objection is taken at face value, the difference theorists, activists and paid professionals are reverting to a public–private distinction that they have spent three decades demolishing. The unacceptability of Muslim identity is no doubt partly to do with the conservative views on gender and sexuality professed by some Muslim spokespersons, not to mention issues to do with freedom of expression as they arose in the Rushdie affair.[11] But these are objections to specific views. As such, they can be contested on a point-by-point basis; they are not objections to an identity. The fundamental objection of radical secularists to Muslim identity as a politicised religious identity is, of course, incompatible with the politics-of-difference perspective on the public–private distinction. It is therefore in contradiction with a thoroughgoing conception of multiculturalism, which should allow the political expression of religion to enter public discourse.

We thus have a mixed-up situation where secular multiculturalists argue that the sex lives of individuals – traditionally, a core area of liberal privacy – are a legitimate feature of political identities and public discourse, and seem generally to welcome the sexualisation of culture (if not the prurient interest in the sexual activity of public characters). Religion, on the other hand – a key source of communal identity in traditional, non-liberal societies – is to be regarded as a private matter, perhaps as a uniquely private matter. Most specifically, Muslim identity is seen as the illegitimate child of British multiculturalism.

Indeed, the Rushdie affair made evident that the group in British society most politically opposed to Muslims, or at least to Muslim identity politics, was not Christians, nor even right-wing nationalists, but the secular, liberal intelligentsia. Muslims are frequently criticised in the comment pages of the respectable press in a way that few, if any, other minority groups are. Muslims often remark that if, in such articles, the words 'Jews' or 'blacks' were substituted for 'Muslims', the newspapers in question would be attacked as racist and, indeed, be vulnerable to legal proceedings. Just as the hostility against Jews, in various times and places, has been a varying blend of anti-Judaism (hostility to a religion) and anti-semitism (hostility to a racialised group), so it is difficult to gauge to what extent contemporary British Islamophobia is 'religious' and to what extent 'racial'.

Even before 11 September 2001 and its aftermath, it was generally becoming acknowledged that of all groups, Asians face the greatest hostility, and many Asians themselves feel this is because of hostility directed specifically at Muslims. In the summer of 2001 the racist British National Party began explicitly to distinguish between good, law-abiding Asians and Asian Muslims (see BNP website). Much low-level harassment (abuse, spitting, name-calling, pulling of headscarves and so on) goes unreported, but the number of reported attacks since 11 September 2001 was four times higher than usual (in the United States it has increased thirteenfold, including two deaths).

The confused retreat from multiculturalism has of course been given an enormous impetus by 11 September 2001. The events of that day led to widespread questioning, once again echoing the Rushdie affair, about whether Muslims can be and are willing to be integrated into British society and its political values, paralleling discourses in most of the EU. The New Labour government was at the forefront of this debate, as were many others who were prominent on the centre-left and had long-standing anti-racist credentials. For example, the Commission for Racial Equality published an article by the left-wing author Kenan Malik, arguing that 'multiculturalism has helped to segregate communities far more effectively than racism'. Hugo Young, the leading liberal columnist of the centre-left *Guardian* newspaper, went further and wrote that multiculturalism 'can now be seen as a useful bible for any Muslim who insists that his religio-cultural priorities, including the defence of jihad against America, override his civic duties of loyalty, tolerance, justice and respect for democracy'. More extreme again, Farrukh Dhondy, an Asian who had pioneered multicultural broadcasting on British television, writes of a 'multicultural fifth column' which must be rooted out, and argues that state funding of multiculturalism should be redirected into a defence of the values of freedom and democracy.[12]

'Faith schools'

One of the specific issues that, as I mentioned, has come to be a central element of this debate is that of 'faith schools', that is to say, state-funded schools run by religious organisations. While they must teach the national curriculum and are inspected by a government agency, they can give some space to religious instruction, though not all do so. They are popular with parents for their ethos, discipline and academic achievements and so can select their pupils, often giving priority to children whose parents can demonstrate a degree of religious observance.

Yet the violent disturbances in some northern English cities in the summer of 2001, in which Asian Muslim men had been among the protagonists, were officially blamed in part on the fact of segregated communities and segregated schools. Some of these were church-run schools and were 90 per cent or more Christian and white. Others were among the most under-resourced and under-achieving in the country and had rolls of 90 per cent or more Muslims. They came to be called, including in official reports,[13] 'Muslim schools'. In fact, they were nothing of the sort. They were local, bottom-of-the-pile comprehensive schools which had suffered from decades of underinvestment and 'white flight' but were run by white teachers according to a secular national curriculum.

'Muslim schools', then, came to be seen as the source of the problem of divided cities, cultural backwardness, riots and lack of Britishness, and a breeding ground for militant Islam. Muslim-run schools were lumped into this category of 'Muslim schools', even though all the evidence suggested that their pupils (mainly juniors and girls) did not engage in riots and terrorism and, despite limited resources, achieved better exam results than local authority 'secular' schools. On the basis of these 'Muslim schools' and 'faith schools' constructions, tirades by prominent columnists in the broadsheet newspapers were launched against allowing state funding to any more Muslim-run schools or even to a church-run school, and demands were made once again that the British state be entirely secular. For example, Polly Toynbee argued in the *Guardian* that a precondition of tackling racial segregation was that 'religion should be kept at home, in the private sphere'.

Reaffirming multiculturalism

The watchword has to be: Don't Panic. Perhaps we ought to brace ourselves for some excesses: I am reminded of the Marxist radicalism of my student days in the late 1960s and 1970s; as we know, that passed and many a radical now holds high office (and fulminates against young radicals!). But we must distinguish between criminal actions and militant rhetoric, between radical Islamists and the wider Muslim opinion; for the former, despite the bewitchment of the media, are as representative of Muslims as the Socialist Workers Party is of working-class politics. We must not give up on the moderate, egalitarian multiculturalism that has been evolving in Britain and has proved susceptible to gradually accommodating Muslim demands.

Other than Muslims themselves, a leading actor in bringing Muslim concerns and racial-equality thinking into contact has been the Runnymede Trust, recognising Islamophobia as one of the chief forms of racism today when it set up its Commission on Islamophobia. The demand for Muslim schools within the state sector was rejected by the Swann Report on multiculturalism in the 1980s and by the Commission for Racial Equality even in the 1990s, but it is now government policy. Adapting the census to measure the extent of socio-economic disadvantage by religious groups has been achieved, as has the outlawing religious discrimination and incitement to religious hatred, although each of the latter is weaker than its 'race' equivalents and the religion question in the Census, unlike the ethnic question, is voluntary. Talk of Muslim identity used to be rejected by racial egalitarians as an irrelevance ('religious not political') and as divisive, but in the last few years Muslim organisations like the Muslim Council of Britain (MCB) and FAIR, mentioned earlier, have co-organised events and demonstrations with groups such as the National Assembly of Black People. The protests against the Anglo-American invasion of Iraq have brought Muslims into the political mainstream, with Muslims sharing the same analysis as many non-Muslims.

Certainly, there must be an emphasis not just on 'difference' but on commonality too. British anti-racists and multiculturalists have indeed been too prone to ignore this; but to do so is in fact less characteristic of Muslims than of the political left (see, for instance, the various statements of the MCB from its inception, and its decision to entitle its newsletter *The Common Good*).[14]

To take up some recent issues, of course, wanting to be part of British society means having a facility in the English language, and the state must be protective of the rights of those oppressed within their communities, as in the case of forced marriages. But blaming Muslims alone for segregation ignores how the phenomenon in the northern cities and elsewhere has been shaped by white people's preferences as individuals, and the decisions of local councillors, not least in relation to public housing.

It is foolish to disparage and dismantle the cohesiveness of Muslim communities. We ought to recognise that there is an incompatibility between radical secularism and any kind of moderate multiculturalism in which Muslims are an important constituent. Integration cannot be a matter of laissez-faire; we must be willing to redefine Britain in a more plural way. The French approach of ignoring racial, ethnic and religious identities does not mean that they, or the related problems of exclusion, alienation and fragmentation, vanish. They are likely, on the contrary, to become more radical; and so the French may actually be creating the unravelling of the republic that they fear.

The *Future of Multi-Ethnic Britain*, the report of the Commission on Multi-Ethnic Britain published in October 2000, is a high-water mark of thinking on these topics. It tried to answer the question: how is it possible to have a positive attitude to difference and yet have a sense of unity? Its answer was that a liberal notion of citizenship as an unemotional, cool membership was not sufficient; better was a sense of belonging to one's country or polity. The report insisted that this 'belonging' required two important conditions: the idea that one's polity should be recognised as a community of communities as well as a community of individuals; the challenging of all racisms and related structural inequalities. Here we have a much more adequate concept of social cohesion than that which has emerged as a panicky reaction to the current Muslim assertiveness and which runs the risk of making many Muslims feel that they do not belong to Britain.

Conclusion

The emergence of Muslim political agency has thrown British multiculturalism into theoretical and practical disarray. It has led to policy reversals in the Netherlands and elsewhere, and across Europe has strengthened intolerant, exclusive nationalism. We should in fact be moving the other way. We should be extending to Muslims existing levels of protection from discrimination and incitement to hatred, and the duties on organisations to ensure equality of opportunity, not the watered-down versions of legislation proposed by the European Union and the UK government. We should target more effectively, in consultation with religious and other representatives, the severe poverty and social exclusion of Muslims. And we should recognise Muslims as legitimate social partners and include them in the institutional compromises of church and state, religion and politics, that characterise the evolving, moderate secularism of mainstream Western Europe, resisting the wayward, radical example of France.

Ultimately, we must rethink 'Europe' and its changing nations so that Muslims are not a 'them' but part of a plural 'us', not mere sojourners but part of its future. A hundred years ago, the African American theorist W. E. B. Du Bois predicted that the twentieth century would be the century of the colour line; today, we seem to be set for a century of the Islam–West line. The political integration or incorporation of Muslims – remembering that there are more Muslims in the European Union than the combined populations of Finland, Ireland and Denmark – has not only become the most important goal of egalitarian multiculturalism but is now pivotal in shaping the security, indeed the destiny, of many peoples across the globe.[15]

Notes

1. Summary Report on Islamophobia in the EU after 11 September 2001, Vienna, European Monitoring Centre on Racism and Xenophobia, 2002.

2. N. Meer and T. Modood, 'The Multicultural State We're In: Muslims, "Multiculture" and the "Civic Re-balancing" of British Multiculturalism', *Political Studies*, forthcoming.

3. For the basis of at least medium-term pessimism about civic equality and multiculturalism in France and Germany, see T. Modood, 'Ethnic difference and racial equality: new challenges for the Left', in D. Miliband (ed.), *Reinventing the Left*, Cambridge, Polity Press, 1994, pp. 87–8. For a less anglocentric view, see R. Brubaker, *Citizenship and Nationhood in France and Germany* (Cambridge, MA: Harvard University Press, 1992); C. Bryant, 'Citizenship, national identity and the accommodation of difference: reflections on the German, French, Dutch, and British cases', *New Community*, vol. 23, no. 2, 1997, pp. 157–72; A. Favell, *Philosophies of Integration* (London: Palgrave, 1998; 2nd edn, 2001); R. Koopmans and P. Statham (eds), *Challenging Immigration and Ethnic Relations Politics: Comparative European Perspectives* (Oxford: Oxford University Press, 2000); R. Kastoryano, *Negotiating Identities: States and Immigrants in France and Germany* (Princeton, NJ: Princeton University Press, 2002).

4. T. Modood, *Not Easy Being British: Colour, Culture and Citizenship* (London: Runnymede Trust/Trentham Books, 1992); T. Modood et al., *Ethnic Minorities in Britain: Diversity and Disadvantage* (London: Policy Studies Institute, 1997).

5. I. Young, *Justice and the Politics of Difference* (Princeton, NJ: Princeton University Press, 1990).

6. For an elucidation of 'even-handedness', see J. H. Carens, *Culture, Citizenship and Community: A Contextual Exploration of Justice as Evenhandedness* (Oxford: Oxford University Press, 2000).

7. For a debate reflecting several sides of the issue and how they have divided liberals, see T. Modood, T. R. Hansen, E. Bleich, B. O'Leary and J. Carens, 'The Danish Cartoon Affair: free speech, racism, islamism, and integration', *International Migration*, 44(5), 2006, 3–57.

8. Forum Against Islamophobia and Racism (FAIR), *A Response to the Government Consultation Paper, 'Towards Equality and Diversity: Implementing the Employment and Race Directives'* (London: 2002); Commission on British Muslims and Islamophobia, *Response to the Commission for Racial Equality's Code of Practice* (London: 2002).

9. I refer to the protests against the offensive character of Salman Rushdie's *The Satanic Verses* as perceived by many Muslims, following its publication in 1988, and the reaction of the West to those protests.

10. T. Modood, 'Muslim views on religious identity and racial equality', *New Community*, vol. 19, no. 3, April 1993, p. 518.

11. Though it is noticeable that Muslim homophobia receives far more condemnation

than does, say, black homophobia, and Muslim sensitivities against offensive literature receive far less sympathetic treatment than do those of radical feminists against pornography and Jews against Holocaust revisionism, not to mention legal restraints against incitements to racial hatred: T. Modood, 'Muslims, incitement to hatred and the law', in J. Horton, (ed.), *Liberalism, Multiculturalism and Toleration* (Basingstoke: Macmillan, 1993).

12. F. Dhondy, 'Our Islamic fifth column', *City Limits*, vol. 11, no. 4, 2001. For a recantation of his Black Panther radicalism, see his 'A Black Panther Repents', *The Times*, 24 June 2002, T2, pp. 2–4.

13. H. Ouseley, *Community Pride, Not Prejudice: Making Diversity Work in Bradford* (Bradford: Bradford Vision, Bradford City Council, 2001).

14. Hence my plea that, even in the time of Mrs Thatcher, anti-racism must relate to a sense of Britishness, not just blackness, Muslimness etc.: Modood, *Not Easy Being British*.

15. T. Modood, *Multiculturalism: A Civic Idea* (Cambridge: Polity Press: 2007).

Acknowledgements

This chapter was originally published in *Political Quarterly* 74(1) and we are grateful to Blackwell Publishing for their permission to reprint parts of this paper here.

ISLAMOPHOBIA IN THE CONSTRUCTION OF BRITISH MUSLIM IDENTITY POLITICS

Jonathan Birt

I am a proud British Muslim. I am close to my community and they are really proud that I am training to be a doctor. I would never give up that heritage. I feel I have nothing in common with all this multiculturalism stuff. Where were all those black brothers and sisters when we were being attacked over Rushdie? Did the CRE say anything to support us? My links are international. We are developing a modern, cosmopolitan Islamic network across the world. (Muslim female, 20 cited in Alibhai-Brown 2000: 25)

As has been commonly observed, questions of identity and, in particular, of identity politics have become central to public deliberation and theoretical debate. It is the contention of this chapter that much debate over identity has been overly concerned with discussions around anti-essentialism and that it should rather focus on the interplay between personal and political agency and its troubled, unstable manifestation as 'identity politics', as Stuart Hall suggests (2000b: 16). But troubling to anti-essentialists is the fact that identity movements conflate personal and public identities and that in the act of mobilisation they cut across other social identities—and herein lies their power to challenge prevailing norms (Werbner 1997). The young woman in the above quote conflates different strands together with proud self-awareness: her Britishness, Muslimness, professionalism, international connections and cosmopolitan modern faith, rejecting what she sees as any pre-packaged multiculturalist or anti-racist identity. An overview of current discussions among British Muslims about Islamophobia and its relationship to their complex identities will be reviewed in this chapter to shed further light upon this debate around 'identity politics'.

Since the *Satanic Verses* affair (see Modood 1992), two main charges have been made against an assertive Muslim identity politics in Britain. The first is political hostility towards the Muslim 'other', which is often deflected into anti-essentialist polemic from those post-structuralist thinkers on the left that singles out collective Muslim assertiveness for particularly strong doses of 'deconstruction', and inveighs against features common to all modern social movements engaged in political mobilisation (Modood 2000, Sayyid 2000). The chief charge is one of reification of an overarching identity, thereby obscuring, or indeed denying, other cross-cutting collective identities, or, simply, existential individuality (e.g. Amit and Rapport 2002, Baumann 1999, Yuval-Davies 1997). It is not insignificant that the same charge of reification was made with respect to 'ethnopolitics' in the 1970s (Rothschild 1981: 252–4); the argument is the same, but the target is now 'religion' and not 'ethnicity'. What is really at issue is a political judgement about the exclusivity or otherwise of Muslim identity politics and its supposed unwillingness to forge broad alliances founded on the core issues of progressive leftist politics, those of anti-racism, tackling poverty and challenging inequality and discrimination.[1]

The second common charge is that local, and later central, government encouraged the creation of a broad 'Asian' identity category, especially through instruments like equal opportunities, which then was further subdivided along religious lines, although it has also been recognised that narratives of black pride developed in the 1970s and 1980s could not, by definition, encapsulate separate 'Asian' post-colonial trajectories and experiences (Hall 1992; Modood 1997). A major culprit in this process of segmentation was seen to be a patriarchal, conservative mosque-centred leadership, which served to divide British Muslims from the anti-racist alliance and later on, encouraged further sectarian segmentation among British Muslims themselves (Baumann 1999; Farrar 2002: 72–94; 265–8; Gilroy 1992). In short, not only is Muslim identity politics seen to be internally and externally divisive and counterproductive, but it is also perceived as the outcome of manipulation by religious conservatives and local and national politicians, an unholy alliance that has come to outflank the progressive politics of the anti-racist left. Both of these charges are open to serious question, although the latter criticism is not the chief focus of this discussion.

Anti-essentialism and agency in identity theory

The contention that Muslim identity movements are, by their very nature, uniquely divisive is unsustainable, because they exhibit features commonly found in all identity movements. They appear to be a general consequence of the expansion of the modern state into new areas of life, which are transformed from 'social' and 'personal' to 'political' and 'public' concerns (Calhoun 1995: 216). This transformation is a direct consequence of the belief that new areas of life, which were formerly seen as personal and prescriptively private, can be rationally organised and reordered by the state. An example from the nineteenth century would be the recognition of workers' rights. In the twentieth century, law and politics came to intrude further upon the private realms of the family, sexuality, health, food and dress, which are now publicly contested and politicised. Therefore, identity movements can be the products either of resistance or of incorporation occasioned by the redrawing of the public–private distinction of the expansionist modern state.

However, if the modern state expands and incorporates new areas of competence into its remit, it does so in distinctive ways. Zygmunt Bauman (1997) argues that there are two major ways in which the modern state defines the stranger as lying outside its vision of order: through either the remaking of parochial, pre-modern diversity by the mass education of the universalising liberal project, or the destruction of those who did not fit into the nationalist-racist project. But neither of these modes appears to describe the multiculturalist praxis that operates in contemporary Britain. Rather, as Pnina Werbner shows, the multicultural liberal state allows for multiple private associations, encouraged by liberal charity provisions that embody all sorts of 'lower-order cultural, religious and national segments' (2002: 73), but does not recognise such small fragments for the purposes of public funding, preferring and in part creating larger, purportedly 'fictive' entities (1997: 241–2).

Crucially, however, the issue is not only that states redraw the boundaries of the public–private distinction, but that identity movements attempt to expand the concreteness of egalitarianism through broadening political sensitivity to diverse forms of human suffering (Rorty 1999: 235–7), giving the figure of the 'neutral' individual citizen in liberal political theory some multicultural colouring. Identity movements drive this expansion of sensitivity through their conflation of what is public and personal, whereby individuals may come to stand for groups: an injustice committed against an individual is a 'wrong' against the whole category to which they belong. The proof offered for the naturalness of this collective identity is personal experience of oppression or discrimination. What might have been prescriptively private has now become one's public face, the classic example being the gay rights movement (Dresch 1995). Similarly, Muslim identity movements, by the very fact of mobilising politically along religious lines, beside the specificities of any religious claims they may make, decentre a foundational public–private distinction of the modern liberal state, which sees religion as a matter of personal concern and private import. In theory at least, even if reality is a little more muddled, religion is to be kept out of the secular public domains of the law, education and politics, domains in which British Muslims have lobbied for the public recognition of their religious distinctiveness. In reaction to Muslim assertiveness, the multiculturalist state in Britain reveals its previously unquestioned secular character (Modood 2002). More broadly, it reveals the Eurocentric character of the liberal idea of the culturally neutral state (Hall 2000a), and perhaps even the decentring of universalising Eurocentric narratives of modernity (Sayyid 2000).

During the high period of nation building in Europe, the modern state, it is often forgotten, strove to break down traditional, local and rooted identities in favour of more homogenising narratives of the new nation (Bauman 1997). Today, however, in the era of globalisation, the state 'no longer has the clout or the wish to keep its marriage with the nation rock-solid and impregnable' (Bauman 2004: 28). In an age of unfettered mass communications, which has coincided with the expansion of global markets and the commodification of patriotism itself in such industries as competitive sports and heritage tourism, the inability of the state to confer rigid national identities is hardly surprising. So, if 'identities' no longer appear to be ascribed by tradition or prescribed by the state, then the burden of choice, of self-invention, of multiple possible selves appears to fall more explicitly upon individuals and social groups, partly in consonance with the needs of 'diversity' in the global marketplace. Manuel Castells concurs:

> Bypassed by global networks of wealth, power, and information, the modern nation-state has lost much of its sovereignty. By trying to intervene in this global scene the state loses capacity to represent its territorially rooted constituencies . . . [and thus to counteract] powerful resistance identities, which retrench in communal havens and refuse to be flushed away by global flows and radical individualism. (1997: 356)

Yet the globally ordering factors that account for the current efflorescence of identity politics – a crisis in the idea of the nation, the further ordering of private life by the expanding modern state, and the impact of global markets and mass communication – seem incomplete to explain the complex processes involved in the mobilisation of identity movements. These explanations seem to underplay the role of identity movements in driving social change. This is linked in part to a post-Marxist loss of hope in a progressive political project (Rorty 1999), in which the rise of Muslim identity movements in the West is viewed as merely symptomatic. In the study of identity politics this political pessimism is expressed as hostility to the 'bourgeois' concept of 'agency', which could only be explained away in terms of Michel Foucault's early work, as an abandonment of the idea of the 'subject' in favour of it having a decentred position within the dominant paradigm (Hall 2000b: 16). But Foucault's later works recognise that 'the decentring of the subject is not the destruction of the subject' and that discursive disciplinary regimes cannot themselves be centred without the constitution of 'subjects' as such (ibid: 26).

To put it in more concrete terms, the aims and goals of identity movements cannot be fully encapsulated by any disciplinary order, for example in any regulatory system of 'multiculturalism' found in the United Kingdom (Baumann 1999), and do not successfully contain the challenges to the nation that multicultural, post-colonial society manifests (Hesse 2000). 'Multicultural', as an adjective, always throws up, in varied contexts, a process whereby culturally disparate meanings and practices are 'invested in the racially marked incidence of contested cultural differences' and the post-colonial period is marked by a long process of formal decolonisation, racial and cultural deseg-regation and 'their ancillary reverberations and reconfigurations' (ibid.: 2, 12). Barnor Hesse's analytical distinction of the discrepancy between a social con-dition of plurality and the ordering practices of multiculturalism emphasises 'the historical antagonism and the social inequality which underlie cultural difference that is represented as marginal or insignificant in dominant discourse, and is conventionally repressed as a subject for discussion or redress' (ibid.: 16). In other words, while the crisis of the nation provides an underly-ing motivation for the statist management of 'multi-culture' as a compensation for a loss of sovereignty, post-colonial identity movements are still able to decentre existing multiculturalist dispensations by operating outside these enfeebled narratives of the nation, and this can only be explained by recourse to the process of collective 'agency'.

Both Anthony Giddens (1991) and Manuel Castells (1997) recognise the possibility of a shift from 'emancipatory' or 'resistance' identities as reactions to structural inequalities, to a 'politics of lifestyle' or 'project identities', which attempt to create new paradigms that shift the current consensus. Yet this process is not the measured self-reflexivity that Giddens proposes, the preserve in any case of a globalised elite, but rather, primarily an agonised reaction against globalisation that dislocates identity in the disjuncture between the local and the global, and thus between experience and power (Castells 1997: 10–11). Yet Castells, while correctly emphasising the weakness of the 'nation' and its legitimising discourses, is unduly pessimistic about how resistance iden-tities might transform themselves to project identities 'aiming at the transfor-mation of society as a whole, in continuity with the values of communal resistance to dominant interests enacted by global flows of capital, power, and information' (ibid.: 357).

As the forgoing discussion has made clear, it is largely the sterility of the debate around essentialism and anti-essentialism (Hall 2000b) which led many not to analyse how and why identity movements may coalesce, conflate older identities and thus in a new configuration upset the old political arrangements. It is precisely in this conflation that identity politics finds its disruptive power and thus the agency to be more than merely reactive (Hesse 2000, Werbner 2002). It is this misconception that has similarly dogged the debate around Muslims (and other social groups) and multiculturalism, by only focusing on how the dominant discourse appears entirely to shape the discourse of com-munity leaders who purport to lead communities with discrete cultures that may be neatly managed, particularly by local government (e.g. Baumann 1996, 1997, 1999).

But in the case of Britain, a demotic return to religion as a primary public identity and a form of political mobilisation, especially in the second and third generations, is widely reported among a number of Muslim communities: Pakistanis in Manchester and North London (Jacobson 1998, Werbner 2002), Bangladeshis in East London (Gardner and Shukur 1994), and multi-ethnic Muslim communities in West London (Ameli 2002) and Leeds (Farrar 2002); similar observations appear to hold true for American Muslims too (Hermansen 2003). The Policy Studies Institute's Fourth National Survey of Ethnic Minorities showed that, of all faith communities, British Muslims were the most likely to view religion as playing a very important part in their lives, a trait shared to a slightly lesser extent by British Hindus and Sikhs (Modood et al. 1997: 301, table 9.7). How this popular religio-political mobilisation among a wide section of British Muslims, regardless of their ethnic heritage, has emerged has been developed further by Pnina Werbner with respect to Manchester's Pakistani Muslims, although her insights seem to be more widely applicable.

Werbner highlights the key role of community-level or subaltern public spheres that by definition may operate outside of the hegemonic public sphere in framing the deep moral and aesthetic senses of an imagined community, which inform its political 'visibilisation' (Werbner 2002: 59) on to the centre stage.

In Werbner's view, three concurrent imagined cultural worlds work in creative tension to constitute 'community' in ethnic diasporic groups. Firstly, *moral community* defines the sense of responsibility for others. It is an act of identification, which, by reaching out, creates and defines the boundaries of a community of co-responsibility, which in its extent often exceeds civic and national limits. An expanding moral solidarity does not need a constitutive outside, for it tends to assume moral parity, not superiority (2002: 61–3). Secondly, *aesthetic community* 'is defined by cultural knowledge, passion and creativity'. It requires cultural experts like intellectuals, writers and religious leaders who all reflect common idioms of humour, tragedy, popular culture, national and religious narratives. Aesthetic values are re-enforced by a multiplicity of voluntary organisations, which reaffirm these values rhetorically and ritually (2002: 63–4). Thirdly, *political community* or the 'community of suffering' which, unlike aesthetic and moral community, must always involve participation in the hegemonic public sphere and invoke more official discourses, albeit often infused with these moral and aesthetic sensibilities. The 'political community' makes two claims on the state: a demand for the recognition of ethnic and/or religious rights and a demand for protection against racism. In opposing a shared experience of racism or xenophobia, which is violent and silencing, a political community has the resources to create new moral and aesthetic communities that sustain new, transversal multi-ethnic alliances (2002: 69–71).

The identification of such arenas hidden from the public gaze emanates from older anthropological insights that destabilise current identity-theory ortho-doxy, the latter promoting a simple narrative of movement from the monocul-ture to multiculture that decentres the old, nineteenth-century European nationalisms. Collective identities are neither essentialised nor hybrid, but rather are relational. Single social agents hold multiple identities, which are selectively emphasised and thus are expressed in terms of opposition to various social others in different contexts. These mobilisations entail not only the pursuit of material interests but also 'the moral values of sociality which *con-stitute* these interests and constraints within given contexts' (Werbner 2002: 56, author's italics). However the very point of multiple identities is their simulta-neous power not only to differentiate but also to conflate. 'It is the fusion of these identities, with all the tensions and contradictions such cross-cutting ties imply, which shapes modes of mediation and overarching processes of dispute settlement and transversal alliances' (ibid.: 56).

Thus, social identities are not simply *reactive*, formed through taking on dominant categories that circulate within hegemonic discourses and inverting their meaning and significance, but rather are *creative*, emerging through the fusion and cross-cutting of multiple identities and making new visions possible. Agency must therefore be a creative act.[2] Liberal theories of the self have been more successful than Marxist or post-structuralist critiques in recognising this creative power and agency, usually expressed in the idea of freedom (Taylor 1991), although they have, at the same time, denied it to the decentring subal-tern. For example, 'strong' liberalism is a 'fighting creed' that seeks to entrench a post-Christian idea of secularity against the allegedly monolithic political claims of Islam (Taylor 1994: 62).

Pace Foucault, this conflation of identities, of multiple moral and aesthetic selves expressed politically, is available to the subaltern at all times, and can form 'a powerful grass-roots basis for ethnic mobilisation', while the cultural is never entirely assimilated to the political (Werbner 2002: 57–8). This points again towards an inherent instability in multiculturalist arrangements. Alberto Melucci's (1989) insights into social movements reminds us that, for the most part, these submerged networks are concerned mostly with the constitution of new cultural codes, except where they have to confront politically a discrimi-natory public policy. Political latency is all too often confused with inactivity by those who solely concern themselves with the hegemonic public sphere onto which British Muslims appeared in 1988, at the outset of the *Satanic Verses* affair.

British Muslim identity formation and Islamophobia

Public debate in Britain over 'Islamophobia' has mostly focused upon the second half of the term: when is criticism of Islam rational and not phobic or irrational and driven by fear and hatred? This emphasis came out of concerns to preserve traditions of free speech while reassessing the impact of ridicule and mockery of the religious symbols of marginalised religious groups, and in turn, whether to extend an old blasphemy law to faiths other than Anglican Christianity. The issue was widely debated in the early 1990s in the wake of the *Satanic Verses* affair, exploring the appropriateness of this tradition of ridicule in a new multicultural and multireligious society (e.g. Webster 1990). A still-influential attempt to distinguish unfounded critiques (defined as negative and essentialising) from founded criticism (defined as open to dialogic virtue and serious enquiry into the diversity of Islam) sought to define parts of this older tradition of ridicule of Christianity as unfounded and therefore prejudicial in the new multi-faith setting (Runnymede Trust 1997). Fred Halliday (2002) points out that this division runs the risk of essentialising an acceptable form of Islam as above unfounded criticism, presupposing the primacy of faith for those who happen to be Muslim, and ultimately stifling genuine debate. However, I would like to contend that British Muslims are just as likely to problematise the first half of the term 'Islamophobia', as they are to debate the second. As Salma Yaqoob, the Midlands peace campaigner, put it in an interview (2004a), 'how you view Islamophobia depends upon how you view Islam'.

Viewing Islamophobia in terms of identity theory allows us to escape a narrow debate designed to define the etiquette for criticism of a minority religion in the hegemonic public sphere. More broadly, Islamophobia can be viewed as a form of cultural racism that specifically attacks the sanctified religious symbols of Islam and seeks to silence collective Muslim voices in the hegemonic public sphere (Werbner 1997: 237). But crucially for my argument, the common experience of Islamophobia creates a unique community of suffering, which conflates ethnically disparate communities as Muslims and creates an assertive Muslim identity politics. In this sense, Islamophobia provokes the constitution of assertive Muslim identities in the hegemonic public sphere. As one Muslim commentator (Yawar 1999) reflected: 'It was Salman Rushdie who . . . made us realise, as a community, that we were primarily Muslims'. Furthermore, in an emergent subaltern public sphere that is at once local, national and global, British Muslims draw on the wide aesthetic and moral resources in the various Islamic traditions to debate the nature of Islam and Islamophobia and the efficacy or otherwise of identity politics.

After 9/11, the more prejudicial media comment portrayed British Muslim communities, and especially their young men, as a dangerous and unpatriotic fifth column, which were sympathetic to anti-West resistance and, indeed, the use of violent terror (Poole 2002: 1–16). Mass communications today shape and order these Islamophobic moral panics and the reactive defence to them (Castells 1997, Poole 2002, Sayyid 2000). These themes were also reflected in government rhetoric about, and political interaction with, British Muslims during and after the Afghanistan war of 2001 that divided them into 'radicals' and 'moderates' (Birt 2005). With regard to a comparable process in France, Laurent Bonnefoy (2004) terms this process of division 'stigmatisation by distinction', which is necessarily part of a post-colonial project of assimilation, replacing older, colonial discourses of racist rejection. Or to put it another way, Islamophobia describes part of a condition internal to the post-colonial state, replacing Orientalism as a metaphor of spatial segregation from an earlier age of imperialism.

Moral and aesthetic debate among British Muslims about Islamophobia reflects their theological diversity,[3] even if their response to 'stigmatisation by distinction' cuts across these differences. The conviction that Islamophobia operates to contrast negatively allegiance to the *umma* (the imagined global Muslim collectivity) with patriotism is widely held. However, the fine characterisation of its causes differs: a 'product of the clash of civilisations' by Hizb ut-Tahrir (Gubra 2003); a function of the war on terror to silence Muslims in the West (Yaqoob 2003); the outcome of defining a new Europe against its Muslims (Sayyid 2003); the result of a failure to incorporate British Muslims into multiculturalism (Sardar 2002) or of too much multiculturalism (Alibhai-Brown 2000); or a xenophobic backlash against an anti-Western, puritanical and politicised Islam (Winter 2003a).

While the breadth and variety of Muslim responses to 9/11 has only been alluded to here, the remainder of the chapter focuses largely upon the example of the Stop the War Coalition (STWC). The movement's analysis of Islamophobia is entangled within the moment of political mobilisation, or the shift from 'reactive' to 'project' identities. Yaqoob (2004a) locates statist Islamophobia not in the tensions of the European project but in the use of Muslims as scapegoats to underwrite a neo-imperialist adventure. Islamophobia is not irrational, but rather a rational process involving the deliberate demonisation of Muslims based upon misinformation used, in the post-9/11 context, to support the war on terror. However, it is important that Muslims should not internalise victimhood, even if they suffer much discrimination. They should not retreat into an exclusive understanding of Islam, but ought to combat all forms of injustice. It was only through the sharing of experiences of suffering, standing on a common platform and taking up other causes that combating Islamophobia became a central plank of the Respect Party's manifesto in 2004.

Muslims in the STWC argued that they had to be part of a broad, anti-imperialist, anti-capitalist alliance (Yaqoob 2003). The STWC was particularly successful between 2001 and 2003 in popularising a model of democratic dissent among younger British Muslims, which almost completely marginalised radical groups who advocated working outside the system and set the agenda for Muslim groups lobbying the government (Birt 2005). Tariq Ramadan (2004) states an intermediate position, offering theological and moral justification for committed citizenship by Muslim minorities, who ought to seek the common good, while still advocating a strong internationalist interest in the affairs of the umma and of other broad cases of inequality and injustice, especially in the poor South. Finally, traditionalists and liberals place British Muslims within the context of the nation-state but draw very different conclusions as to their political response. The first wish broadly to preserve the status quo and to find the means to integrate and embed a British Islam without recourse to identity politics, while the second, as Muslim members of the global elite (see Castells 1997 for a definition), have a much more ambitious project to frame a post-national cosmopolitan Britishness. The traditionalists are not prepared at present to develop a new definition of citizenship, unlike the reformers, preferring the older metaphor of the courteous, but presumably temporary, guest who does not seek to annoy his host (Winter 2003b). The reformer's charge is that this creates an attitude of short-termism (Ramadan 2004).

These debates are set against the background of widespread political mobilisation among British Muslims, including intensified lobbying, the support of a popular anti-war movement, the creation of a Muslim-centred political party (the Respect Party, founded in January 2004) and, most importantly, the accelerated integration of British Muslims into the entirety of the political spectrum. While British Muslims have for the most part been a Labour loyalist community for the past forty years, polling indicated that the Labour share of the Muslim vote fell from 75 per cent in 2001 to 32 per cent in 2004, mostly because of sharp disagreement with the government's support for the US-led invasions of Afghanistan and Iraq.[4] A rapid shift towards more ideological and tactical voting was palpable and was also reflected in public debate (Asaria 2004, Yaqoob 2004b).

British Muslims from the subaltern to emancipatory politics: a case study of the Stop the War Coalition and the Respect Coalition

It has been suggested that in the study of subaltern politics 'we need . . . to probe further . . . into what makes for key moments of social transition from fabulations to political mobilisation, from mere consciousness to emancipatory politics, from the grand oratory of the diasporic public sphere to open public protest' (Werbner 2002: 270). The STWC that sprung up in the wake of 9/11, with a large Muslim component, mobilised the largest street protest in British history in 2003, and contained enough momentum to support the creation of a new political party in January 2004.

One of the few detailed personal accounts to emerge after 9/11 suggests that the moment between the shock of racist violence and abuse, dislocation and disorientation and the channelling of subaltern discourses into bridging and progressive politics can be sharply compacted:

Within a few hours [after 9/11], Muslims were being blamed for the terrible attacks, and the words 'Islamic terrorism' were being screamed from every media outlet. Suddenly I was not Salma any more, but a terrorist somehow connected with these despicable acts. My fear was very real and I felt isolated and a stranger for the first time.

Returning to my home, I was spat upon in the street. I was shaking with anger. I had my three year old son with me and I feared for his safety. Nobody said or did anything – they just looked and passed by . . .

My friend, on her way home from work, had overheard people saying, 'I want to stab all Muslims.' She was later humiliatingly sprayed with a can of beer, while onlookers stood by and did nothing . . . These racist attacks were particularly upsetting as I have lived in Birmingham, a thriving multicultural city, all my life and had never experienced such racism before . . . We had all watched the events in Bosnia . . . When I sat with my friends and family we all experienced the same fear and panic. The ethnic cleansing of Muslims had just taken place in the 1990s on our doorstep in modern Europe . . . I had taken my place in this society for granted, and now this assumption had been badly shaken . . . All those things I took for granted – my home, my children, our future, my hopes – all were now in question. Nothing seemed stable or safe. The irony of this was that we were feeling so afraid with our very existence being threatened, yet we were being portrayed as the threat.

It was not until a friend of mine, quite by coincidence, came across a group of Socialist Worker Party activists campaigning in the city centre against the proposed bombing of Afghanistan, that things began to turn around. At a time when we were feeling powerless and were being told to keep our heads down, it was reassuring to be approached by people who [were] sympathetic to our stance and predicament. She told me of an anti-war meeting . . . That meeting was a ray of hope, and my friends and I had a renewed sense of optimism. For the first time our views and thoughts were being heard and taken seriously, and the fear and frustration of being constantly mis-understood began to lessen. I was encouraged to become a member . . . and soon thereafter found myself with the responsibility of being the chairperson.

Within eighteen months we were at the head of [a] vibrant coalition that involved thousands through local and national demonstrations, public meetings and direct action. (Yaqoob 2003)

The movement did not gain its real momentum during the Afghanistan conflict of 2001, or in reaction to the Israeli incursion into the Palestinian city of Jenin in the West Bank, but when it became clear during 2002 that an invasion of Iraq was in the offing. According to the organisers' own figures, while the national march on 28 September 2002 attracted 400,000 protestors, more than the entire series of historic anti-Vietnam marches, there were some two million at the march on the eve of war in Iraq on 15 February 2003 (German 2003: 273). At its height, it represented a clear instance of the 'multitude' defined as 'productive, creative subjectivities of globalization . . . They are in perpetual motion and they form constellations of singularities and events that impose continual global reconfigurations on the system' (Hardt and Negri 2000: 60).

A key organiser within the movement noted the wide participation, that crossed traditional lines of ethnicity, age, sexual orientation and creed, and that despite the 'varied' politics, there were key themes that united this particular manifestation of the multitude: a sense of betrayal on the left at Labour going to war, cuts in public services, the sharp inequalities produced by global capitalism and cynicism about geopolitical priorities in the Middle East. At the core of a concerted mobilisation were the old socialist activist parties, the peace movement, the trade union movement and the Muslim community. But it could not equally condemn the regimes of the Taliban or Ba'athist Iraq for fear of splitting the coalition and alienating its Muslim element, and so concentrated on a platform that was exclusively anti-imperialist, anti-racist and against the erosion of civil liberties (German 2003: 274–5).

The second generation of British Muslims, particularly women (overturning leftist stereotypes of passivity in the process), played a key role in mobilising Muslim support and providing political leadership, and in certain areas, like the West Midlands, constituted the mainstay of the movement's support. Muslim involvement created a sharp debate among British socialist activists, echoing the European left, about the ethics of an alliance with those of the Muslim community who defended their 'clothing, culture or religion' and who could not therefore be 'an ally but must be in some way "fundamentalist"' (German 2003: 276, see also Murray and German 2005: 57–63). An early example of this was at a key rally in Birmingham in November 2001, which aimed to bring in the local Muslim community. The involvement of an *imam* on a panel was viewed by some on the ideological left as retrograde, although it provided a vital endorsement for the many Muslims new to this sort of coalition politics (Yaqoob 2003). It was precisely a blank resistance to the idea that Muslims, and particularly devout ones, could play any meaningful role in progressive left politics, which was viewed by these young Muslim activists as inherently Islamophobic:

> Looking back it seems . . . almost inevitable that a large anti-war movement took shape across Britain . . . However, there was nothing inevitable in the coming together of so many different people . . . It was also certainly not without its challenges . . . Although initially we [Muslims] were welcomed . . . it became apparent very quickly that not everyone saw our involvement in positive terms and as being unproblematic. Our relief turned to disappointment when labels such as 'reactionary fundamentalists' and ridiculous accusations regarding our beliefs and motives were thrown at us . . . The accusers did not know me, had not asked me or the other Muslims about our beliefs and stance, clearly had no knowledge of Islam itself, and yet were publicly denouncing our involvement with derogatory and negative statements about Muslims and Islam . . . Our critics could not conceive of any notion of Islam other than an

extreme one. The mere fact we were Muslims, some of us visibly so because we wore the *hijab*, meant that we must be extremists. (Yaqoob 2003)

Alongside a part of the ideological left, Hizb ut-Tahrir also attempted to derail Muslim involvement in STWC, but at an early stage both wings were completely marginalised in the voting that took place in autumn 2001 to elect a leadership for the fledgling movement. Leaving aside stereotypes of a mono-lithic Muslim block, good Muslim participation was far from assured. To take the example of Birmingham, it needed the money and leadership of the more politically committed mosques like Birmingham Central Mosque, and the lead-ership of second generation Muslims, who were mainly women, to galvanise less politically minded congregations to attend rallies, mainly by providing free coach transport. At all times, the Muslim leadership of the STWC aimed to and largely succeeded in building an intra-Muslim component that crossed kinship networks, and sectarian, ethnic and generational cleavages (Yaqoob 2003).

In Salma Yaqoob's view, Muslims had to reject victimhood and a retreat into a narrow, intolerant interpretation of their faith. The whole anti-war movement can be interpreted as a creative response to the Islamophobic moral panic after 9/11. Here young British Muslims, especially women, were able to be at the centre of a new political movement, in some ways similar to the rainbow coali-tions of the 1980s, and to open up new political space for themselves. In so doing they have taken on the political analysis of neo-imperialism favoured by the ideological left, in which Islamophobia is cast merely as an instrumentalised rhetorical effect of the war on terror. They have also attempted to frame a broad, humanitarian Islam that no longer focuses on Muslim-only issues.[5] One example of this was the fundraising by Birmingham Central Mosque for the firefighters' strike in 2003. In return, the left has taken up new human rights causes centred in the Muslim world, like Palestine and Kashmir (Murray and German 2005: 81–9), with even greater seriousness and it now respects what was once seen as Muslim cultural and religious alterity on the basis of freedom of conscience and personal choice. For example, the wearing of the hijab is no longer seen automatically as a matter of patriarchal enforcement.

Together they found a shared passion to tackle injustice. One result has been to put anti-Islamophobia at the centre of British anti-racism, which was certainly not true five years ago. For Yaqoob, the time has come for British Muslims to hammer out and resolve differences face to face, and to leave behind the old style of ineffective politics of the pioneer generation. These young Muslims have gone, in a very short time, from being perceived as fun-damentalist outsiders to being partners in the radical politics of the age. It might be too easy to deride the new Respect Party, formed in January 2004, as 'Taliban and Trotskyists', but in only six months they were able to get 1.5 per cent of the vote in the European elections in June and more than the Scottish National Party (although considerably less than the British National Party).[6]

At the very least, even if the Respect Party turns out to have been short lived, many capable young Muslims, in a generation that is danger of being disenfranchised, will have learned invaluable lessons in alliance building and democratic dissent.

The compromise platform reached by the Respect Party in February 2004 unsurprisingly appeared to be broadly socialist, anti-imperialist and anti-racist. None of this is very new for the ideological left, except for the finding of a *modus vivendi* with conservative Muslims on issues of personal morality, who have agreed to join a platform that opposes all forms of discrimination. They will not be taken to task for failing to promote all aspects of this agenda, such as gay rights, if they agree to keep any objections personal and private for the purposes of party discipline and to uphold the right to individual self-determination in sexual choices.[7] To some this might look like the death of progressive politics (Cohen 2003); but for others, it is a work in progress (Gray 1995), as is further evidenced by the 'pragmatism' of other progressives, who, despite a clear stand against 'fundamentalism', are prepared to work with religious conservatives when campaign goals are shared (Gupta 2003).

Concluding remarks

The title of Salma Yaqoob's (2003) account of the Stop the War Coalition is revealing: *Global and local echoes of the anti-war movement: a British Muslim perspective*. Britishness is only partly constitutive of modern Muslim identities but this observation hardly applies to them alone, so the question then becomes, why are Muslims being so singled out in the first place for what is a general phenomenon? There was a sharp bifurcation of British Muslims into loyal moderates and disloyal radicals after 9/11, part of an Islamophobic assimilationist discourse, but it could not be sustained to the same degree after the emergence of a large, third space for democratic dissent that British Muslims helped to shape in the run up to the Iraq war. This third space was anti-imperialist, anti-Islamophobic and internationalist in outlook, and represented the emergence of a creative response in which new, hybridised identities and alliances could emerge.

If identity is understood to be constituted by its outside, where Islamophobia and its impact on Muslims are concerned, it would not only constitute their reactions but also fundamentally shape who they are. Fortunately, this dismal scenario is neither true of identity theory in general nor of British Muslims in particular. Rather, with the Islamophobic shock after 9/11, they have sought to ask new questions about their political role and built new alliances, which, in the words of Salma Yaqoob, have been 'transformative' of their approach to Islam as well. In short, the idea of creative agency should be put at the heart of identity formation, and to do this more attention must be paid to the way British Muslims seek to confront new challenges by revisiting their central moral and aesthetic values. In short, the contention of this chapter is that Islamopobia merely creates anti-Islamophobia, and that it cannot permanently define the British Muslim experience.

Notes

1. The major reservations from the ideological left to politicised Islam, and to Islam in general, are expressed with a rare religio-cultural sensitivity in Tariq Ali's 'Letter to a Young Muslim' (2003: 329–39).
2. I owe this insight to Dr S. M. Atif Imtiaz.
3. Ameli (2002) and Modood (2000) also view distinctions by theology as important in understanding British Muslim differences.
4. Dr Asifa Hussain and Professor Bill Miller, Glasgow University; Guardian/ICM Poll, November 2004.
5. Yaqoob (2003) in her account draws parallels between her understanding of Islam and the liberation theologies of South America.
6. Percentages of the national vote achieved in the June 2004 European elections were: Conservative 26.7%, Labour 22.6%, UK Independence Party 16.1%, Liberal Democrat 14.9%, Green 6.3%, British National Party 4.9%, Respect 1.5%, Scottish National Party 1.4%, Paid Cymru 1.0%; see BBC News (2004).
7. The relevant, carefully worded clauses from the Respect Party (2004) are as follows: '(1) Opposition to all forms of discrimination based on race, colour, gender, ethnicity, religious beliefs (or lack of them), sexual orientation, disabilities, national origin or citizenship, and (2) The right to self-determination of every individual in relation to their religious (or non-religious beliefs) as well as sexual choices.'

References

Ali, T. (2003), *The Clash of Fundamentalisms: Crusades, Jihads and Modernity*, London: Verso.

Alibhai-Brown, Y. (2000), *After Multiculturalism*, London: Foreign Policy Centre.

Ameli, S. R. (2002), *Globalization, Americanization and British Muslim Identity*, London: Islamic College for Advanced Studies.

Amit, V. and Rapport, N. (2002), *The Trouble with Community*, London: Pluto.

Asaria, M. I. (2004), 'Towards a Muslim electoral strategy in the UK', *Muslim News*, 183, p. 12.

Bauman, Z. (1997), 'The making and unmaking of strangers', in P. Werbner and T. Modood (eds), *Debating Cultural Hybridity: Multi-Cultural Identities and the Politics of Anti-Racism*, London: Zed, pp. 46–57.

Bauman, Z. (2004), *Identity*, Cambridge: Polity Press.

Baumann, G. (1996), *Contesting Culture: Discourses of Identity in Multi-ethnic London*, Cambridge: Cambridge University Press.

Baumann, G. (1997), 'Dominant and demotic discourses of culture: their relevance to multi-ethnic alliances', in P. Werbner and T. Modood (eds), *Debating Cultural Hybridity: Multi-Cultural Identities and the Politics of Anti-Racism* London: Zed, pp. 209–25.

Baumann, G. (1999), *The Multicultural Riddle: Rethinking National, Ethnic, and Religious Identities*, London: Routledge.

BBC News (2004), 'European election: United Kingdom result', BBC News, http://news.bbc.co.uk/1/shared/bsp/hi/vote2004/euro_uk/html/front.stm, 14 June, accessed 1 January 2005.

Birt, J. (2005), 'Lobbying and marching: British Muslims and the state', in T. Abbas (ed.), *British South Asian Muslims: Politics and Society in a Post-September 11 World*, London: Zed.

Bonnefoy, L. (2004), 'Modalities and limits of stigmatisation: French public institutions and Muslims after 11th September 2001', paper presented at seminar Challenging Islamophobia: New Perspectives and Contemporary Agendas', 14 September, Islamic Foundation.

Calhoun, C. (1995), *Critical Social Theory: Culture, History, and the Challenge of Difference*, Oxford: Blackwell.

Castells, M. (1997), *The Information Age: Economy, Society and Culture, Volume II: The Power of Identity*, Oxford: Blackwell.

Cohen, N. (2003), 'The lesson the left has never learnt', *New Statesman*, 21 July, www.findarticles.com/p/articles/mi_m0FQP/is_4647_132/ai_106059005 accessed 4 January 2005.

Dresch, P. (1995), 'Race, culture and – what?: Pluralist certainties in the United States', in Wendy James (ed.), *The Pursuit of Certainty: Religious and Cultural Formations*, London: Routledge, pp. 61–91.

Farrar, M. (2002), *The Struggle for 'Community' in a British Multi-Ethnic Inner-City Area*, Lampeter: Edwin Mellen.

Gardner, K. and Shukur, A. (1994), ' "I'm Bengali, I'm Asian and I'm living here": the changing identity of British Bengalis', in Roger Ballard (ed.), *Desh Pardesh: The South Asian Presence in Britain*, London: Hurst, pp. 142–64.

German, L. (2003), 'Anti-war movement', in F. Reza (ed.), *Anti-Imperialism: A Guide for the Movement*, London: Bookmark, pp. 273–80.

Giddens, A. (1991), *Modernity and Self-Identity: Self and Society in the Late Modern Age*, London: Polity Press.

Gilroy, P. (1992), 'The end of anti-racism', in J. Donald and A. Rattansi (eds), *'Race', Culture and Difference*, London: Sage, pp. 49–61.

Gray, J. (1995), *Enlightenment's Wake: Politics and Culture at the Close of the Modern Age*, London: Routledge.

Gubra, W. (2003), ' "Islamophobia" – the product of a clash of civilisations', *Al-Khilafah* (London), www.khilafah.com/home/printable.php?DocumentID=7941, 20 July, accessed 31 December 2003.

Gupta, R. (ed.) (2003), *From Homebreakers to Jailbreakers: Southall Black Sisters*, London: Zed.

Hall, S. (1992), 'New Ethnicities', in J. Donald and A. Rattansi (eds), *'Race', Culture and Difference*, London: Sage, pp. 252–9.

Hall, S. (2000a), 'Conclusion: the multi-cultural question', in B. Hesse (ed.), *Un/settled Multiculturalisms: Disaporas, Entanglements, Transruptions*, London: Zed, pp. 209–41.

Hall, S. (2000b), 'Who needs identity?', in P. du Gay, J. Evans and P. Redman (eds), *Identity: A Reader*, London: Sage and the Open University, pp. 15–30.

Halliday, F. (2002), *Two Hours that Shook the World: September 11, 2001: Causes and Consequences*, London: Saqi, pp. 121–31.

Hardt, M. and Negri, A. (2000), *Empire*, Cambridge, MA: Harvard University Press.

Hermansen, M. (2003), 'How to put the genie back in the bottle: "Identity" Islam and Muslim youth cultures in America', in O. Safi (ed.), *Progressive Muslims: On Justice, Gender, and Pluralism*, Oxford: Oneworld, pp. 306–19.

Hesse, B. (2000), 'Introduction', in B. Hesse (ed.), *Un/settled Multiculturalisms: Disaporas, Entanglements, Transruptions*, London, Zed, pp. 1–30.

Jacobson, J. (1998), *Islam in Transition: Religion and Identity Among British Pakistani Youth*, London: Routledge.

Melucci, A. (1989), *Nomads of the Present: Social Movements and Individual Needs in Contemporary Society*, ed. by J. Keane and P. Mier, London: Hutchinson.

Modood, T. (1992), 'British Asian Muslims and the Rushdie affair', in J. Donald and A. Rattansi (eds), *'Race', Culture and Difference*, London: Sage, pp. 260–77.

Modood, T. (1997), ' "Difference", cultural racism and anti-racism', in P. Werbner and T. Modood (eds), *Debating Cultural Hybridity: Multi-Cultural Identities and the Politics of Anti-Racism*, London: Zed, pp. 154–172.

Modood, T. (2000), 'Anti-essentialism, multiculturalism, and the "recognition" of religious groups', in W. Kymlicka and W. Norman (eds), *Citizenship in Diverse Societies*, Oxford: Oxford University Press, pp. 175–95.

Modood, T. (2002), 'The place of Muslims in British secular multiculturalism', in N. Alsayyad and Manuel Castells (eds), *Muslim Europe or Euro-Islam*, Lanham, MD: Lexington, pp. 113–30.

Modood, T. et al. (1997), *Ethnic Minorities in Britain: Diversity and Disadvantage*, London: Policy Studies Institute.

Murray, A. and German, L. (2005), *Stop the War: The Story of Britain's Biggest Mass Movement*, London: Bookmarks.

Poole, E. (2002), *Reporting Islam: Media Representations of British Muslims*, London: I. B. Tauris.

Ramadan, T. (2004), *Western Muslims and the Future of Islam*, New York: Oxford University Press.

Respect Party (2004), 'The founding declaration of Respect – the unity coalition', *Respect – The Unity Coalition*, www.respectcoalition.org/?ite=3, 1 February, accessed 27 January 2005.

Rorty, R. (1999), *Philosophy and Social Hope*, London: Penguin.

Rothschild, J. (1981), *Ethnopolitics: A Conceptual Framework*, New York: Columbia University Press.

Runnymede Trust (1997), *Islamophobia: A Challenge for Us All*, London: Runnymede Trust.

Sardar, Z. (2002), 'The excluded minority: British Muslim identity after 11 September', in P. Griffith and M. Leonard (eds), *Reclaiming Britishness: Living Together After 11 September and the Rise of the Right*, London: Foreign Policy Centre, pp. 51–5.

Sayyid, S. (2000), 'Beyond Westphalia: nations and diasporas – the case of the Muslim *Umma*', in B. Hesse (ed.), *Un/settled Multiculturalisms: Diasporas, Entanglements, Transruptions*, London: Zed, pp. 33–50.

Sayyid, S. (2003), 'Muslims in Britain: towards a political agenda', in M. S. Seddon, D. Hussain and N. Malik (eds), *British Muslims: Loyalty and Belonging*, Leicester: Islamic Foundation, pp. 87–94.

Taylor, C. (1991), *The Ethics of Authenticity*, Cambridge, MA: Harvard University Press.

Taylor, C. (1994), 'The politics of recognition', in Amy Gutmann (ed.), *Multiculturalism*, Princeton, NJ: Princeton University Press, pp. 25–73.

Webster, R. (1990), *A Brief History of Blasphemy: Liberalism, Censorship and 'The Satanic Verses'*, Southwold: The Orwell Press.

Werbner, P. (1997), 'Essentialising essentialism, essentialising silence: ambivalence and multiplicity in the constructions of race and ethnicity', in P. Werbner and T. Modood (eds), *Debating Cultural Hybridity: Multi-Cultural Identities and the Politics of Anti-Racism*, London: Zed, pp. 226–54.

Werbner, P. (2002), *Imagined Diasporas among Manchester Muslims*, Oxford: James Currey.

Winter, T. J. (2003a), 'Muslim loyalty and belonging: some reflections on the psychosocial background', in M. S. Seddon, D. Hussain and N. Malik (eds), *British Muslims: Loyalty and Belonging*, Leicester: Islamic Foundation, pp. 3–22.

Winter, T. J. (2003b), 'Tradition or extradition? The threat to Muslim-Americans', in A. A. Malik (ed.), *The Empire and the Crescent: Global Implications for a New American Century*, Bristol: Amal Press, pp. 142–55.

Yaqoob, S. (2003), 'Global and local echoes of the anti-war movement: a British Muslim perspective', *International Socialism Journal*, Autumn, http://pubs.socialistreview index.org.uk/isj100/yaqoob.htm accessed 21 May 2004.

Yaqoob, S. (2004a), telephone interview, 24 May.

Yaqoob, S. (2004b), 'Vote for Respect, an alternative political party', *Muslim News*, 185, p. 7.

Yawar, A. (1999), 'Seven years of Q-News', *Q-News*, 302–3, March, p. 54.

Yuval-Davies, N. (1997), 'Ethnicity, gender relations and multiculturalism', in P. Werbner and T. Modood (eds), *Debating Cultural Hybridity: Multi-Cultural Identities and the Politics of Anti-Racism*, London: Zed, pp. 193–208.

AFTERWORD

Peter Hopkins and Richard Gale

Muslims in Britain shape their geographies; geographies shape their experiences. Documenting some of the ways in which place, locality and neighbourhood influence and are influenced by Muslims in Britain, the aim of this book is to contribute to understanding the ways in which these geographies intersect and interact with everyday life. The chapters make it clear that – from the home to the neighbourhood, the labour market to the community and from the nation to the experiences of transnational mobilities – the intersections and interactions of different geographies matter to the complex ways in which Muslims in Britain negotiate their everyday lives, structure their social relationships and navigate their experiences of inequality.

The contributors to this collection include human geographers, sociologists, educational researchers, religious studies scholars and others who sit between these and other disciplines. A key contribution of this collection is the way in which it highlights the importance of geographical issues – such as locality, neighbourhoods, communities and mobilities – in the lives of Muslims in Britain. Reflecting upon the different disciplinary backgrounds of the contributors leads us to question the various benefits of different geographical approaches and possible advantages of adopting an interdisciplinary perspective to our work in this field. In particular, there is scope for more intensive, reciprocal dialogue between geography and religious studies in exploration of the spatiality of Muslim identities, along the lines charted in the pioneering work of Kim Knott (2005).

Furthermore, as well as critically reflecting upon the disciplines that influence our work, it is crucial that we also think carefully about the concepts and theories we use when undertaking research with Muslims in Britain. Much work in this field adopts anti-racist and feminist approaches, thereby highlighting the salience of processes of racialisation and gendering in the lives of Muslims in Britain. Although these works – and the theoretical and conceptual approaches that characterise them – have made significant critical insights into the lives of Muslims in Britain, future research could usefully seek to adapt elements of a wider range of approaches, to capture different aspects of British Muslim experiences, including the religious, the economic and the post-colonial.

The research methodologies and practices of researchers who work with Muslims in Britain are also a key topic for future consideration. The majority of the contributions to this collection use a mixture of qualitative research methods – such as ethnography and interviews – reflecting their interests in exploring the experiences, attitudes and feelings of the people they are research-ing. There has, however, been little discussion within existing literature about the methods and methodologies best suited for researching Muslims in Britain, and there appears to be a disjuncture between quantitative work – some of which is documented in the introduction - focusing on census analysis and mon-itoring of levels of segregation, and the qualitative work highlighted in this col-lection. Future research could usefully seek to combine quantitative and qualitative approaches in exploring the lives of Muslims in Britain and reflect upon the advantages and disadvantages of adopting a mixed methods approach (Hopkins, 2007). For example, some of the traditional work that seeks to measure, monitor and map varying levels of residential segregation could use-fully be combined with qualitative investigations that explore the experiences, values and attitudes of Muslims living in segregated neighbourhoods. Conversely, much of the already rich research on Muslim gender identities could be further developed through being brought into touch with quantitative analysis of gender differentials in the labour market (as achieved in Bowlby and Lloyd-Evans's chapter above).

As well as reflecting upon the methods used to research Muslims in Britain, there are also important issues throughout the research process that require critical engagement and reflection, yet there has to date been little work explor-ing such issues. Concerns here include negotiating access, ethics in research, providing feedback to communities and how researchers negotiate issues about their positionality in the research. Sanghera and Thapar-Bjokert (2008: 544) have reflected upon the role of various gatekeepers in their work with Muslims in Bradford, noting that 'Arguably this relationship is important as the gate-keeper is often the first point of contact in the field research process, yet it is a relationship that is fraught with inconsistencies and instabilities.' This is one of the few contributions to understanding methodological issues in researching Muslims in Britain, clarifying that this is a key topic of consideration for future work. Questions here might include: how do researchers go about accessing Muslims for participation in research and what are the ethical and political issues involved? What are the various positionalities of those conducting the research and how are these interpreted, managed and negotiated during the research process? How do researchers work with Muslims in Britain, offer them feedback on research, or seek to help improve the experiences of individuals and communities? In this context, a principal concern for researchers working with Muslims in Britain should be to continue to seek out ways of balancing the unfolding preoccupations of the academy with an ethic of care for research participants, as well as the wider social networks in which they are embedded.

References

Hopkins, Peter (2007), 'Young people, masculinities, religion and race: new social geographies', *Progress in Human Geography* , 31(2), 163–77.

Knott, K. (2005), *The Location of Religion: A Spatial Analysis*, London: Equinox Publishing.

Sanghera, Gurchathen and Thapar-Bjokert, Suruchi (2008), 'Methodological dilemmas: gatekeepers and positionality in Bradford', *Ethnic and Racial Studies*, 31(3), 543–62.

INDEX